REVISED AND ENLARGED
THIRD EDITION

More About
This Business
of Music

REVISED AND ENLARGED
THIRD EDITION

More About
This Business
of Music

SIDNEY SHEMEL AND
M. WILLIAM KRASILOVSKY
original edition edited by Lee Zhito

BILLBOARD PUBLICATIONS, INC.   NEW YORK

Copyright © 1967, 1974, 1982 by Sidney Shemel and M. William Krasilovsky

Revised and enlarged third edition first published 1982 in New York by
Billboard Publications, Inc.
1515 Broadway, New York, N.Y. 10036

Library of Congress Cataloging in Publication Data
Shemel, Sidney.
  More about this business of music.

  Includes index.
    1. Music trade—United States.   2. Music—
Economic aspects.   3. Copyright—Music—United
States.   4. Music, Popular (Songs, etc.)—
United States—Writing and publishing.
I. Krasilovsky, M. William.   II. Title.
ML3790.S49   1982   338.4′778′0973   82-1119
ISBN 0-8230-7567-2   AACR2

Manufactured in the U.S.A.

First Printing, 1982

1 2 3 4 5 6 7 8 9/87 86 85 84 83 82

*To our children
with affection*

Preface

THIS book consists of additional topics and material not contained in *This Business of Music,* written by the same authors. The third edition contains a new chapter, "This Business of Jazz" and an enlarged treatment of religious music. The present updated text has been written to help participants in the music and recording industries comprehend the intricacies of the business and their rights and obligations. Economic facts deemed significant for daily operations as well as common legal concepts which guide business decisions are presented. The book is not designed to be a substitute for expert legal and accounting advice.

The Third Edition

In respect to prior editions and the present third edition, the authors have received generous and valuable assistance from many business associates and industry leaders. As to the third edition, the authors wish to acknowledge their particular indebtedness to the following people: Paul S. Adler, Albert Berman, Stephen L. Cotler, Sylvia Goldstein, Lisa Gonzalez, John Gross, John Hammond, Ben Hoagland, Margaret Jory, Edward J. Slattery, and Theodora Zavin. Special appreciation is due to Roma Baran for her research and editorial assistance, and to Marisa Bulzone for her editorial and production guidance. Barbara Adams was most helpful with the many details involved in the handling of the manuscript.

Contents

Jazz Arrangements
Jazz Repertory
Performance Income
Mechanical License Fees
Publications
Jazz Organizations

Types of Printed Music
Indexes to Printed Music
Fake Books
Preparation for Printing
Independent Folio Licensees and Selling Agents
Folio Licensee Royalties
Folio Selling-Agent Commissions
Sheet Music Licensees
Selling Agency
Term of Licensee or Selling-Agent Agreements
Joint Ventures
Personality Folios
Lyric Licenses
Copyright Notice
Return Privileges
Discounts
Prices of Printed Music
Foreign Sales
Mailing Privileges

Background Music Services
Muzak
3M
Licenses from Copyright Owners
Compulsory Licenses and Transcriptions
1976 Copyright Act Changes
Public Performance Licenses for Musical Compositions
Performing Rights Organization Distributions
Film Music
Synchronization Licenses
Performing Rights Licenses
ASCAP and BMI Distributions for Background Music
Composers of Television Music
Sound Track Libraries
Union Standards
Radio Broadcast Transcriptions

PART THREE   **Appendixes**   **127**

PART ONE
The Business of Serious Music

1

Background

THE field of serious music is commonly considered to include symphonies, chamber music, operas, choral works, oratorios, piano sonatas, and other recital pieces. There are the established repertoire works of Bach, Beethoven, and Brahms and the more contemporary compositions of Bartok, Shostakovich, Stravinsky, Schoenberg, Barber, Copland, Ives, Carter, Cage, and Boulez. Included is the traditional opera repertoire of Mozart, Rossini, Puccini, Verdi, and Wagner, and the more recent operas of Berg and Gian-Carlo Menotti.

Symphony Orchestras

America is considered to be a country of quality symphony orchestras. Among the symphony orchestras of worldwide reputation are the New York, Philadelphia, Boston, Cleveland, and Chicago orchestras. They are compared favorably with such leading European orchestras as the Vienna and Berlin philharmonics and the Amsterdam Concertgebouw. Even the orchestras from the smaller American cities are regarded well in comparison with their European counterparts. Annual attendance in America at symphony concerts was in excess of 23 million for the 1978–1979 season.

There is generally an economic plight for serious musicians. Most musicians in orchestras do not earn their main source of income from orchestra work. Only the major orchestra players are engaged on a full-time basis for so many weeks a year, with such employment furnishing their major income. Most symphony orchestras have seasons that are less than 30 weeks.

However, during the 1979–1980 season, year-round contracts were offered by the Philadelphia, Boston, New York, Chicago,

Cleveland, Houston, Cincinnati, Los Angeles, Pittsburgh, Minnesota, San Francisco, National (Washington, D.C.), Detroit, St. Louis, and Dallas orchestras: an increase of six over the 1973–1974 season. For example, the Chicago Symphony had 339 concerts by full orchestra and ensembles composed of orchestra personnel during the 1979–1980 season. In the early 1960s, Chicago had a 41 week season, with a minimum weekly salary of $200. By the 1979–1980 season, the season had increased to a full 52 weeks, with musicians receiving a minimum weekly salary of $550 and seven weeks of paid vacation.

In the more than 1,500 orchestras in the United States and Canada in 1980, most of the players were professionally trained, but relatively few were full-time professionals. Of these orchestras, approximately 392 are college and university orchestras; some 906 are community and youth orchestras with operating budgets under $70,000; 83 are urban orchestras with budgets between $70,000 and $150,000; 111 are metropolitan orchestras with budgets between $150,000 and $600,000; 36 are regional orchestras with budgets between $600,000 and $2.25 million; and 35 are major orchestras with budgets as high as $16 million in 1980. An area which experienced phenomenal growth during the 1970s was the chamber orchestra (15 to 30 musicians), numbering 159 in 1980, with operating budgets ranging from $0 to $3 million.

A classification and description of orchestras as presented by the American Symphony Orchestra League are in Appendix 1.

Opera Groups

In the 1978–1979 season, there were 966 opera-producing groups. Of these groups, 451 were within the music departments of universities and 551 were opera companies. The 551 companies included 95 major professional companies with budgets over $100,000. In 1978–1979, these 95 major professional companies spent a total of $111.5 million. Fifteen of these companies expended more than $1 million each, and an additional 15 spent over $500,000 apiece.

Together, the above opera companies gave approximately 8,500 performances during the 1978–1979 season (of which 64 were world premieres) to audiences totaling almost 10 million.

The New York Metropolitan Opera Company expended $500,000 in 1979 for a series of eight public park performances. In the same period, it received subsidies of $925,000 from New York State funds. Its financial report for the preceding year showed that it was one of the relatively few opera production companies whose ticket sales brought in 50 percent or more of their operating costs. Only 11 companies had ticket sales of 50 percent or more of their operating budgets.

Deficits of Orchestras and Opera Groups

Most performing arts organizations, including symphony orchestras and opera companies, operate at a deficit and depend on grants and contributions to survive. For the 32 largest American symphony orchestras, between 1970 and 1980 concert attendance rose 56 percent, from approximately 9 million to more than 14 million. However, concert production expenses rose 215 percent.

For the 35 major orchestras in the United States and Canada, their earned income in the 1979–1980 season amounted to approximately 59 percent of their total expenses. Such earned income, for which services were required, included ticket sales and fees, tax-supported and foundation grants, radio, television, and recording income. Of their total gross expenses of some $199 million, about $77 million (or some 39 percent), was raised from sources other than earned income. Of this, almost $12.1 million came from tax-supported grants from city, county, state, and national sources. Maintenance fund campaigns and other fund-raising projects raised $45.1 million and income from endowments and investments was $19.8 million.

Broadcasting and recording receipts in the 1979–1980 season brought 24 American major orchestras and three Canadian major orchestras income of $7.8 million. It should be noted that of the gross expenses of $199 million of these major orchestras, the artistic personnel expenses, including the regular salaries of musicians and the fees paid to guest conductors and artists, totaled $107.1 million.

Government's Interest

Composer Aaron Copland has stated that "Music as everybody knows has always been the last of the arts to flower in any country. In its primitive or folk form, there is nothing more natural to man, but in its cultivated form it seems to need more coddling than any of its sister arts."

Many countries in the Western world, including Great Britain, France, Germany, Italy, Sweden, and Canada, directly subsidize serious music. This has not been true of the United States government until fairly recently.

The United States government's concern for the performing arts was indicated by the enactment on September 29, 1965, of a federal statute establishing a National Foundation of the Arts and the Humanities. Its purpose is to develop and promote a national policy for the arts and humanities.

The statute marks a significant departure from the prior policy of depending almost entirely on private philanthropy and state activities, although some indirect assistance from the federal government was extended through income tax benefits to private individuals and firms for their contributions in support of the arts.

Government Endowments

Under the statute, the foundation has two major branches, called endowments: a National Endowment for the Arts and a National Endowment for the Humanities. Each endowment is given guidance and advice by Councils of Private Citizens, appointed by the President. For the Arts Endowment, the advisory body is the National Council on the Arts, established by statute and composed of 26 private citizens plus its chairman. The council chairman serves as the chief executive officer of the endowment. Coordination between the two endowments is provided through a Federal Council on the Arts and the Humanities.

The general guidelines for the activities to be supported by the National Endowment for the Arts are broad in scope and include the following:

1 Productions which have substantial artistic and cultural significance, giving emphasis to American creativity and the maintenance and encouragement of professional excellence.
2 Productions meeting professional standards or standards of authenticity, irrespective of origin, which are of significant merit and which, without such assistance, would otherwise be unavailable to our citizens in many areas of the country.
3 Projects that will encourage and assist artists and enable them to achieve standards of professional excellence.
4 Workshops that will encourage and develop the appreciation and enjoyment of the arts by our citizens.
5 Other relevant projects, including surveys, research, and planning in the arts.

For the purpose of the Arts Endowment, the definition of "arts" is comprehensive and includes the following:

Music (instrumental and vocal), dance, drama, folk art, creative writing, architecture and allied fields, painting, sculpture, photography, graphic and craft arts, industrial design, costume and fashion design, motion pictures, television, radio, tape and sound recording, and the arts related to the presentation, performance, execution, and exhibition of such major art forms.

Appropriations by Congress to the Arts Endowment are made in the following categories:

1 Program Funds: This is the source of most direct grants to organizations and individuals. The grants must be matched dollar for dollar by private funds.

2 Treasury Fund: This money is used to match private donations dollar for dollar. Grantees must then match the combined total of the donors' pledge and the Treasury Fund disbursement.

3 Challenge Grants: These funds are awarded for projects that contribute to the long-term financial stability of grantee organizations. Each grant must be matched on a three-to-one basis.

The Arts Endowment appropriations have generally escalated over the years. For its first fiscal year, 1966, $2.5 million was appropriated. By fiscal year 1981 the appropriation had risen to $158.5 million.

In the fiscal year 1980, the funds obligated for music awards constituted $13,572,300 plus challenge grants of $11,880,000. In the same period there were additional funds obligated for opera–musical theater in the sum of $5,597,000, plus challenge grants of $3,700,000.

Music grants cover aid to orchestras, opera companies, jazz organizations, choruses, individuals, and other musical activities. There are grants to assist services to the art of music and to aid new music performances. In the case of orchestras, generally the grants for a future fiscal year do not exceed 5 percent of an organization's total income for the previous fiscal year. For the fiscal year 1981, orchestras that employed professional musicians on a full-time basis for at least 26 weeks a year received grants ranging between $45,000 and $315,000.

The Arts Endowment initiated a Music Recording Program in fiscal year 1981. It offers assistance to nonprofit organizations for the recording and distribution of American music.

A new area of endowment grants for the 1980s may be the funding of nonprofit companies to record, tape, film, or videotape outstanding works by American composers of classical, jazz, and folk music.

Employment Outlook

The prospects for employment of musicians and singers are indicated in a 1980–1981 report by the U.S. Department of Labor on the employment outlook for the performing arts occupation. The sections relating to musicians and singers are included in Appendix 2. For musicians and singers the report states in part: "Employment . . . is expected to grow faster than the average through the 1980s, but competition for jobs will be keen."

Union Scale

The difficult, intermittent, and seasonal employment situation of symphony orchestra musicians, the supply of which is generally larger than the demand for their services, has been recognized by the American Federation of Musicians (AFM) in its agreement with phonograph record companies.

The following table compares the American Federation of Musicians standards for symphonic and popular music for 1981:

	SYMPHONIC	POPULAR
Minimum session	3 or 4 hr	3 hr
Permissible recording at session	45 min. (3 hr) 60 min. (4 hr)	15 min. (3 hr)
Pay scale per session *	$155.62 (3 hr) $207.49 (4 hr)	$146.81 (3 hr)
Overtime pay per ½ hr	$38.90	$48.93

There is a minimum-call basic session of 3 hours for both symphonic and popular recordings. However, in a 3-hour session a record company can complete 45 minutes of recorded symphonic music, in contrast to only 15 minutes of popular album music. In 1981, the musicians' pay scale of $155.62 for a symphonic session is 6 percent higher than the $146.81 payable for a popular music session. The ½ hour overtime rate of $38.90 for symphony orchestra musicians is some 20 percent lower than the $48.93 for popular music musicians.

In reality the 6 percent difference in basic session pay is on the low side, in terms of productivity as measured by the greater amount of finished music that can result from the symphonic music session.

The American Federation of Television and Radio Artists (AFTRA), which represents singers who make phonograph recordings, also makes concessions with respect to serious music. In its agreement with phonograph record companies, the union predicates hourly pay on an average of up to 5 minutes of finished recorded music for each hour of a serious music session, whereas for popular music an hour's pay is due for each 3½ minutes of

---

* At this writing, a new agreement between the AFM and the recording industry was being negotiated. It has been reported that under a new agreement the pay scales for both symphonic and popular music sessions are likely to include increases of 15 percent over a 2 year period, with 8 percent in the first year and 7 percent in the second year.

finished music. For finished recorded music in excess of these limits, a singer receives ¼ hour's pay for each additional 1¼ minutes of classical music or part thereof. For popular music, an additional 50 percent of the 3½ minute rate, applicable to singles only, is paid for each 60 seconds or portion thereof over three and one-half minutes. For recordings of popular music, other than singles, e.g., LPs, finished music over 3½ minutes, but not in excess of 7 minutes, is treated as requiring an additional hour's pay.

A distinction is also made as to the pay scale for a coach rehearsal of singing groups of 25 or more. For serious music recordings, there may be a coach rehearsal with a minimum call of 2 hours within 48 hours of the recording session. The scale pay is $7.75 per hour per singer, which is approximately 50 percent of the regular recording pay. For popular music, rehearsal pay is the same as regular pay.

Group singer scale rates for serious music per hour or per side, whichever is higher, under the agreement with the American Federation of Television and Radio Artists as of April 1, 1981 were:

NUMBER IN GROUP	RATE
3 to 8	$39.75
9 to 16	$32.00
17 to 24	$28.81
25 or more	$53.50 for a 3 hour minimum call, for up to 20 minutes of recorded music

Union scale payments for musicians alone have aggregated some $50,000 for an average symphonic long-playing record. This is based on a scale of approximately $150 per session for a session of 3 hours. French symphony musicians receive about 40 percent; English symphony musicians approximately 60 percent; and German symphony musicians about 70 percent of that amount for a similar 3 hour session. In view of the difference in costs, it can be seen why more new symphony recordings are made in Europe than in the United States.

Despite the disparity in costs, companies with principal offices abroad, such as Deutsche Grammaphon and London Records, are making some symphonic recordings in the United States. Deutsche Grammaphon has a recording agreement with the Boston Symphony Orchestra, and London Records has agreements with the Chicago Symphony and the Los Angeles Philharmonic orchestras. They can justify their expenditures on the sales appeal in Europe of new serious works in their repertoire.

It has been stated that the Philadelphia Orchestra is "without question, the best-selling orchestra of all time." In the period since 1917, when it recorded two of Brahms' Hungarian dances conducted by Leopold Stokowski for the old Victor Talking Machine Co., the Philadelphia Orchestra has recorded thousands of records, including, according to one estimate, more than 800 under the baton of Eugene Ormandy. It has three gold records awarded for sales over $1 million, for Handel's "Messiah," "The Lord's Prayer," and "The Glorious Sound of Christmas."

Amateur Instruments and Players

An essential element in the review of music in America is the availability of musical instruments in the hands of amateur musicians from whose ranks professional musicians are drawn. In 1980, the American Music Conference Review of the music industry indicated that about 50 million Americans say they can play an instrument, and nearly three-fourths of this group play regularly. The report estimated that over one-half of all American households has at least one amateur musician. In 1979, retail sales of musical instruments, accessories, printed music, and sound reinforcement equipment sold through music stores are estimated to have reached $2,353,609,000.

A more detailed review of data published by the American Music Conference is shown in the following table:

What The Amateurs Are Playing

	1978-1979 [1]				1969-1970 [1]			
INSTRUMENT	Number of Amateurs [2]	% Male	% Female	Median Age	Number of Amateurs	% Male	% Female	Median Age
Piano	18,188,000	21	79	28	14,800,000	23	77	27
Guitar [3]	15,140,000	65	35	23	7,000,000	70	30	21
Organ	6,196,000	29	71	31	4,700,000	32	68	37
Clarinet [4]	2,948,000	31	69	19	2,600,000	45	55	16
Drums [4]	2,748,000	94	6	19	1,900,000	86	14	17
Flute [4]	2,548,000	17	83	19	630,000	38	62	14
Trumpet	2,299,000	86	14	19	2,200,000	88	12	15
Violin	1,799,000	32	68	27	1,250,000	45	55	19
Harmonica [5]	1,549,000	86	14	25	750,000	90	10	44
Saxophone	1,549,000	82	18	22	not included this year			
Accordion	not included this year				1,400,000	44	56	28

1. These figures represent national projections based on the results of a 1978 survey of 1,521 U.S. households by The Gallup Organization. The figures should be read as numbers of Americans (between the ages of 5 and 75) who say they play these instruments—and not an indication of instrument ownership. 1969-1970 figures are projections from a survey of 1,520 families by The National Opinion Research Center.
2. Half of all amateur musicians play more than one instrument.
3. Includes acoustic and electric guitars.
4. Median age for active players in these three categories is: clarinet—14; drums—16; and flute—18.
5. This number reflects those who consider themselves experts on harmonica. Since several million harmonicas are sold annually, the number of players is probably much higher.

Recording Industry Trust Funds

For many years, the producers of phonograph records, electrical transcriptions, and television film have been contributing to the Recording Industries' Music Performance Trust Funds pursuant to agreements negotiated with the American Federation of Musicians. Most of the contributions have been made by the phonograph record industry on the basis of percentages of the suggested retail list price of records sold.

Payments to the Trust Funds have grown in recent years, and for the 12-month period ending April 30, 1981, they totaled $18,719,673. They are expended for free concerts in the United States and Canada to encourage work by musicians at union scale and to foster the educational and cultural life of the nations. The concerts are given in parks, schools, hospitals, convalescent homes, prisons, museums, libraries, and other places. The administration of the Trust Funds involves the approval and presentation of approximately 75,000 live music performances. As a result of its operation, about 65,000 checks are issued each year to individual musicians. Programs are frequently cosponsored by state arts councils, municipalities, museums, banks, and other companies.

The following is a summary of allocations made by the trustees of the Trust Funds for services of performing musicians in each of the fiscal years 1950–1981:

Fiscal year	Amounts allocated
1950	$ 900,000
1951	1,400,000
1952	1,700,000
1953	1,950,000
1954	2,200,000
1955	2,300,000
1956	2,800,000
1957	3,900,000
1958	4,850,000
1959	6,325,000
1960	5,650,000
1961	6,150,000
1962	5,820,000
1963	5,040,000
1964	5,855,000
1965	5,410,000
1966	5,235,000
1967	5,210,000
1968	5,650,000
1969	6,935,000
1970	7,370,000
1971	7,255,000
1972	8,085,000

Fiscal year	Amounts allocated
1973	9,000,000
1974	8,700,000
1975	8,982,306
1976	9,430,340
1977	10,700,272
1978	12,338,522
1979	16,029,653
1980	17,621,557
1981	18,492,347
Total	$219,284,997

Pursuant to the agreement between the American Federation of Musicians and the recording industry, half of the contributions of the phonograph record industry go into a special fund for distribution to the musicians who participated in creating the new recordings. The balance referred to in the above summary of allocations is used for free concerts.

2

Organizations and

Representatives

THE field of serious music includes a number of important unions and other organizations, some of which have been previously mentioned.

The American Federation of Musicians (AFM) takes jurisdiction over musicians in symphony, opera, and ballet orchestras.

Solo operatic singers, solo concert artists (both instrumentalists and singers), and choral singers in the operatic and concert fields are members of the American Guild of Musical Artists (AGMA).

Singers engaged in light opera and musical comedy are members of Actors' Equity Association (AEA).

Vocal performers who sing for phonograph records are under the aegis of the American Federation of Television and Radio Artists (AFTRA), irrespective of their membership in other unions. Similarly, instrumentalists who record for phonograph records, whether or not they are members of other unions, belong to the American Federation of Musicians.

All the above unions except the AFM are branches of the Associated Actors and Artistes of America (AFL-CIO).

An organization of serious music composers is the American Composers Alliance, incorporated in 1938, which is a publisher-affiliate of Broadcast Music, Inc. (BMI), a performing rights organization. Another organization of serious music composers is the American Music Center, Inc., which acts as an information center and as a loan library for its members' works. Both organizations are described more fully below.

The American Guild of Authors and Composers (AGAC) is open to both popular and serious music writers. It has a present membership of about 3,500 writers. AGAC has promulgated a standard form of contract to be used by its writers when entering into agreements with music publishers. Because of the special problems of serious music writers, the guild has been studying the advisability of a different form of contract for these composers.

The guild provides a service for its members through which it watches over copyrights; it notifies members when renewal applications should be filed and gives them the option to file the application or to use the guild's services for such purpose. All AGAC members permit the guild, for a service fee of 5 percent, to collect and audit the royalties payable to AGAC members by publishers.

The guild has an administrative publisher service for its writers who also publish their own material. This service includes registration of copyrights at the U.S. Copyright Office; filing notices of use; recording of any assignments; clearing the songs at the appropriate performing rights society (see following section) and with The Harry Fox Agency, Inc.; collecting performance royalties from a performing rights society and mechanical royalties from The Harry Fox Agency; collecting sheet music income; and accounting to the publisher and writers. AGAC will not engage in any exploitation or promotion of a catalog, nor negotiate print or foreign rights. For its services the guild charges 7.5 percent of the gross income, except for 2 percent of domestic small performance royalties, against a minimum semi-annual charge that depends on the size of the catalog. There is also a one-time-only setup charge of $2.00 per song. The writer in AGAC is not charged the 5 percent royalty collection fee on statements rendered to him or her under this administrative service plan.

The organization of the standard music publishers is the Music Publishers' Association of the United States (MPA), to which most of the important publishers belong. A list of the leading music publishers prepared as a service by MPA is in Appendix 3.

Performing Rights Societies

There are three performing rights organizations in America, the American Society of Composers, Authors and Publishers (ASCAP), Broadcast Music, Inc. (BMI), and SESAC, Inc. ASCAP is a membership organization of over 20,000 composers and 7,700 publishers. It was founded in 1914 and shares revenue equally between writers and publishers.

BMI, a competitor of ASCAP, represents about 39,000 writers and approximately 22,000 publishers. BMI is owned by over 300 broadcasting stations. It was established by broadcasters in 1940 to increase the broadcasting industry's bargaining power with ASCAP. Except for operating expenses and a reserve, all BMI's collections are paid to its affiliated publishers and writers, with no dividends to the owners of BMI.

SESAC is a private performing rights licensing organization that has been owned by the Heinecke family for over 30 years. SESAC reports an affiliation with about 1,000 writers and over 750 publishers, whose catalogs contain some 150,000 compositions. It is generally accepted that SESAC's position is relatively minor in comparison with that of ASCAP or BMI.

Other Organizations

The American Symphony Orchestra League, founded in 1942, is a nonprofit, membership, service and research organization in which voting memberships are held by major, regional, metropolitan, urban, community, college, and youth symphony orchestras. About two-thirds of the symphony orchestras in the United States are represented within the membership. Nonvoting individual memberships are held by symphony orchestra boards and symphony women's associations, educational organizations, music business firms, and libraries.

The National Music Council, founded as a nonprofit membership corporation in 1940 and chartered by the U.S. Congress in 1957, is comprised of some 60 member musical associations of national scope. These represent an aggregate individual membership of more than 1,500,000.

It was organized, and provides a forum, for the discussion of United States' national musical affairs, and it acts to enhance the importance of music in the national life and culture. As a clearinghouse for the opinions and decisions of, and information concerning, its member organizations, it also coordinates their efforts. In the *National Music Council Bulletin,* issued 3 times a year, it publishes news about its member organizations, accounts of governmental activities in the field of music, digests of proposed congressional legislation regarding music, lists of national and international musical competitions and contests, and articles on music in industry.

The National Music Council is the sole musical society among the national groups represented on the U.S. Commission for UNESCO. A list of the organizations that belong to the National Music Council is included in Appendix 4.

The Central Opera Service is sponsored by the Metropolitan

Opera National Council, with offices at Lincoln Center in New York City. It is primarily a cooperative information service that supplies information or sources thereof for such areas as:

Repertory: Musical requirements and
                            suggestions for standard,
                            modern, and rarely
                            performed operas
Translations: Those available, where
                            performed, and rights
Performances: When, where, and by whom
Musical materials: Availability of scores,
                            parts, and orchestrations;
                            publishers
Scenery, costumes,   Rental, sale, or exchange
props: opportunities; new
                            production devices
Publicity: Public relations methods
                            and suggestions for
                            fund raising

A list of its publications is in Appendix 5.

Managers and Agents

Performing artists in the field of serious music usually obtain employment through managers, who are sometimes referred to as "booking agents." Included in this field are large firms such as Columbia Artists Management, Inc.; Hurok Attractions, Inc.; Shaw Concerts, Inc.; and the William Morris Agency, Inc.; as well as a considerable number of individual managers with more limited facilities.

The largest of these firms is Columbia Artists Management, Inc. It has some 110 employees in New York, 10 in Los Angeles, and 85 to 90 on the road who work in its community concert program. Its roster includes almost 300 solo artists, some of whom are Leontyne Price, Mstislav Rostropovich, and Andre Watts. It represents almost 100 groups, including most of the important symphony orchestras in the world, the Bolshoi Ballet, the Martha Graham Dance Company, the Black Watch, The Chamber Music Society of Lincoln Center, as well as many of the bus and truck companies of Broadway's outstanding hits. Its clients include 70 orchestra conductors, among whom are Eugene Ormandy, James Levine, and Herbert von Karajan. According to the president of Columbia Artists, its function is primarily to coordinate the overall management of the artist's career rather than to book for particular engagements.

Another large management organization is Shaw Concerts, Inc., which manages over 75 artists and attractions, including the Royal Winnipeg Ballet, the Dallas, Toronto, and Milwaukee Symphonies, and artists such as Vladimir Horowitz and Janet Baker.

As previously noted, artists in the fields of opera, concert, recital, and oratorio, as well as dance and ballet, are represented by the American Guild of Musical Artists (AGMA). By an agreement between managers and artists, the union regulates managers' relationships with its members.

A list of firms and people who as concert managers have entered into an agreement with AGMA is in Appendix 6. The term for any management contract, including renewal and option obligations, cannot exceed 4 years, and there are minimum terms under which an artist can be made available for engagements. The artist has the right to terminate the agreement with a manager if specified personnel leave the manager's staff.

The standard form of artist management contract required by AGMA for its members is in Appendix 7. This form provides that maximum fees of managers range from 10 percent of gross receipts for operatic and ballet engagements to 20 percent of gross receipts for regular concert engagements. A maximum fee of 15 percent of gross receipts is applicable to civic, community, and similarly organized concert engagements.

AGMA does not regulate its members in their dealings with personal representatives who are not also managers. Such people, who handle accounting, investments, and other career guidance matters, do not necessarily duplicate the role of managers whose functions center on the negotiation of employment agreements and related activities, such as collection of payments.

When an AGMA member deals with a major institutional employer, such as the Metropolitan Opera Company, the basic terms are laid out by the union and the employer in a collectively bargained agreement covering all union members. In the Fall of 1979, AGMA announced that for the first time in its history it had achieved national negotiations for a repertory opera company basic agreement. Negotiations were aided by federal mediation and were conducted with a consortium of major regional opera employers. A three-year agreement resulted which provides for soloist performance rates of $237 as of August 1, 1980, and $256 as of August 1, 1981. Provision is made for supporting role payments, as of the respective dates, of $162 and $175, and for a solo bit role payments of $70 and $75.

The AGMA standard artist's form of contract for employment is in Appendix 8. This standard agreement is subject to modifications contained in basic agreements between AGMA and a particular employer.

Occasionally a concert artist, although an AGMA member, will find it necessary to join other unions. For example, vocal recording artists are governed by the American Federation of Television and Radio Artists. When duplicate union membership is required among the performing unions that are branches of the Associated Actors and Artistes of America (AFL-CIO), arrangements are made for the first union joined ("parent" union) to receive its full initiation fee and dues and for the second union to accept less than its usual fees and dues.

3

Recording Industry Aspects

LOVERS of serious music are wooed by various record companies, some of which are well known for the quality of their classical recordings. Many serious music recordings, both excellent and of lesser quality, originate in Europe. This is due to the traditional European interest in such music, and also because Europe's lower musician wage scales make it more economically feasible to record large symphony orchestras and choral and operatic groups there.

Sale of Recordings

Serious music accounted for about 4 percent of America's $3.7 billion record and tape sales at retailer's list price in 1979. The following, based on a 1979 study by the National Association of Recording Merchandisers, Inc., indicates the shares of various music categories in total United States record sales.

TYPE OF PRODUCT	% OF DOLLAR VOLUME
Rock Pop	48.7
Country	11.9
Disco	9.2
Soul	10.2
Middle of the Road	5.1
Jazz	4.1
Classical	4.1
Children's	5.3
Comedy	1.4

Various American and European record labels share in the serious music sales in the United States. Lists of serious music labels and LPs are found in the *Schwann Record and Tape Guide-1*. It is issued on an updated monthly basis, and covers about 45,000 available recordings that are primarily in the serious category. Analysis of a 1980 edition shows that Current Popular and Jazz listings were limited to about 50 pages compared with the 184 pages on serious recordings listed by composer, with another two pages for an opera and ballet title cross-index. The *Schwann Record and Tape Guide-1* covers 600 record labels, 250 tape labels, and 70 in the quadrophonic category. Its basic listing is supplemented by price lists. Schwann also releases on a three-year basis a compilation of the recordings of particular groups or artists such as orchestras, trios, quartets, conductors, instrumental soloists, choral groups, operatic groups, and vocalists. The most recent issue in 1979 included 25,000 entries in the field of classical recordings. Of the 1979 new releases of serious music, the classical composer most recorded was Beethoven, followed by Mozart and Bach. Conductors with the most new listings were Marriner, Karajan, and Dorati.

Famous serious music labels from Europe include Deutsche Grammophon and Telefunken from Germany, L'Oiseau-Lyre from France, Cetra from Italy, and Angel and London from England. Most important of the American labels releasing classical records are Columbia, RCA, and Capitol.

Small serious music labels in this country continue to hold their own. These include companies that encourage unknown young artists and composers on labels such as Musical Heritage Society, Connoisseur Society, and Composers Recordings, Inc. Higher-priced audiophile recordings are issued by companies such as Desmar Delos and Telarc, which is the most commercially successful of the labels releasing custom-made digital disks. An economic study of the recording industry, prepared in 1980 for the Recording Industry Association of America, Inc., found that 94 percent of classical LPs do not break even. The comparable figure for pop LPs is 84 percent.

Price Categories

Higher-priced serious music recordings usually have suggested list prices averaging approximately $8.98 to $9.98 for single stereophonic LPs. Budget-line suggested list prices vary widely from about $5.98 and up. RCA affixes its Red Seal label to its higher-priced recordings and uses Gold Seal for budget releases. Capitol issues higher-priced recordings on the Angel label and its budget recordings on the Seraphim label; CBS Masterworks represents the higher-priced category and Odyssey the budget line of CBS. Deutsche Grammophon uses the Privilege label for its lower-priced works.

Budget lines, which are released by both large and small

companies, do not necessarily signify lower quality. Frequently they are top-grade recordings of older vintage with established artists and conductors. They also include new recordings. Some budget lines, such as Nonesuch and Turnabout, specialize in esoteric recordings, or in recordings of music of a particular period.

It is possible to find the identical artists and conductors being featured in both price categories at the same time. In fact, the discriminating record buyer who is not seeking the most recent recordings may find that he or she can build an excellent record library on the lower-priced recordings.

Price discounting is as rampant in serious music recordings as it is in other types of recordings. The *New York Times* Sunday edition frequently runs advertisements of cut-price sales. Sam Goody, Inc., King Karol, and J & R Music World are stores that advertise such sales from time to time.

Record Clubs

The importance of record clubs has diminished somewhat over the past decade. Both of the major remaining mail-order record clubs, RCA Victor Record Club and Columbia House, handle classical records. Both clubs make their offerings by means of magazine inserts published 18 to 20 times yearly. Members may elect to receive six records for 1 cent if they agree to purchase four more records at regular club prices over the next three years in the case of RCA Victor, or thirteen records for 1 cent and nine more at regular club prices in the next three years as a member of the Columbia House.

The clubs handle the records of several record labels, including those of their namesake record company. These clubs ordinarily take master tapes from their licensing record companies and then press records based on the tapes. They pay royalties to the licensing record company and mechanical copyright license fees to the copyright proprietor. They make payments on sales due to the Music Performance Trust Fund and the Special Fund. The licensing record company pays any artist royalties that become due.

Recordings of new classical albums by leading record companies have been encouraged by the additional sales anticipated through their record club affiliations.

Trade Reviews

New serious music recordings are reviewed in *Billboard* and in *Record World,* record and music publishing weekly trade papers. *Variety* and *Cash Box,* which review popular music recordings weekly, do not usually contain serious music reviews.

Billboard, in its weekly "Album Reviews," rates recordings as "Top Album Picks." These constitute a product predicted for the top half of the "Top LPs & Tape" chart, in the opinion of the review panel. There is a category of classical among the "Top Album Picks." There is also a category of "Billboard's Recommended LPs," which are predicted to land in the second half of the "Top LPs & Tape" chart. Among recommended LPs is a classical subgroup. *Billboard* prints a monthly chart listing "Best Selling Classical LPs" in retail outlets. A typical chart issued by *Billboard* is reproduced on pages 38 and 39.

Record World has a "Classical" section that contains a weekly "Classical Retail Report" showing, among other things, "Best Sellers of the Week" and the "Classic of the Week."

Consumer Publication Reviews

Reviews of classical albums are carried in various magazines, including *High Fidelity, Stereo Review,* and *American Record Guide;* in the Sunday edition of the *New York Times;* and other key daily newspapers. There are also reviews by FM radio station magazines such as *Dial* and *Ovation.*

Recording Artists

The factor of prestige may loom large in negotiations by record companies for the services of renowned serious music artists and orchestras. Their recordings draw public attention to the company, and may also attract interest in other albums in the record company's catalog.

Another element in negotiations is the long active life of many serious music recordings; this is in contrast to the short life of most popular music LPs. However, serious music LP sales may be considerably slower than the sales of a popular music album, so that it may take much longer to recoup the recording company's investment.

Serious music has charms for the listening public in many countries of the world, whereas the sales of a popular album may be restricted to only a few countries. An Arturo Toscanini-conducted symphony orchestra LP will sell for years and has a wide international market. In its calculations, the record company may also be influenced by the fact that no mechanical license royalties will be payable for public domain music contained in an album and that copyrighted serious music can be customarily licensed at rates lower than those applicable to popular music.

A recording contract with a serious music artist is similar in many respects to the contract entered into with a popular music artist. The contract will provide that the artist's services are exclusive to the record company for all phonograph record recordings. The term of the agreement will be at least 1 year, and there are likely to be a number of 1-year extension options in favor of the record company. These options are exercisable by a notice in writing to the artist before the expiration of the current 1-year term.

The popular artist and the serious music artist are treated differently in a number of respects. The serious music artist is usually only an album seller, and there is little or no expectation that he will have sales of other types of records. The minimum number of recordings set forth in the agreement with a serious music artist will be in terms of the number of LPs rather than, as in the case of the popular artist, the number of single sides to be recorded.

Another difference may relate to the recoupability of the recording costs of the album from the artist's royalties. Such costs are usually recoupable from the artist's royalties in the case of a popular artist. If the serious music artist is a solo pianist performer, such as Artur Rubinstein or Claudio Arrau, there are no recording costs of consequence other than studio costs. A similar observation might apply to instrumentalists or vocalists who may use only a piano accompaniment.

However, the musician costs alone (without studio charges) of recording the average album by a symphony orchestra come to about $50,000. Whether recording costs of serious music recordings are recoupable from the artist royalties is the subject of negotiations in each instance. However, as compared with popular music recordings, it is more common to find that, except for the union scale paid to a featured artist, the record company has waived the right to recoup out of the artist royalties. This is more prevalent in the case of established performers and the better symphony orchestras that have devoted record audiences that assure the company of substantial sales.

Royalties payable to serious music artists, as in the case of popular music artists, tend to vary with the stature of the artist. Royalties to the serious music artist of 10 percent of suggested retail list price, less the price of packaging, for recordings of public domain music are not unusual. A provision is often made that the royalty rate for recordings of copyrighted music will be lower.

Here again the more favorable terms will be given to the artist or orchestra that has an extensive record following. As a part of the negotiations, the company and the artist will also discuss whether payments will be based on 90 percent (as is common for popular artists) or a higher percentage of sales and whether the royalty rate will be reduced for sales outside the United States.

Survey For Week Ending 1/23/82

(Published Once A Month)

Billboard ®

Best Selling

Classical LPs ™

This Week	Last Report	Weeks on Chart	TITLE, Artist, Label & Number
1	1	111	**PACHELBEL: Kanon** Paillard Chamber Orchestra, RCA FRL 1-5468
2	4	15	**THE UNKNOWN KURT WEILL** Teresa Stratas, Nonesuch Digital D 79019
3	2	37	**60th ANNIVERSARY GALA** Stern, Perlman, Zukerman, New York Philharmonic (Mehta), CBS Masterworks IM 36692
4	3	24	**LIVE FROM LINCOLN CENTER** Sutherland, Horne & Pavarotti, New York City Opera Orchestra (Bonynge), London Digital LDR 72009
5	9	28	**BEETHOVEN: Complete Symphonies** Berlin Philharmonic (Karajan), DG Bargain Box 2740-241
6	7	10	**PLACIDO DOMINGO GALA OPERATIC CONCERT** (Guilini), DG 2532009
7	16	10	**BEETHOVEN: VIOLIN CONCERTO IN D** (Perlman, Guilini), Angel DS-37471
8	19	6	**HOLST: THE PLANETS** (Karajan), DG Digital 2532019
9	17	10	**BOLLING: TOOT SUITE FOR TRUMPET & JAZZ PIANO** (Andre, Bolling), CBS SM 36731
10	12	89	**PAVAROTTI'S GREATEST HITS** London, PAV 2003/4
11	13	150	**ANNIE'S SONG: Galway** National Philharmonic Orchestra (Gerhardt), RCA ARL 1-3061
12	5	311	**JEAN-PIERRE RAMPAL & CLAUDE BOLLING: Suite for Flute & Jazz Piano** CBS Masterworks M 33233
13	6	115	**O SOLE MIO: Neapolitan Songs** Pavarotti, London OS 26560
14	14	24	**VIVALDI: Four Seasons** Karajan, DG 2530 296
15	15	6	**PAVAROTTI SINGS EARLY VERDI ARIAS** Pavarotti, CBS M37228
16	8	24	**MAHLER: Symphony No. 2** Solti, London Digital LDR 72006

17	10	15	**POPS ON BROADWAY** Boston Pops (Williams), Philips Digital 6302 124
18	28	6	**WAGNER: MUSIC FROM THE RING OF THE NIBELUNGEN** (Tennstedt), Angel DS 37808
19	11	10	**MENDELSSOHN: SYMPHONIES NOS. 3 & 4** (Marriner), Argo ZRG-926
20	NEW ENTRY		**BRAHMS: German Requiem** (Haitink), Vienna Philharmonic, Philips Digital 6769-055
21	18	15	**BAROQUE AND ON THE STREETS** Fred Hand, CBS Masterworks FM 36687
22	20	24	**BRAHMS: Symphony No. 4** Vienna Philharmonic (Kleiber) DG 2532-003
23	32	171	**HITS FROM LINCOLN CENTER: Pavarotti** London OS 26577
24	NEW ENTRY		**WAGNER: Ring** (Boulez), Philips Digital 6769-074
25	36	6	**HANDEL: Messiah** (Hogwood), L'Oiseau Lyre D 189 D3
26	21	49	**A DIFFERENT KIND OF BLUES: Perlman & Previn** Angel DS-37780
27	38	6	**BARTOK: CONCERTO FOR ORCHESTRA** (Solti), London Digital LDR 71036
28	29	24	**PACHELBEL: CANON: Galway** RCA AFL 1 4063
29	35	15	**HOLST: THE PLANETS** The Philharmonia and Ambrosian Singers (Rattle), Angel DS 37817
30	31	45	**PAVAROTTI'S GREATEST HITS, Vol. 2** London PAV 2006
31	NEW ENTRY		**MAHLER: Symphony No. 8** (Ozawa), Philips 6769-069
32	22	24	**ORFF: Carmina Burana** Atlanta Symphony (Shaw), Telarc 10056
33	23	10	**IT'S A BREEZE** (Ithzak Perlman & Andre Previn), Angel DS-37799
34	24	98	**SONG OF THE SEASHORE: James Galway** RCA ARL 1-3534
35	25	19	**MOZART: Complete Symphonies Vol. V** Academy of Ancient Music (Hogwood), L'Oiseau Lyre D171D4
36	26	63	**POPS IN SPACE** The Boston Pops (Williams), Philips 9500921
37	37	15	**PHASES OF THE MOON: Traditional Chinese Music** CBS Masterworks M 36705
38	27	58	**MOZART: Symphonies, Vol. IV** Academy Of Ancient Music (Hogwood), L'Oiseau Lyrie D170D3
39	30	10	**HANDEL: WATER MUSIC** (Hogwood), L'Oiseau Lyre DSLO-543
40	33	10	**DEL TREDICI: FINAL ALICE** (Hendricks, Solti), London Digital LDR-71018

4

Publishers and Composers

SERIOUS music performers base much of their repertoire on the standard works by composers such as Bach, Beethoven, Brahms, and Mozart. Much of this repertoire is in the public domain, and no performance fees or mechanical license fees can be collected for their performance or mechanical reproduction, but there is a steady and continuing interest in this music by students and performers. This is the foundation of the business of printing and selling editions of public domain serious music. Those engaged in this business know that they have no monopoly and that they may anticipate competition from other publishers.

Composers

A singularly qualified observer of the role of the symphony orchestra in relation to contemporary composers is Leonard Bernstein. A prime reason for his resigning as conductor of the New York Philharmonic Orchestra was to be able to devote time to composing works such as "Mass." He has stated in an interview in *ASCAP Today* that he "wanted to write music . . . to be involved in the lifestream of music, and that was not to be found in the orchestral hall . . . (that) basically, the symphony orchestra is still a vehicle for performing the great works of Mozart, Beethoven, Brahms, Strauss, Mahler and so on." By devoting more time and energy to composing, Bernstein has hoped to create a counteraction to what he calls "a bad moment for music," in that new music is not being fed sufficiently to the symphony orchestras in the same way that great music was fed to the symphony orchestras in the period "roughly from Mozart to Mahler."

The work of a creative composer has been described by Leonard Bernstein as "hard work," subject to "dry spells." The creative process, he said, is "a very mystic thing . . . this *Dybbuk* enterprise." He acknowledged that he throws away "at least ten times as much music as I save." His criterion for discarding early drafts is his recognition that the work was not "coming from a really deep place, spontaneously and profoundly" (or that it is) "imitative or trying to be something I'm not." He states: "To be perfectly honest, I collect fragments, bits, ideas, and many of them are apparently unrelated to one another; and then suddenly comes the magic moment when I find that idea A is related to idea P, skipping B, C, D, and so on in between and A and P suddenly go together, or F and X, or whatever it is."

Old and New Music

Bernstein's successor as conductor of the New York Philharmonic was Pierre Boulez. He has spoken of "works of the past as a permanent manifestation to explore and discover." As for new fields of music, Boulez cautioned against "fear of the unknown."

The composer Charles Wuorinen has noted that "the vast bulk of hostility to new music would pass if genuinely representative performances . . . were available to listeners who are now averse." However, Wuorinen has claimed that union rehearsal demands make it harder for a new work to compete with a well-known old standard and that, therefore, the performance of new music is rare.

A statistical view of the symphony orchestra as a "museum" is shown in studies made by BMI in association with the American Symphony Orchestra League. This study found that, within a relatively recent year, some 25,000 works of serious music were being performed. However, a full 7,592 were old masters by only ten composers: Bach, Beethoven, Berlioz, Brahms, Dvorak, Haydn, Mendelssohn, Mozart, Tchaikovsky, and Wagner. It is of historic interest to note that Wagner himself considered that he had to actively promote his own "contemporary" music, which was in competition with the established earlier masters.

With respect to recordings of serious music, contemporary composers must still compete with the recordings of well-rehearsed and familiar old standard works. Even the avant-garde successful synchronizer recordings have often relied on old master works such as the Bach music in "Switched-on Bach."

Music Publishers

There are a few established music publishers in the United States that specialize in serious music. These include Theodore Presser Co., G. Schirmer, Inc., Carl Fischer, Inc., Galaxy Music Corp.,

Boosey & Hawkes, Inc., C.F. Peters Corp., and Oxford University Press, Inc.

Other large publishers have substantial serious music educational departments. Among these are MCA Music, Chappell & Co., Inc., Warner Bros. Music, Belwin-Mills Publishing Corp., and Southern Music Publishing Co., Inc.

Publishers of serious music tend to be relatively more involved with printing operations than popular music publishers because the music is complex and the printed edition is important as educational material for students and for use by orchestras and individual performers.

All rights under copyright are available to publishers and writers of most twentieth-century serious music. In the United States, for music written before 1978, there is copyright protection for the original 28-year period of copyright, and there is a copyright renewal and extension period of an additional 47 years. Music composed in 1978 and thereafter is protected for the life of the author plus 50 years. Outside the United States, the duration of copyright is normally the author's lifetime plus 50 years.

The more important rights under copyright are those of mechanically reproducing, performing, and printing the music. These will be considered in greater detail later. A form of publishing contract for serious music is shown in Appendix 9. A special rider to adapt a popular song writer's contract form to apply to serious music has been prepared by AGAC and is in Appendix 10. For a discussion and a copy of the basic AGAC popular song writer's contract form, see *This Business of Music.**

Mechanical Rights

A composer will grant to a publisher the right to license the reproduction of the music by mechanical means, including tapes and records. In music trade parlance, the publisher grants a mechanical license to a record company.

In addition, the mechanical right is the basis for collecting synchronization fees. These are payable by the producers of motion pictures and television films for a license from the publisher to include copyrighted compositions in the soundtracks.

Nondramatic music, whether serious or popular, is subject to the so-called compulsory licensing provisions of Section 115 of the 1976 Copyright Act of the United States. Pursuant to the terms thereof, including the rate determination effective July 1, 1981, by the Copyright Royalty Tribunal formed under the act, when phonographic records of any nondramatic musical composition have

---

* Sidney Shemel and M. William Krasilovsky, rev. ed. (New York, 1979), pp. 527-539.

been distributed to the public with the authorization of the copyright owner, any other person may record and distribute phonorecords of the work upon giving certain notice and paying a specific royalty of 4 cents for each record made and distributed, or ¾ cents per minute or fraction thereof, whichever is larger.*

A person who intends to rely upon the compulsory license provision must serve a notice of such intention by registered or certified mail on the copyright owner before any records are distributed with service to take place before or within 30 days of making the record. If the files of the Copyright Office fail to identify the copyright owner and his or her address, then the notice requirements can be met by sending the notice to the Copyright Office together with a $6.00 fee.

In practice, users request and copyright owners grant mechanical licenses for serious music at the rate for each minute of playing time on a record. Thus, for an entire 40-minute album of serious music that is protected by copyright, the record company would pay a mechanical license fee of 30 cents at a rate of ¾ cent for each minute of playing time, although good faith negotiations between the record company and the publisher sometimes result in higher rates. For a comparable popular music album containing 10 songs, a mechanical license at the license rate of 4 cents per composition would result in an aggregate license fee of 40 cents, or 33⅓ percent higher than the 30 cent rate for the serious music LP. This difference in the cost of mechanical license fees is an important factor in warranting higher royalty rates to the serious music artist.

Ordinarily, record companies do not resort to the compulsory licensing provisions of the Copyright Act. A negotiated license will usually permit quarterly accountings and payments, instead of the monthly ones under oath called for by the 1976 statute, and will probably dispense with the requirement under the 1976 act for cumulative annual statements certified by a certified public accountant. Many serious music publishers are represented by The Harry Fox Agency, Inc. in New York City as their agent-trustee to administer mechanical licenses on their behalf.

Film Synchronization Right

The Harry Fox Agency frequently acts for the publisher in negotiating and issuing synchronization and performance licenses for theatrical and television motion pictures.

* The rates will increase on January 1, 1983, to 4.25 cents (or 0.8 cents per minute of playing time or fraction thereof, whichever is larger); on July 1, 1984, to 4.5 cents (or 0.85 cents per minute of playing time or fraction thereof, whichever is larger); and on January 1, 1986, to five cents (or 0.95 cents per minute of playing time or fraction thereof, whichever is larger).

The agency can be most helpful to producers of films in their obtaining proper licenses. It can and will supply a wealth of information about the owners and proper licensors of copyrighted music.

It is not unusual for serious music to be in the public domain in the United States but be under copyright elsewhere. The Harry Fox Agency represents many European publishers, one of whom may control the music for which film licenses are sought. A film producer will ordinarily apply for both a synchronization license and a United States performance license. He may rely on performance licenses granted to theaters outside the United States by local performing right organizations. He may also depend on the blanket licenses issued by such organizations to television stations in the United States and throughout most of the world. In the United States, the theaters, under a court antitrust decree, are not required to be licensed for ASCAP music. It may be assumed that the precedent also covers BMI music. For a further discussion of the functions of The Harry Fox Agency, see *This Business of Music.**

As in the case of popular music, the serious music composer under music industry standards will contract with the contracting ("original") publisher to receive 50 percent of the mechanical-license and synchronization-license fees collected by the original publisher. Foreign subpublishers frequently retain 50 percent of the mechanical-license and synchronization-license fees collected by them, remitting only the balance to the original publisher, and in such instances the composer can expect to be paid one-quarter of the collections by the foreign subpublisher.

ASCAP

ASCAP and BMI have recognized that serious music composers are a cultural asset and should receive special consideration over and above the number of logged performances of their works. Composer Virgil Thomson has said that both ASCAP and BMI "have found they need the intellectual support, the prestige, of the serious composer, and have now come round to collecting and distributing in quite impressive amounts performance fees for serious music." He has paid tribute on behalf of the serious composers "to the composers of light music that we get paid at all for our performing rights, since it is they who have always organized the society for exacting such payment and furnished the funds for fighting infringers in the courts."

Stanley Adams, a former President of ASCAP, has said that

* Sidney Shemel and M. William Krasilovsky. rev. ed. (New York. 1979). pp. 45. 96. 195–196. 220. 243. 282. 287.

ASCAP "has long recognized the importance of symphonic and concert works to the culture of the nation, and the Society's duty to encourage the creation of symphonic and concert works and to help ensure that the public will have continued access to them. In keeping with this objective, the Society adopted rules providing for additional credit for performances of serious works in symphony and concert halls."

Multiple Credits

In the past, ASCAP, in its distributions to serious music composers for the performances of their works in symphony and concert halls, allocated to them amounts equal approximately to 15 times the society's collections for those performances. Later, the multiple was reduced to 5 times.

Having undertaken an effective campaign of educating the users of serious works to obtain licenses to perform the compositions, the society noted that it had added many new licensees. The license fees paid by old and new licensees climbed to the point of a substantial increase in the distributions to writers of serious music. The society therefore has placed a present maximum limitation of twice the regular credits on added credit provisions that the society applies to performances of serious works in symphony and concert halls.

ASCAP also uses multiple credits in connection with loggings of performances of serious works of 4 minutes' or longer duration. The ASCAP Weighting Formula calls for multiple credits in relation to the minutes of actual performance. For example, for a 5-minute performance, the multiple is 2; for a 10-minute performance, 6; for a 20-minute performance, 20; a 40-minute performance has a multiple of 60; and a 60-minute performance a multiple of 100.

Appendix 11 contains extracts from the ASCAP Weighting Formula with respect to credit for performances of serious works.

Qualifying Works

ASCAP favors serious works in another respect. The weighting formula provides that for works which in their original form were composed for a choral, symphonic, or similar concert performance credits required to classify such a work as a "qualifying work" shall be reduced to 20 percent of the number of feature performances required for other musical compositions. Under the "qualifying work" concept applied in the ASCAP system of credits, a popular song with a history of over 20,000 feature performances, of which the most recent 5 years contributed an aggregate of at least 2,500 feature performances, is given special higher credits when used in nonfeature roles such as background, cue, bridge, or theme; not more than 750 feature performances are to be counted in any 1 of the 5 years to meet the 2,500 requirement. There is also a partial qualification for higher credits if a work that passes the 5-year test has accumulated 15,000 or 10,000 feature performance credits.

Although a qualifying work employed as a theme is accorded half a feature credit, an unqualified work in the same form is granted only one-tenth of a feature credit. Half a feature credit is given to any background use, regardless of duration, of a qualifying work, while an unqualified work requires a 3-minute use for 30 percent of a feature credit with reduction for lesser use. For example, a 20-second use of an unqualified work would earn only 6 percent of a feature credit. As noted previously, serious works will be regarded as qualifying works although they log only 20 percent of the number of feature performances required of other compositions.

Special Awards

Further special consideration for composers of serious music is given by ASCAP in certain other respects. In the distribution of monies collected for the performance of symphonic and concert works, ASCAP does not deduct any administrative expenses. This is unlike the treatment of popular music.

ASCAP has a Special Awards Panel that through its Popular-Production Panel makes special monetary awards to popular music composers and through its Standard Awards Panel to composers of symphonic and concert music. The panels are composed of people of standing who are not ASCAP members.

Applications for awards are filed by writers or by others on behalf of writers; the staff of ASCAP does not generally initiate applications. The Standard Awards Panel has stated as its goal "to provide encouragement and recognition to ASCAP members and to stimulate the composition and performance of contemporary music." Among the factors considered by the panel are a member's current productivity, prizes, honors, grants, fellowships, commissions, performances by contemporary music groups, and creative leadership. These factors are judged by two basic criteria, i.e., unique prestige value for which adequate compensation would not otherwise be received and substantial performances in media not surveyed by the society.

The aggregate sums awarded to both popular music and serious music composers, in excess of $1 million, are shared in approximately equal amounts by serious and popular music recipients. In 1980–1981, awards were made to John Cage, Philip Glass, and Ned Rorem.

A spokesman on behalf of the Standard Awards Panel has stated that the awards give "special recognition to talented new composers whose creative contributions are just beginning to be felt, as well as to outstanding established writers who have had a significant influence on our musical culture." Appendix 12 is an extract from the ASCAP Writers' Distribution Formula relating to special awards.

In its efforts to encourage the performance of contemporary serious works, ASCAP gives annual awards aggregating about $15,000 to various symphony orchestras. The selection is by a panel chosen by the American Symphony Orchestra League, and the awards are in recognition of the use of contemporary works.

Even the Articles of Association of ASCAP are designed to encourage the writers and publishers of serious music. They provide that the Board of Directors of ASCAP shall consist of 24 directors, 12 of whom shall be writer-members and 12 of whom shall be publisher-members. At all times, three of such writer-members shall be "standard" writer-members, and at all times, three of such publisher-members must be "standard" publishers.

BMI

BMI uses a multiple credit system in compensating the composers and publishers of serious music. Each *minute* of performance of a serious work receives a payment that is generally equal to or higher than the payment for a full popular song. This multiple credit structure is not, however, applicable to background usage or popularized versions of a serious work. In recognition of the fact that serious music is not as widely programmed as popular music, a special "concert universe" of stations is used for logging broadcast performances of such works. BMI has agreements with many concert composers by which they receive guaranteed annual payments. In addition to the special payment rate available for serious compositions licensed through BMI, the organization takes an active part in bringing publishers and composers together and keeping orchestras and other performing groups advised of contemporary works. Catalogs of the BMI concert repertoire are distributed to orchestras, colleges, and universities. Brochures containing both biographical and catalog information with respect to prominent concert composers are prepared and distributed. For over 29 years, BMI has presented annual cash awards to student composers. Five of the recipients of this coveted award subsequently received Pulitzer Prizes. These awards, aggregating

$15,000 annually, are available to students under the age of 26 who live in the Western Hemisphere. Award recipients are selected by a panel composed of distinguished composers, musicians and publishers. William Schuman, the former President of Lincoln Center and a Pulitzer Prize winner himself, serves as chairman of the panel.

Promotional Publications

BMI, from 1951 to 1969, compiled and published a pamphlet entitled "Concert Music USA." There were 15 revised editions, up to the issue entitled "1969 Concert Music USA." The publication surveyed in brief, and with emphasis on statistics of recent growth, the activities of symphony orchestras, classical recordings, concert music, broadcasting, opera groups, and music instruction.

Both BMI and ASCAP have separately issued a catalog of the serious music of their respective members or affiliates licensed through the performing rights organization.

Biographical profiles of its more prominent serious music composers are released from time to time by BMI. For years there was cooperation between BMI and the American Symphony Orchestra League on annual orchestra surveys.

It has been estimated that BMI spends about $1 million a year in the sphere of serious music, for writer and publisher distributions.

Other Performing Rights Aspects

It is customary for ASCAP and BMI publishers to negotiate directly the premiere concert performance of a serious music composition.

The ASCAP publishers arrange for an appropriate music score and parts rental fee. Performance rights licensing is handled by ASCAP. Under licenses issued by ASCAP to symphony orchestras and other nonbroadcasting users of serious music, ASCAP is entitled to restrict the first United States performance of a composition. In that event, ASCAP acts on the publisher's request. It appears that ASCAP's practice of restricting the first performance until cleared by its publishers enables its publishers to negotiate appropriate terms for score rentals and other elements of the concert. A form of the ASCAP symphony license applicable to community orchestras is included as Appendix 13. There are several ASCAP forms of a license for colleges and universities, namely, "one tier," "two tier," and "minimal user." Under the two-tier form, as set forth in Appendix 14, there is a fee per student based on full-time student enrollment (8 cents for 1981–1982), plus a fee for each major concert, which is defined in the form.

BMI publishers, in addition to renting the music score and parts, may, if they so desire, license the premiere performance directly. BMI normally licenses all other performances, as well as the premiere performance, in the event the publisher does not prefer to do so directly.

It has been noted that certain publishers, especially in the symphonic field, tend to increase the rental fees for scores and parts if a performance is intended to be broadcast. The user may argue that the greater fee for broadcast rights is difficult to justify since radio and television stations appear to be covered by the blanket licenses issued by BMI and ASCAP. The publisher may contend that a single broadcast can be equivalent, in respect to audience, to many concert hall uses and may diminish the opportunities for other rentals of parts. Publishers have also expressed concern about whether the sampling method of ASCAP or BMI for logging will catch the broadcast and result in actual credits when the broadcast is a nonnetwork performance. See a further discussion under the heading, "Rental Income" on page 51.

The Music Publishers' Association in collaboration with the American Symphony Orchestra League has prepared a brochure entitled "Hire of Materials for the Performance of Musical Compositions" to guide nonprofessional orchestral librarians in renting musical materials from publishers. The brochure includes a suggested standard order form to be used when ordering music on a rental basis that sets forth the information required by publishers in order to quote proper fees. A copy of the brochure is in Appendix 15.

Foreign performing rights societies, as a rule, give extra weight to performances of serious music. Through their arrangements with foreign societies, ASCAP and BMI are able to collect from abroad for American members or affiliates. The writers and publishers of American serious music thereby benefit from the favorable weighting accorded to serious music performances by the foreign societies.

Grand Rights

Serious music composers who create music for dramatic productions will be interested in the distinction between dramatic performance rights (frequently called "grand rights") and non-dramatic performance rights ("small rights"). Grand rights cover the dramatic renditions of operas, operettas, musical comedies, ballets, revues, sketches, and like productions, in whole or in part.

A separate composition that does not originate in an opera or other dramatic production may also involve a grand right if it is woven into, and carries forward, the plot of a broadcasting program and its accompanying action.

ASCAP obtains from its members only nondramatic small performance rights.

BMI acquires from its writer and publisher affiliates the right to license dramatic performances of selections from operas, operettas, and musical comedies. Not included is the right to perform more than one song or aria from an opera, operetta, or musical comedy, or more than 5 minutes from a ballet if such performance is accompanied by the dramatic action, costumes, or scenery of that opera, musical comedy, or ballet. The publishers and writers of a work may jointly, by written notice to BMI, exclude from BMI the right to license performances of more than 30 minutes of a work which is an opera, operetta, or musical comedy. Where there are restrictions on BMI's right to license, BMI's licensees must obtain special permission from copyright owners or their representatives. There is no restriction on the radio performance of an entire cast album, even if it exceeds 30 minutes, in the case where all the works in the album have been cleared by BMI, with no limitations by the publishers and writers in the BMI clearance. BMI licenses to broadcasters also permit the dramatization of a nondramatic individual song.

The standard SESAC license excludes grand rights, which are licensed separately by SESAC. If the performing rights organization does not license a dramatic performance, the prospective user must seek a license from the publisher or from the writer if he or she has reserved the dramatic right.

Printed Editions

In the case of an opera, a printed edition means a vocal score. For other works, there will be a full score in a large edition or a pocket-sized study edition. Costs for the copying and other preparation may vary from $2,000 to $35,000, with many major works falling in the $10,000 range. The high cost of copying in the United States has led to the referral of a considerable amount of such work to lower-cost European and Asian experts. Many contemporary composers become their own copyist or use students or aspiring composers as copyists in order to encourage the inexpensive printing and performance of their work.

Particularly in regard to new music, it becomes difficult to justify on a purely business basis the expense of launching printed editions of serious works. The Rockefeller Panel Report on The Performing Arts stated (p. 104):

> . . . a review is required of the entire system of publishing and distributing new music. As economic patterns have changed, this can no longer be done adequately by publishers, commercial or nonprofit, without some form of outside assistance.

A printed opera vocal score will be priced at about $200. There is extensive use of facsimile editions instead of engraved or notation system editions. Symphony scores usually have a lesser duration, involve fewer pages, and are priced in accordance with the number of pages. There are few prospective purchasers. Rentals, rather than purchases, of parts have tended to become the prevailing practice. In addition, the publisher charges a dramatic performance fee for the performance of the opera. With respect to minor opera works frequently performed at schools, the single fee quoted may include both the rental and the performance fee. ASCAP, as noted previously, does not license dramatic performance rights of dramatic works, and BMI acquires only limited rights to issue such licenses.

Music Sales Royalties

For sales of serious music editions in the United States and Canada, the standard royalty payable to the composer is 10 percent of the suggested retail list prices established by the publisher. Contrast this with a usual royalty for popular music approximating 10 percent of the wholesale price. Some representatives of serious music composers contend that the royalty should be a minimum of 12½ percent of the suggested retail price and should increase to not less than 15 percent after a stipulated number of sales.

The composer will be entitled to receive 50 percent of the receipts of the publisher from sales of printed editions through subpublishers outside the United States and Canada. The publisher frequently is paid 10 to 15 percent of the suggested retail list prices in the foreign countries.

Rental Income

With regard to the publishers' income from rentals, the share of such rentals payable to the composer will frequently depend on whether the publisher or the composer pays the expense of extraction and preparation of parts on master sheets. This may run to about $10,000 for a major work. If the publisher pays the expense, the composer commonly receives 25 percent of the rental income. In the event the expense is borne by the composer, his share is likely to be 50 percent of the rental income. Composers may contend that rental payments to them should never be less than 50 percent irrespective of whether the composer or the publisher bears the expense of extraction and preparation of parts. The position of AGAC is that the publisher must prepare rental material and shall pay the composers 50 percent of the rental income.

One of the advantages to the publisher of rentals, as opposed to sales, is that the publisher may achieve a greater voice in selecting the performers of the work and thereby avoid poorly timed competing performances. In addition, the publisher is able to exercise better control in checking the loggings by ASCAP and the reports of record companies. For frequently played scores, it is not unusual to have 15 to 20 rental sets in use at any one time. For example, Aaron Copland's "Lincoln Portrait" is the subject of many rentals.

Printing

The printing of a serious work is of preeminent importance when obtaining performances and recordings of the work.

An important problem of the serious music composer is the contractual obligations of publishers for printing and rentals. The writer will wish to ensure that his or her work is printed and made available for sale to the public. Because of the expense of printing and the thinness of the prospective market, the publisher may avoid a firm commitment to print. This is a subject for bargaining between the composer and publisher. They may compromise by providing that all rights will revert to the composer if the publisher fails to print within a stipulated period, such as 1 year after the first performance.

A publisher, although averse to a printing commitment, may agree to provide rental copies. These are often ozalid reproductions from transparencies originally prepared by the composer. The cost to the publisher is considerably less than the expense of printing. Composers may be dissatisfied with only rental copies since they are relatively few in number and the public will be unable to purchase copies of the serious music work. In the absence of printed editions, copies are generally unavailable to amateurs, and promotional distribution to encourage performances and recordings is restricted.

Prospects for New Works

A characteristic of the opera world is its adherence to the standard works, the established performers, and the accepted style of presentation.

Relatively few contemporary works are presented by the renowned opera companies. Together with the emphasis by symphony orchestras and many performers on traditional repertoire, it can be easily seen that the opportunities for contemporary composers and enterprising new publishers in the field of serious music tend to be limited.

It has been said that the business of publishing new serious works rivals the new Broadway stage productions in the risks involved. Demand must be generated from a public that appears generally unwilling to buy enough records to warrant commercial recordings of new works. Orchestras which operate at serious deficits and have limited funds for rehearsals are loath to incur the expense and risk in sponsoring new works.

The need to subsidize contemporary compositions has been recognized by various groups. Certain foundations have paid the recording costs for phonograph records of new compositions. Orchestras and opera groups associated with colleges and universities and supported by educational funds have assumed a commanding position in performing new works. BMI's annual guarantees to serious music publishers and to writers are in effect a form of subsidy of serious works, as are the multiple credits applied by ASCAP and BMI in evaluating serious music performances.

Too often, aspiring composers invest time and money in sending manuscripts to the wrong publisher for consideration. The selection of an appropriate publisher and the manner of submitting a proposed manuscript are essential first steps in reaching a professional status. As a helpful guide, the Music Publishers Association of the United States and the National Music Publishers Association have prepared a booklet with "some suggestions for getting your music published," entitled "The MSS Market," which can be obtained from these associations at 130 West 57th Street, New York, New York 10019 and 110 East 59th Street, New York, New York 10022, respectively. A copy of the booklet is in Appendix 16.

American Composers Alliance

Cooperative and self-help ventures by composers are a feature of the serious music field. The American Composers Alliance

(ACA), founded in 1938, acts as a publisher for its members through its American Composers Edition, which arranges for the reproduction of its members' works at the request of either the composer or a performer or group. Reproduction is by the ozalid process from transparencies furnished by the composers and deposited with ACA. There is a Special Edition series which is printed outside the ACA office by offset method and advertised nationally. This series is selected for publication each year by a committee of ACA members.

ACA maintains a library of its members' works, making available for sale or rental pieces that other publishers, who must print in quantity, cannot afford to handle. The organization acts in behalf of its members in arranging for synchronization licenses for films and mechanical licenses for records. ACA has helped to found an orchestra of sixty players, known as the American Composers Orchestra, which is devoted to performing American symphony music. This orchestra is an independent nonprofit operation that gives three concerts annually in Alice Tully Hall in New York City. Concerts are broadcast live on WNYC–FM to 200,000 listeners and are rebroadcast on both the National Public Radio and Voice of America networks.

Performing rights of ACA members are vested in BMI. ACA is a publisher-affiliate of BMI, and each ACA member holds concurrent membership in BMI. ACA claims to be the oldest and largest national service organization for composers of concert music.

Composers Recordings, Inc.

Composers Recordings, Inc. (CRI), established in 1954, is a nonprofit recording company devoted exclusively to contemporary concert music. CRI is headquartered at ACA, which helped to found it.

CRI produces and distributes many recordings of contemporary American works, most of which have not been previously recorded. The CRI catalog lists over 350 records on which more than 450 composers are represented. CRI's catalog is increased by 18 records each year. As with many domestic record companies, many orchestral works have been recorded outside the United States by lower-cost orchestras in countries such as Japan, Norway, England, and Italy. Chamber music has been recorded by leading American musicians.

Among the American orchestras recorded have been the New York, Boston, Chicago, San Francisco, Knoxville, Indianapolis, and Oklahoma City symphony orchestras, as well as Leopold Stokowski and the American Symphony Orchestra. There are recordings by the American Composers Orchestra, founded by ACA. Often recordings are made after a work has been rehearsed thoroughly for a live concert, resulting in a substantial saving in rehearsal expenses.

Funds for the recording budget of CRI are received from the National Endowment for the Arts, the New York Council on the Arts, private foundations, universities, and individual patrons. Sources include ACA, the American Academy and Institute of Arts and Letters, the Walter W. Naumburg Foundation, the Alice M. Ditson Fund of Columbia University, the Jerome Foundation, the Ford Foundation, the Andrew W. Mellon Foundation, and the Martha Baird Rockefeller Fund for Music, Inc. All styles, media, and professional affiliations are eligible for CRI recordings. A committee of distinguished musicians passes on all recording projects. CRI recordings are distributed by mail and through record distributors and retailers. In 1979 CRI became the sole distributor of the Louisville Orchestra First Edition Records, previously available only through mail order. CRI states that it has become the largest record company devoted to twentieth-century concert music.

American Music Center

The American Music Center, Inc. (AMC), which has been designated as the official United States Information Center for Music, was founded in 1940. It is a nonprofit organization of some 1,200 members, including composers, publishers, performers, patrons, critics, and institutions.

The AMC maintains a large circulating library of 15,000 scores of serious American music, which are available on loan to any qualified person, without charge, for thirty days. The library of scores, largely unpublished, does not include performance parts. The material is often unavailable elsewhere. The organization is supported by membership dues, sales of periodicals and catalogs, and grants from both the public and the private sectors.

A program, funded in part by the Martha Baird Rockefeller Fund for Music and the New York State Council on the Arts and administered by the American Music Center, assists composers in meeting expenses incurred in copying performance materials, provided there is a guarantee of performance by a professional organization. From time to time, the Center administers a program offering commissions to performers for solo recital pieces.

The AMC administers the Nonesuch Commission Awards and, from time to time, other award-giving contests or competitions. The AMC offers technical assistance to composers and to performing ensembles of all sizes on commissions, grants and fellowships, organizations of performing groups, repertoire, performance opportunities, recording and publishing of contemporary music, and, most importantly, the promotion of contemporary works. The unique biographical files on American composers and the information on contemporary American performing groups are available from the AMC to any person or organization. The organization's librarians offer equivalent service in a variety of fields to approximately 200 people a week.

The *Newsletter,* which is published quarterly, is available to subscribers and to members. This publication contains information of interest and importance to composers and performers of new music, such as competitions, awards, recent recordings, first performances, and publications.

Commissioned Works

Just as Frederick the Great subsidized composers of his day, we find foundations, corporations, and individuals commissioning concert works today. This granting of commissions to composers for new works is a distinctive characteristic of the field of serious music.

A commission involves several aspects. The composer agrees to write a specific work or type of work. The commissioning party undertakes to make a payment to the composer, or to guarantee a concert performance, or both. In fact, the assurance of a first performance may often be more attractive to the composer than a payment, and will be a deciding factor in negotiations about the amount of the payment.

The consideration to the commissioning party frequently entails the dedication of the piece to the patron. If the patron is a performer, he or she may be granted the exclusive rights to perform and/or record the new work, not only for the premiere performance but also for a period of years. Rarely will the patron reserve the right to designate the publisher of the piece.

A question may arise about whether the patron or the composer is vested with the ownership of the copyright in a commissioned work. The parties may contract freely in this regard. The foundation, philanthropist, or performer acting as patron may be expected to have no interest in the copyright proprietorship. But a serious music publisher who is a patron may seek the copyright ownership, subject to the payment of writer royalties.

Under customs and usages applicable to commissioned serious music works, in the absence of a definitive agreement, a composer is regarded as an independent contractor, rather than an employee-for-hire, and is deemed to be the copyright proprietor.

A commission is considered to be an honor to the composer of serious music, worthy of mention along with references to the winning of contest prizes, fellowships, and awards.

Cecil Taylor, the pianist, has been recently commissioned to write and perform music for the Munich Symphony and the Brooklyn Harmonia as well as for the Alvin Ailey Dance Company. The National Symphony Orchestra commissioned eleven composers, including William Schuman, Ulysses Kay, and Benjamin Lees, to write original musical works for performance by the orchestra in its 1975–1976 and 1976–1977 seasons in honor of the nation's bicentennial celebration.

Some other examples of commissioned works of contemporary serious music are:

Virgil Thomson	"The Mother of Us All": When commissioned by the Alice M. Ditson Fund to write a new opera, Thomson decided to revive his collaboration with Gertrude Stein. Stein agreed and provided a political fantasy based upon the career of Susan B. Anthony. The work was introduced at Columbia University in 1947.
Igor Stravinsky	"Abraham and Isaac": This is a sacred ballad for baritone and chamber orchestra. It was commissioned by the state of Israel for its 4th Annual Festival and was introduced in Jerusalem in 1964.
Paul Creston	"Symphony #4, Opus 52": This was commissioned by Viola Malkin as a memorial to her husband, Joseph D. Malkin. It was introduced in 1952 by the National Symphony Orchestra in Washington, D.C. "Toccata for Orchestra, Opus 68": This is a symphonic work commissioned by the Cleveland Orchestra for its 40th anniversary. It was introduced by that orchestra in 1958. "Concerto #2 for Violin and Orchestra, Opus 78": This was commissioned by the Ford Foundation for the violinist

Michael Rubin who introduced it in
1960 in Los Angeles as a soloist with
the Los Angeles Philharmonic.

Gunther Schuller   "The Visitation":
This is an opera to the text of
Kafka's *The Trial.* In
1962 Rolf Lieberman, director of the
Hamburg Opera, commissioned
Schuller to write a jazz opera
for his company.

Composer Earnings

Serious music composers, as all serious musicians, are frequently
unable to support themselves from the proceeds of their work.
Referring to the increased performance fees for serious music
paid by ASCAP and BMI, Composer Virgil Thomson has written:
"As a result, and also as a result of enlarged foundational patronage, today's young composers get commissioned, paid, played
and even published. They are not yet living on their take; only
five standard composers in America can do that. The rest still
teach, mostly in universities."

Aaron Copland, describing Dr. Serge Koussevitzky, then
leader of the Boston Symphony Orchestra, has written: "He has
been profoundly disturbed at the realization that the great major-
ity of our composers devote the major part of their time, not to
writing music, but to the gaining of a livelihood. He can never
accustom himself to the thought that in this rich country of ours
no plan exists that would provide composers with a modicum of
financial security for the production of works of serious music."

The increase since 1965 in governmental subsidies in the
United States has been previously referred to on pages 19 and 20.

The magazine *ASCAP in Action* carries news of the pre-
mieres of many serious music works. For example, in 1980, the
Baltimore Symphony Orchestra premiered Morris Moshe Cotel's
"Harmony of the World." The Shreveport Symphony Orchestra
in that year offered the first performance of Arnold Freed's "Win,
Place or Show." The magazine also contains information about
current contests in which serious music composers may compete.
In 1981 there was reference to the annual NISSIM Composers
Competition for ASCAP members, which features a cash prize of
$5,000 for the score of an orchestral work. The competition is
sponsored by the ASCAP Foundation, which states its hope that
the award-winning composition will be given its first professional
performance by a leading American symphony orchestra. To
encourage such performance the ASCAP Foundation will make

supplementary funds available to the orchestra for proper rehearsal preparation.

The magazine *BMI The Many Worlds of Music* offers news of the premieres of certain serious music works. Thus an issue in 1980 referred to the premiere by The Atlanta Symphony of a work by T. J. Anderson entitled "Messages." The magazine carries information about the annual BMI Awards to Student Composers competition, which was established in 1951. As noted previously, prizes total $15,000 and range from $500 to $2,500 at the discretion of the judges. The competition is designed to encourage the creation of concert music.

The *National Music Council Bulletin* occasionally offers information about contests for serious music composers. The *Musical America International Directory of the Performing Arts* lists contests and awards for serious music composers. A typical page is shown in Appendix 17.

A list and description of foundations, trusts, and other sources of funds for grants and awards for music, as well as schools offering graduate fellowships and scholarships in music, may be obtained from The Music Educators National Conference, The National Education Association, 1902 Association Drive, Reston, Virginia 22091. Another source is the annual edition of *The Musicians Guide*.

5

Religious Music

MUSIC plays an essential role in the services of some 300,000 local United States congregations with approximately 100 million adherents.

An estimate given to the National Music Council has placed the total of hymns in various languages as 500,000. It would seem normal to consider hymns to be unchanging through the years. In actual fact, analysis shows that there is a constant creation, revision, and discard of liturgical music. Methodists have dropped 200 hymns from their 1935 book, the Episcopal Hymnal of 1940 eliminated 193 hymns from its earlier contents, and the Lutherans removed about one-third of the hymns from their earlier books. In each case, new hymns have been brought forth to replace those discarded. New hymns cover fields such as: world order, social welfare, marriage and family life, and ecumenical concepts. Selection of editorial content and arrangements of church hymnals is frequently the province of a board of qualified editors.

Some churches have encouraged the use of jazz in special religious services; for instance, the late Duke Ellington performed his original sacred works in Westminster Abbey in a concert recorded by RCA Records.

A prominent change has been the Catholic Church's reshaping and reevaluation of its liturgical and musical life, in keeping with the 1963 promulgation of the Second Vatican Council Constitution on Liturgy. As a result of this decree, the congregation, and not just the choir, participates in church music. This has created a need for major revisions in choral repertoire, resulting in new publishing ventures. As part of the decree, vernacular language has replaced Latin in liturgical services throughout the world.

Nonchurch Usage

Religious music is not limited to church and synagogue usage. There are many religious broadcasts throughout the country in which music is an essential part.

There is an outpouring of religious-oriented serious music during the Christmas and Easter seasons. The Christmas list of one New York radio station included "Sancta Civitas" ("The Holy City") by Vaughn Williams, "A Ceremony of Carols" by Benjamin Britten, "Laud to the Nativity" by Respighi, "Veni Creator Spiritus" by Orff, "Christus" by Liszt, "El Pessebre" ("The Manger") by Casals, and "Christmas Oratorio" by J. S. Bach. This largely religious programming was interspersed with other serious music such as Menotti's "Amahl and the Night Visitors," Rachmaninoff's "The Bells," and Anderson's "A Christmas Festival."

Appreciation of religious music is shown annually in numerous Christmas and Easter season concerts: for example, there are frequent presentations of Handel's "Messiah" and Bach's "Christmas Oratorio." There has grown up a tradition of "do-it-yourself" Messiah choruses, with mostly amateur singers and musicians, held in concert halls in New York, Chicago, San Francisco, London and in churches in many other areas.

Education

Scholarly pursuit of liturgical music has long been a tradition. Currently, divinity schools, such as the Yale Divinity School and Catholic University, have a special liturgical music section. Cantorial music for synagogue use is a matter for study at the Union Theological Institute and at the Rabbi Isaac Elchanan Theological Seminary, an affiliate of Yeshiva University.

Standard Religious Works

There is a rich repertoire of sacred works in classical music. Among these are masses, magnificats, oratorios, cantatas and motets, as well as a very substantial number of organ solos.

Classical composers whose works continue to be performed in religious music programs include Bach, Beethoven, Berlioz, Brahms, Bruckner, Handel, Liszt, Mahler, Mendelsohn, and Schubert.

Contemporary Religious Works

An apt illustration of the range and significance of religious musical works by contemporary composers is the program of a 1965 concert of ecumenical symphonic and choral works attended by Pope Paul VI. The concert presented works by composers of four faiths. The program included Sibelius's "Two Solemn Melodies" for violin and orchestra; Darius Milhaud's "Psalm CXXIX" for baritone and orchestra; Gian Francisco Malipiero's "Saint Francis of Assisi" for baritone, orchestra, and chorus; and Igor Stravinsky's "Symphony of Psalms."

Among contemporary additions of note to sacred repertoire are works of Leonard Bernstein and Benjamin Britten. The latter's contributions encompass "Ceremony of Carols," "Hymn to St. Cecilia," and "Rejoice in the Lamb." A major work by Bernstein is "Chichester Psalms," which was originally written for a full English Cathedral orchestra, with texts in Hebrew to be sung by a major chorus; Bernstein also prepared an alternative version for use by a chorus accompanied only by organ, percussion, and harp.

Folk Religious Works

In addition to other folk-inspired religious music, there are spirituals such as "Swing Low Sweet Chariot," "Mary Had a Baby," "Ezekial Saw the Wheel," "I've Got Shoes," and "Give Me That Old Time Religion." Odetta, Johnny Cash, and Bob Dylan are examples of prominent contemporary artists who have given renditions of folk religious music.

Oscar Brand's experience in developing a standard out of his "Burgundy Carol" is notable. It was introduced by the Weavers in a folk music setting, performed on a record by Joan Baez, and was later recorded by the Mormon Tabernacle Choir and others. Brand has reported receiving a special commission to write 13 songs dealing with the life of Christ, with each directed to one of thirteen different important feast days. At the premier performance of the songs, each was introduced by a 1-minute sermon by one of 13 separate ministers; the same repertoire was later utilized at liturgical conventions and conferences.

Gospel Music

There is a commercially successful marriage between church music and popular music in gospel music, usually identified, in racial terms, as black gospel or white gospel. According to *Soul* magazine, which concentrates on the various forms of black music, there are three basic types of gospel music: traditional, crossover, and contemporary. The last has been described as Christian music with a beat. John Lomax, 3rd said in 1981 that "Ten years ago, gospel was composed of but two types: Southern gospel and black gospel. Today gospel has scattered into a myriad of forms: contemporary black gospel, 'Jesus-rock', Catholic gospel, inspirational gospel, and traditional gospel, as well as gospel comedians and bands which play gospel lyrics set to jazz, soul and even 'new wave' rhythms."

The rural South has been the mainstay and natural home of much of the black gospel field. With black migrations northward, great gospel sources such as Ohio, which spawned the Reverend James Cleveland, and Detroit, which has been the training ground for Aretha Franklin and others, have come to the fore.

White gospel has also looked to the rural South for its natural home and origins. Touring groups, like the LaFevre Family (now called the Rex Nelson Singers), the Gaither Trio, the Blackwood Brothers, and The Statesmen Quartet have attained major commercial acceptance and success.

To critics of the commercialism of gospel music the retort sometimes made is Jesus's admonition: "Go unto the highways and byways" to preach the gospel. Gospel music groups can claim the fulfillment of this instruction. A late 1970s Gallup poll reported that almost half of the United States population listens to at least one religious broadcast a week.

Gospel Music Records

Gospel music record sales account for over $100 million per year. There are some 500 performing groups and solo gospel artists who fill more than 50,000 hours of gospel broadcasting throughout the United States. Over 300 record labels specialize in gospel music.

There are approximately 1,400 religious-oriented radio broadcasting stations, which program at least six hours of gospel music per week. Radio centers for gospel music are traditionally Nashville, Birmingham, Orlando, and Jacksonville. There are also major centers in Waco, Texas, northern and southern California, Kansas, and Grand Rapids, Michigan.

About a dozen record companies dominate the field of gospel music. Among the more important is Word, Inc., located in Waco, Texas. Word is a division of ABC, Inc., the entertainment conglomerate. Record labels owned by Word include Canaan, Word, Myrrh, and Day Spring, and it distributes A & S, Good News, Image VII, Lamb & Lion, Light, Maranatha, Newpax, New Song, Paragon, Seed, and Solid Rock. Another significant record firm is The Great Circle Record Company, a division of The Benson Company of Nashville, Tennessee. The record labels it possesses are Heart Warming, Impact, Greentree, and Cross Country. It distributes the DIP and Jim labels, as well.

Nashboro Record Co., of Nashville, is an important black gospel company, which is the proprietor of the Creed, Excello, and Nashboro record labels. It distributes the Kenwood label. Savoy Records is also a leading black gospel record company, headquartered in Elizabeth, New Jersey, and distributed by Arista Records of New York City.

MCA Records with its custom Sparrow label and CBS Records with its custom Salvation label and its own gospel label, Priority, are indicative of the recognition by major secular record companies of the significance and growth of the gospel field.

Gospel Music Publishing

According to the Gospel Music Association, there are over 130 gospel music publishers. Word, a giant among the publishers, services some 4,000 Christian bookstore outlets. Most major gospel publishers such as Word, Manna, Gaither Music, Benson, Lexicon, Lillenas, and Singspiration are members of the Church Music Publishers Association. It is estimated that sales of gospel printed editions in the form of hymnals, compilations, choral music, and sheet music, amount to approximately $75 million annually.

Crossover Recordings and Artists

A number of secular artists have achieved success in the religious music field and vice-versa. Leading crossover artists are B. J. Thomas, Barry McGuire, Andrae Crouch, Paul Stookey of Peter, Paul, and Mary, Willie Nelson, Barbara Mandrell, Pat Boone, and Debby Boone. "You Light Up My Life" was the vehicle for Debby Boone's capturing the secular market after having recorded several Christian projects.

Andrae Crouch records secular releases for Warner Bros., while also under contract to Word Records for Christian albums. He is a successful artist in both religious and secular markets, having sold more than a million albums.

B. J. Thomas, an outstanding crossover artist, has a record contract with MCA and records as well for the Myrrh label of Word Records.

Performance Income

Based on loggings by performing-rights organizations, performance fees are paid by them to composer and publisher affiliates which, respectively, compose and publish religious music.

For years religious works which are four minutes or longer in their original duration have received special treatment from

The American Society of Composers, Authors and Publishers (ASCAP) when broadcast in any form on a religious program sponsored or produced by a religious organization or on a religious program of an exclusively devotional nature such as a program of hymns or other religious works. Prior to October 1, 1981, ASCAP accorded the performance three times the otherwise applicable credits, but the multiple was reduced to two times effective October 1, 1981, and no multiple is applicable as of October 1, 1982. If religious works were originally written for a choral, symphonic, or similar concert performance, ASCAP will grant additional credits which are the higher of (1) the applicable multiple referred to above or (2) the applicable multiple in a table which ranges upwards in relation to the minutes of actual performance; for a 5-minute performance the multiple in the table is 2, for a 10-minute performance, 6, and for a 20-minute performance, 20. For a further discussion of ASCAP increased credits for serious works see "performance income" on page 79.

Broadcast Music, Inc., (BMI) has also been favorable to religious music. For broadcast performances of serious religious music written originally for concert performances, BMI grants credits over and above the credits allotted for popular songs. The extra credit is allowed only for feature performances and not for popular arrangements of the works. BMI has promulgated a schedule showing the additional payments for such a "concert work," which are discussed in further detail under "performance income" on page 79. For example, in the case of network radio feature performances, the payment for a concert work is 8 cents for each station compared with payment for a popular work of 6 cents for each station on network radio.

BMI also may reward with additional credits a religious work not originally written for a concert if it exceeds seven minutes in length as commercially recorded; an application for extra credit must be made at the time a clearance form for the work is submitted to BMI.

Religious Music Arrangements

Much religious music, especially of a choral or symphonic nature, was composed many years ago and is in the public domain, and therefore unprotected by copyright.

Performers of religious music may make substantial additions to, or revisions in, the basic work, either in the music or lyrics, or both. By such material variations, a new version of the work is produced and a "derivative work" created under the 1976 Copyright Act. Such a derivative work is protected by copyright under the act insofar as there are material additions, changes, or revisions in the music or lyrics of the underlying public domain work. However, the basic work continues in the public domain.

In the event the new version is of a work not in the public domain, the new material in the resulting derivative work is protected by copyright only if created by the copyright owner of the original work or with his or her consent. A mechanical license to record, granted by the copyright owner, is generally construed to mean there will be no objection to performances which adjust the work to the performer's style or manner of interpretation. It is not meant to denote a grant of the right to create a copyrightable derivative work. The mechanical license does not justify a copyright claim in the new version by the performer or by the original copyright owner. For a further discussion, see "jazz arrangements," on page 77.

Mechanical License Fees

The owner of copyright in a composition possesses the exclusive right to reproduce the work in the form of recordings. A record company, in the case of a previously recorded copyrighted work, may either obtain a negotiated mechanical license from the copyright owner or resort to the compulsory license provisions of Section 115 of the 1976 Copyright Act.

Under that section the license fees for each record manufactured and distributed amount to 4 cents per composition or ¾ cent per minute or fraction thereof, whichever is larger.*

In practice, the formula for compulsory license fees tends to act as a ceiling on royalty rates in licenses negotiated in the United States for a previously recorded, copyrighted musical work. For a further discussion of mechanical license fees, see "Mechanical License Fees" on page 80.

Trade Publications

In the music trade press in the United States, coverage of religious music is ordinarily confined to what is generally known as "gospel" music. *Billboard* periodically devotes a page to gospel music. From time to time it publishes a column of 40 best selling "Inspirational LPs" and at other times a column of 17 best-selling "Spiritual LPs." The former covers white gospel, and the latter,

---

* The rates will increase on January 1, 1983, to 4.25 cents (or 0.8 cents per minute of playing time or fraction thereof, whichever is larger); on July 1, 1984, to 4.5 cents (or 0.85 cents per minute of playing time or fraction thereof, whichever is larger); and on January 1, 1986, to five cents (or 0.95 cents per minute of playing time or fraction thereof, whichever is larger.)

black gospel. For the week ending October 17, 1981, the five top LPs in the *Billboard* "Spiritual LPs" chart were:

Title	Artist	Record Label
Amazing Grace	B. J. Thomas	Myrrh
Hearts of Fire	Sweet Comfort Band	Light
In Concert	Amy Grant	Myrrh
Priority	The Imperials	Day Spring
It's Time to Praise the Lord	Praise Five	Maranatha

Cash Box, in its gospel coverage, separates the 40 best-sellers into 20 top "Spiritual" albums and 20 best-selling "Inspirational" LPs.

Record World, in addition to gospel music news, prints two gospel music charts, each with a listing of 40 top-selling albums. One is called "Soul & Spiritual Gospel" and the other "Contemporary & Inspirational Gospel." *Record World* rates the better new album releases of gospel music as "Gospel Album Picks."

Organizations

The Gospel Music Association of Nashville, Tennessee, is the leading organization in the field of gospel music. During its sponsored Gospel Music Week, the association makes its Dove awards for top albums in the inspirational category and for top albums in the spiritual category. Awards also cover leading inspirational male and female vocalists and groups, and there are comparable awards in the spiritual field. Further Dove awards are made for songs and their writers.

Other organizations of note are the Church Music Publishers Association, composed of gospel music publishers, and National Religious Broadcasters, comprised of leading gospel broadcasting stations.

6

This Business of Jazz

As stated by Les Ledbetter in the *New York Times,* ". . . jazz has always been the stepchild of the arts and has always had to remain lean and tough because of the inattention it gets from the general public." Although recognized as a truly indigenous American art form, jazz musicians have been besieged with business advice to "compromise principle" and to dilute their music in an attempt to gain general public acceptance. Some business success has been achieved by jazz thinly disguised as rock or Latin music. At other times jazz has been sold to the public as background music for exciting television detective programs or as musical settings for dances.

The threat of mere academic appreciation without appropriate financial rewards has not deterred a large number of jazz musicians who prefer to live *for* their art rather than *on* it. As in the case of composers and performers of serious music, many jazz artists and composers have learned to exist in a world of foundation grants, foreign appreciation, and moonlighting employment. Others, however, such as Benny Goodman, Duke Ellington, and Louis Armstrong, have achieved tremendous success and made lasting cultural contributions. Some well-known jazz artists and their fields of jazz follow.

Bebop	—Charlie Parker or Dizzy Gillespie
Fusion	—Billy Cobham or Mahavishnu Orchestra
Jazz-Rock	—Miles Davis
Swing	—Benny Goodman
Avant-Garde	—Ornette Coleman or Cecil Taylor
New Music	—AACM

Latin Jazz   —Stone Alliance or Mongo Santamaria
Modern Jazz   —Modern Jazz Quartet
Pop Jazz   —Chuck Mangione

A good reflection of the more commercial side of jazz appears in the special Jazz chart issued weekly in *Billboard,* indicating the best-selling LP recordings. The weekly listing of jazz hits from *Billboard* is as follows for a week ending October 3, 1981.

Billboard Best Selling Jazz LPs

Survey For Week Ending 10/3/81

This Week	Last Week	Weeks on Chart	TITLE Artist, Label & Number (Dist. Label)	This Week	Last Week	Weeks on Chart	TITLE Artist, Label & Number (Dist. Label)
☆	1	6	**BREAKIN' AWAY** Al Jarreau, Warner Bros. BSK 3576	26	29	28	**DIRECTIONS** Miles Davis, Columbia KC2-36472
★2	2	4	**SIGN OF THE TIMES** Bob James, Columbia FC 37495	27	15	10	**PIED PIPER** Dave Valentine, Arista/GRP GRP 5505
☆	3	5	**FREE TIME** Spyro Gyra, MCA MCA 5238	28	20	18	**HUSH** John Klemmer, Elektra 5E-527
4	4	11	**THE MAN WITH THE HORN** Miles Davis, Columbia FC 36790	★29	39	30	**MOUNTAIN DANCE** Dave Grusin, Arista/GRP 5010
5	7	16	**AS FALLS WICHITA SO FALLS WICHITA FALLS** Pat Metheny & Lyle Mays, ECM 1-1190 (Warner Bros.)	☆	42	4	**AUTUMN** George Winston, Windham Hill C 1012
6	6	46	**WINELIGHT** ▲ Grover Washington Jr., Elektra 6E-305	31	21	8	**INVOCATIONS THE MOTH AND THE FLAME** Keith Jarrett, ECM-D-1201 (Warner Bros.)
7	5	25	**VOYEUR** David Sanborn, Warner Bros. BSK 3546	32	27	19	**SECRET COMBINATION** Randy Crawford, Warner Bros. BSK 3541
8	8	22	**RIT** Lee Ritenour, Elektra 6E-331	33	32	9	**THIS TIME** Al Jarreau, Warner Bros. BSK 3434
★9	14	8	**FUSE ONE** Fuse One, CTI CTI 9003	34	35	20	**TARANTELLA** Chuck Mangione, A&M SP-6513
10	11	18	**FRIDAY NIGHT IN SAN FRANCISCO** John McLaughlin, Al DiMeola, Paco De Lucia, Columbia FC 37152	35	33	4	**MISTRAL** Freddie Hubbard, Liberty LT 1110
11	12	6	**MAGIC MAN** Herb Alpert, A&M SP-3728	★36	46	2	**SLINGSHOT** Michael Henderson, Buddah BDS 6002 (Arista)
12	13	13	**APPLE JUICE** Tom Scott, Columbia FC 37419	37	37	21	**RAIN FOREST** Jay Hoggard, Contemporary 14007
13	9	11	**MECCA FOR MODERNS** Manhattan Transfer, Atlantic SD 16036	38	38	3	**SHOGUN** John Kaizan Kneptune, Inner City IC 6078
14	16	7	**BLUE TATTOO** Passport, Atlantic SD 19304	★39	47	84	**HIDEAWAY** David Sanborn, Warner Bros. BSK 3379
☆	25	2	**REFLECTIONS** Gil Scott-Heron, Arista AL 9566	40	40	10	**MY ROAD OUR ROAD** Lee Oskar, Elektra 5E-526
16	19	19	**LIVE** Stephanie Grapelli/David Grisman, Warner Bros. BSK 3550	41	44	15	**SOCIAL STUDIES** Carla Bley, ECM/W11 (Warner Bros.)
17	17	10	**LIVE IN JAPAN** Dave Grusin & the GRP All Stars, Arista/GRP GRP 5506				

18	18	21	**THE CLARKE/DUKE PROJECT** Stanley Clarke/George Duke, Epic FE 36918	42	30	20	**EXPRESSIONS OF LIFE** Heath Brothers, Columbia FC 37126
☆19	24	9	**YELLOW JACKETS** Yellow Jackets, Warner Bros. BSK 3573	43	45	5	**VINTAGE SESSIONS** Sonny Rollins, Prestige P-24096
20	22	12	**THREE QUARTETS** Chick Corea, Warner Bros. BSK 3552	44	31	33	**YOU MUST BELIEVE IN SPRING** Bill Evans, Warner Bros. HS 3504
21	23	9	**CLEAN SWEEP** Bobby Broom, Arista/GRP GRP 5504	45	36	5	**GOLDEN LADY** Abbey Lincoln, Inner City IC 1117
22	10	11	**WORD OF MOUTH** Jaco Pastorius, Warner Bros. BSK 3535	46	48	2	**LIVE AT THE NORTH SEA JAZZ FESTIVAL** Oscar Peterson, Pablo 2620115
23	26	2	**ORANGE EXPRESS** Sadao Watanabe, Columbia FC 37433	47	49	16	**THREE PIECE SUITE** Ramsey Lewis, Columbia FC 37153
☆24	34	21	**THE DUDE** ● Quincy Jones, A&M SP-3721	48	41	25	**GALAXIAN** Jeff Lorber Fusion, Arista AL 9545
				49	50	8	**MELLOW** Herbie Mann, Atlantic SD 16046
25	28	4	**BLYTHE SPIRIT** Arthur Blythe, Columbia FC 37427	50	43	13	**MY DEAR LIFE** Sadao Watanabe, Inner City IC 6063

★ Stars are awarded to those products showing greatest sales strength. ☆ Superstars are awarded to those products showing greatest upward movement on the current week's chart (Prime Movers). ● Recording Industry Assn. Of America seal for sales of 500,000 units. (Seal indicated by dot.) ▲ Recording Industry Assn. Of America seal for sales of 1,000,000 units. (Seal indicated by triangle.)

Record Labels for Jazz

Jazz has somewhat unique characteristics in the record marketplace. It is distinguished from serious and popular music in its frequent length of marketability, its adaptability to lower-cost concert or live renditions and in the large number of available and licensed master recordings.

There are numbers of small jazz specialty record labels that are content with low-budget, long-selling LPs with sales volumes as low as a few thousand copies per LP; these sales volumes would generally be disastrous for conventional popular record labels. On the other hand there are high-budget, large-selling records by a select group of artists such as Weather Report, Herbie Hancock, Stanley Turrentine, Hubert Laws, and Chick Corea, who appear on conventional commercial labels such as Capitol, Impulse-MCA, Elektra-Asylum, Columbia, and Arista. Jazz artists in larger number, including the highly respected Anthony Braxton (Arista-Freedom), Oregon (Vanguard and ECM), Joanne Brackeen (Tappan Zee/Columbia), Ursula Duziak (Inner City), and Abby Lincoln (Inner City), appear on small jazz-oriented labels with their new product.

Specialty jazz labels that handle reissues and licensed master recordings abound in the marketplace. Examples are Pacific,

Impulse-MCA, Inner City, P.M., Biograph, Contemporary, Bee-hive, and Zanadie. Jazz masters can often be obtained on a term license or lease from a foreign originating label or from an artist who owns a concert tape. These masters cost as little as $1,000 to record and, inclusive of mastering, jacket costs, and the initial pressing order, the investment up to initial release can be under $10,000. Prices rarely reflect this limited investment, although discounts to wholesalers of specialty jazz product are commonly greater than to those of conventional broad interest products. Royalties paid on jazz masters of a specialty nature range from about 8 to 15 percent of the retail list prices.

Of the 1,114 new listings in the 1979 Schwann Jazz sections (1,258 in 1978), there were 774 LPs (up from 699 in 1978), 168 cartridges (279 in 1978), and 172 cassettes (121 in 1978). Among the most frequently listed jazz performers were:

Anita O'Day	5
Thelonious Monk	4
Art Pepper	4
Cannonball Adderley	3
Art Ensemble of Chicago	3
Ron Blake	3
Stan Getz	3
Charles Mingus	3
Art Tatum	3

The year 1979 saw an abundance of previously unreleased material by Duke Ellington, Miles Davis, Lennie Tristano, John Coltrane, Thelonious Monk, and Johnny Hodges. The 5-record set of Charlie Parker's Complete Savoy Studio Sessions was a landmark reissue. Jazz bassist Charles Mingus died in 1979, and singer Joni Mitchell completed the album alone on which they were collaborating. Mingus was further immortalized by the release of two multiple record sets spanning his recording years. Jazz traditions were carried on with the release of new albums by Oregon, Weather Report, Pat Metheny, Cedar Walton, Art Pepper, and Jeff Lorber.

Background of Jazz

Nat Hentoff, in his book *The Jazz Life,* tells of the early days around the turn of the century, when jazz was sometimes called "ragtime," and was played at parades, funerals, store openings, dances, and brothels, as well as its seemingly continuous use "to complement the joy, rage, or sorrow of whiskey in the blood." Hentoff reports that before jazz audiences included formal critics, the best jazz critics were the after-hours musicians who would jam together after the drinkers, dancers, and more casual audience would depart. Eventually, in the 1930s, trade magazines such as *Down Beat* began to supply formal criticism and popularity charts.

Leonard Feather's *Encyclopedia of Jazz* disputes as "common misconceptions" the theories that New Orleans was the exclusive nursery of jazz, that jazz was originally African music, or that it is a peculiar racial domain of blacks. He states that "The music we recognize today as jazz is a synthesis of six main sources: rhythms from West Africa; harmonic structure from European classical music; melodic and harmonic qualities from nineteenth-century American folk music; religious music; work songs and minstrel show music; with, of course, a substantial overlapping of many of these areas."

With respect to the recording industry history of jazz, Feather writes that there was an early start in "race records" aimed at the black market of the 1920s with such recording artists as King Oliver (whose band included Louis Armstrong and Johnny Dodds), recording for the early Gennett company, and Jelly Roll Morton, Fletcher Henderson, and Fats Waller. An historic development which brought jazz to a white public was Paul Whiteman's introduction at Aeolian Hall in 1924 of George Gershwin's "Rhapsody in Blue." Record buffs, according to Feather, have considered the years 1926 to 1929 as the golden years of jazz recording, leading into the era of white jazz recordings by Benny Goodman, Joe Venuti, Ben Pollack, and the Dorsey Brothers.

International acclaim of jazz as an authentic black American musical tradition is of long duration. Willis Conover's "Voice of America" jazz programs were so successful that many generations of foreigners were won over to jazz. The White House has proudly presented jazz as a American cultural asset in programs for foreign visitors. George Wein, founder of the Newport Jazz Festival and promoter of its traveling versions, including the *Grande Parade du Jazz* at Nice, France, received the award of The Order of Arts and Letters from the French government for furthering "Franco-American friendship and understanding."

Jazz in Serious Music

Jazz was "discovered" in the 1920s by Stravinsky, Milhaud, Ravel, Copland, Carpenter, Gruenberg, and Gershwin. Uses within serious music included Milhaud's "La Creation de Monde" of 1923 and Gershwin's "Rhapsody in Blue," "American in Paris," and "Concerto in F."

In some instances there is a mere inclusion of portions of

existing jazz in a symphonic work. Other uses comprise a fusion or synthesis of jazz with a more conventional serious composition. There is also the full development of jazz in its own symphonic form. The Modern Jazz Quartet has pioneered by appearing at nonjazz festivals. Gunther Schuller is one of the most active participants in the process of combining jazz elements with, rather than into, serious music. He says, in a contribution to the *Jazz Encyclopedia,*

> The bringing together into a positive relationship of the spontaneity and sense of timing in jazz with the disciplines of classical music is recognized as desirable by most forward-looking musicians, although it is decried (as usual) by the cavilling jazz purists.

Jazz in the Religious Setting

Mary Lou Williams, the late jazz pianist, presented her musical mass in the sedate setting of Saint Patrick's Cathedral, attended by an archbishop and other church luminaries. Duke Ellington had such regular church settings for his specially prepared sacred music that he formed a special corporate division for this portion of his jazz repertoire. Jazz vespers were scheduled for many Sundays at Park Avenue's Central Presbyterian Church.

Employment

"Paying your dues" is a phrase particularly applicable to jazz musicians. The "dues" of years of knocking on doors and accepting low pay or inadequate conditions are generally a jazz musician's career necessities. But even the opportunity to work for low pay and under poor working conditions requires contacts and connections. In contrast to dance companies and theater performers, no open auditions are available for jazz bands. Union membership is ordinarily a necessary key to working as a musician. However, the union hiring hall is not run by lottery but by contractors. Knowing the contractor is usually the key.

In the 1930s, a new arrival in the jazz scene could hang around jazz night clubs and occasionally "sit-in" with the jazz band during regular shows or after-hours jam sessions. He would thereby obtain a form of audition and a chance to become associated with established jazz musicians. Today a concert hall jazz appearance is in a setting where the performers are distant from the audience, and a visiting musician is only a member of the audience. Night club jazz bands and after-hours jam sessions may still sometimes permit casual self-introductions, but the opportunities presented are fewer than in the past. More often, the new jazz musician will get a start by membership in rock and roll groups and will establish connections and a reputation while in that genre by occasional jazz-rock playing.

The formation of new jazz groups is common, but it is a struggle for a group of new jazz musicians to be heard and to be adequately compensated. One respected jazz group, even after releasing a well-received LP recording, had a few members who "played the streets" in the 1970s for nickels, dimes, and quarters. It is a social commentary that they earned more from such voluntary street appearances than many an older jazz musician made in the 1930s from rolling cigars or other moonlighting jobs. The actual hourly average on a good street has been reported at over $10 per person.

Having a record released is a goal of the new musician. Being selected by a featured artist to appear on a record date as a sideman results not only in minimum union scale, in 1981, of $146.81 per 3-hour session but also an album name credit. With such a credit, it is an easier task to obtain employment on future record dates or for live performances. Securing a record contract for a new group or a new leader is a nearly impossible task without prior album credits or favorable concert reviews.

However, some jazz musicians have achieved a first record release by arranging for a live concert to be recorded and then selling the master recording to a record company. The investment in the master recording, for engineering crew and equipment, union scale to musicians, and related mastering expense can amount to thousands of dollars. This may represent wasted moneys since such masters are rarely purchased and released by a record company, irrespective of the offering price. The American Federation of Musicians has condemned speculative recording sessions where the musicians are paid only if the master is successfully sold: Without such a saving, the minimum cost for a live concert LP would be several thousand of dollars.

Such standards as "Sweet Georgia Brown," "My Funny Valentine, "I Got Rhythm," or "I Left My Heart in San Francisco" will be found in numerous jazz forms on records and in concert repertoire. Ordinarily an original jazz composition by even the great jazz artists such as Thelonious Monk, Elvin Jones, or Illinois Jacquet will be recorded solely by the originating artist. An exception is Duke Ellington's theme "Take the A Train," written by the late Billy Strayhorn, which, although identified as an Ellington classic, is recorded by numerous jazz players.

Jazz records may have longevity often uncharacteristic of the "top 40" hits of popular music, but commonly there is a lack of current income. A jazz recording may reach relative hit status in

Billboard's top jazz charts with a mere forty thousand in sales, whereas higher levels of sales are required for a comparable chart position of easy listening or popular records. A jazz LP may earn royalties for the artist in the long run but, during the artist's active life, it is likely that a follow-up LP will be made before session costs for the earlier LP are recouped. Thus, for many years the only revenue realized by the jazz artist may be union scale for making the recording and, in the case of original compositions written by the artist, songwriting or publishing income resulting from the limited LP sales. In many instances, the jazz artist is asked by the record company to cross-collateralize writer or publisher accounts with artist accounts, and in such cases the limited writer or publisher income will be used to recoup session costs. Fortunately, however, for record companies as well as artists, the frequency of unrehearsed live sessions makes recording costs for jazz relatively cheap. An acceptable jazz LP master can be delivered for less than $6,000, which may be compared with session costs of many times that amount for rock and roll or popular LPs.

Foreign tours of individual bands or those in connection with overseas jazz festivals (e.g. Montreux) have been a mainstay of the jazz arts and jazz performers. Countries such as West Germany, England, France, Japan, and Sweden have been very receptive to American jazz artists. International cultural exchange programs have often used American jazz compositions and performers, although it is rare that foreign jazz musicians appear in the United States.

Jazz Festivals

Jazz is noteworthy for the large number of jazz festivals throughout the world. For example, in the period from June to December of 1980, there were known festivals in the United States, Canada, England, West Germany, Holland, Belgium, Denmark, Norway, Switzerland, Hungary, Austria, and Poland.

George Wien, in 1980, presented major jazz festivals in Boston, New Orleans, Los Angeles, New York, Nice, Munich, and London. In addition, he provided a good percentage of artists for festivals in The Hague, Pori, and other European festivals. His 1980 budget for dollars paid to musicians was over $2 million and approximately 750,000 people were estimated to attend his festivals in that year.

Festivals are often regarded as prestige builders and a form of public service rather than a self-supporting venture able to pay more than minimum union scale. For its 16 years at Newport, Rhode Island, the Newport Jazz Festival tottered near bankruptcy. Its move to New York City in 1972 has been a positive one, with growing attendance at the several dozens of events at each festival. In 1980 the festival, which was initially dedicated to Charlie Parker, the genius alto saxophonist, ran for ten days and was held primarily in New York City at Carnegie Hall, Avery Fisher Hall, Town Hall, and other places, including the Staten Island Ferry and a street fair on 52nd Street. Its program included 37 concerts by some 800 musicians. Its main sponsor, with a generous subsidy, was the Brown and Williamson Tobacco Co., which manufactures Kool cigarettes and which now calls the festival in New York the "Kool Jazz Festival." At the festival the company announced the establishment of a $5,000 scholarship to the Juilliard School for a promising young jazz musician.

In 1981, the Newport Jazz Festival was revived in Newport, Rhode Island, by George Wien on a much smaller scale than that of the 1960s. Wien has stated that he decided to resume the festival in Newport in order to protect his legal right to the name.

Governmental Grants

An active organization in the field of jazz is the Universal Jazz Coalition, Inc., a nonprofit service organization for the jazz artist and community. In its publication, the *UJC Jazz Catalyst* for the Spring of 1979, it listed the year's grants in support of jazz by the federal National Endowment for the Arts. The *UJC Jazz Catalyst* segregated the federal grants into certain categories as follows:

1   Nonmatching fellowship grants to established professional jazz artists of exceptional talent to advance their careers through composition, arrangement, or performance. The maximum grant amount is $10,000; 70 grants were issued, totaling $331,000. Examples of recipients of the grants are Cecil P. Taylor, $5,000; Andrew Hill, $5,000; Manny Albam, $7,500; and Leon Konitz, $5,000.

2   Nonmatching fellowship grants to enable young musicians of exceptional talent to study with individual professional artists for concentrated instruction and experience. The maximum grant is $5,000; 55 grants were issued, totaling $104,145.

3   Matching grants to organizations for jazz presentations, educational programs, short term residencies by jazz specialists, and carefully planned regional or national festivals or tours. The maximum grant amount is $25,000 for organizations with annual expenditures of more than $100,000 for jazz programming. The maximum grant amount is $15,000 for organizations with annual expenditures of less than $100,000 for jazz programming; 74 grants were issued, total-

ing $460,685. Examples are: Alley Theatre, Houston, Texas, $6,000 to support a Summer Jazz Festival featuring local artists; Central Missouri State University, $2,000 for residency by the Woody Herman Band; Creative Music Foundation, Inc., Woodstock, New York, $4,500 for performances and workshops; and Las Vegas Jazz Society, $15,000 for a concert series and jazz instruction in Las Vegas schools.

4 Grants to individuals and organizations to carry out projects not covered by the established categories of support: 3 grants were issued, totaling $37,500, including $24,000 to the Jazz Consortium of Organizations and Artists, of New York, New York.

The National Endowment for the Arts makes additional grants in categories of Expansion Arts, namely, instruction and training, arts exposure, and special summer projects.

The *UJC Jazz Analyst* also reported that for the fiscal year 1978–1979, the New York State Council on the Arts, in support of jazz, gave subsidies to at least 18 organizations totaling in excess of $500,000. Among the largest awards were: Jazzmobile, Inc., $118,500; New Muse Community Museum, $104,000; National Jazz Ensemble, $44,500; and International Art of Jazz, $44,500.

For the year 1978 the *UJC Jazz Analyst* stated that the Creative Artists Public Service Program (CAPS) had given fellowships of $3,500 each to 14 fellows chosen from 338 applications. CAPS is an arts service program funded by the New York State Council on the Arts, the National Endowment for the Arts, and corporate sponsors. The fellowships are awarded to New York State artists.

Jazz Arrangements

The essence of jazz is its improvisation, its variety, and its spontaneity. A basic jazz rendition may well take the form of an interpretation of a popular work such as "Embraceable You" which, as performed, may be almost unrecognizable. Jazz performers may make such substantial revisions of the basic song as to require an expert musicologist to track down the popular song source.

Under the 1976 Copyright Act, by his variations a jazz performer is deemed to have made an arrangement of the basic work and to have created a "derivative work." The act permits derivative works to be copyrighted only if made by the copyright owner of the original work or with his consent. When a copyright owner grants a common mechanical license to record, this in practice is construed to indicate there will be no objection to arrangements which adjust the work to the performer's style or manner of interpretation. The license does not denote a grant of rights to arrange, but is rather an agreement not to object. Ordinarily no claim to copyright is made in the arrangement by the performer or by the copyright proprietor of the basic material.

Despite the arrangement, full copyright credit will belong to the original basic work and none will be accorded to the jazz contribution.

Jazz Repertory

In view of the improvisational nature of jazz, it is not ordinarily thought of as a repertoire item except for recordings and transcriptions. Printing of jazz scores has not been encouraged.

Nevertheless, the mid-1970s saw the founding of the New York Jazz Repertory Company by the National Endowment of the Arts, The New York State Council on the Arts, and Carnegie Hall. Its founding leaders—Stanley Cowell, Gil Evans, Billy Taylor, and Sy Oliver—recognized as the basic "company" some 100 or more acclaimed jazz musicians, representing all periods and styles of jazz. Some of these musicians are Art Blakey, Sam Rivers, Bobby Hackett, Elvin Jones, and Illinois Jacquet.

George Wein, as Executive Director, observed that

One of the benefits of having such a huge and varied company of musicians available is that those who are writing material for the concerts can compose with a much wider concept that they might if they were writing for a specific orchestra. The depth of available talent allows a jazz composer writing for the company to insert a solo for one of the company who might not be playing in the regular section for other parts of the piece.

The purposes of the repertory company include the presentation of new music specially written for large jazz orchestras. The company maintains a library of new works, as well as transcriptions of old arrangements. Through the library, a particular musical piece can be made available for repeat performances not necessarily rendered by prior performers.

Establishment of accessible jazz repertoire is also a purpose of the Berkeley School of Music printing program which presents jazz arrangements in printed form and compositions suitable for large aggregations of jazz musicians. With its catalog, the Berkeley School of Music services hundreds of other schools and colleges.

Performance Income

When jazz music is played on radio or television, the performing rights organizations log the performances. Based on the credits, performance fees are paid by the organizations to the composer and publisher affiliates.

Broadcast Music, Inc., (BMI) has been historically supportive of jazz and has established minimum annual earnings guarantees, usually of a modest nature, for jazz composer affiliates. BMI grants additional credits for a "concert work," which is determined to include jazz originally written for concert performances. For a concert work performed as a feature on local radio there is a payment for each Group 1 station performance of 8 cents per minute as compared with a total of 6 cents for a popular song. For Group 2 stations, the payment is 3½ cents per minute versus 2½ cents in toto for a popular song. Under BMI standards, a Group 1 station is one which in the latest calendar year paid BMI $4,000 or more as an annual license fee, whereas a Group 2 station has paid less than $4,000.

For a concert work feature performance on television, the remuneration from BMI is 24 cents per minute for performances on local television, $2.25 per minute for each station carrying Group A network programs, and $1.25 per minute for each station showing group B network programs. A Group A network program is one broadcast between 7:00 P.M. and 1:00 P.M. Programs broadcast at all other times are deemed to be in the Group B category. This may be compared to total payments for a popular song performed on a local television station of 24 cents, and $2.25 and $1.25, respectively, for performances on each network Group A and Group B station.

A nonconcert jazz work which exceeds 7 minutes as commercially recorded may be eligible for additional credit. When a clearance form for such a work is submitted to BMI, it should be accompanied by a letter applying for consideration for additional credit.

ASCAP favors jazz works which in their original form were composed for a choral, symphonic, or similar concert performance. These are sometimes referred to as serious works.

Multiple credits are allotted by ASCAP to logged radio or television performances of serious works which are 4 minutes or longer in duration. The credits are awarded in relation to the minutes of actual performance. Thus for a 5-minute performance the multiple is 2; for a 10-minute performance, 6; and for a 20-minute performance, 20.

ASCAP, instead of merely distributing the license fees received from concert and symphony halls, multiplies such fees by 5 in determining the credits to be awarded for concert and symphony hall performances. Extra credits are also allotted for serious works based on the number of instruments for which a work was written and the actual duration of the performance.

Under the ASCAP system of credits, a "qualifying work" is granted special higher credits when used in nonfeature roles such as background, cue, bridge, or theme music. Only 20 percent of the number of feature performances necessary to classify other music as a "qualifying work" is required in the case of serious works.

Performance income paid by the performing rights organizations to jazz composers is limited. AM radio stations ordinarily regard jazz as too academic for a general audience and do not favor jazz performance. FM radio stations which feature jazz cater to select audiences and are not numerous.

Mechanical License Fees

Record companies which issue jazz recordings must apply for mechanical licenses to the owners of the copyrights or their designated agents. For many owners, the agent is The Harry Fox Agency, Inc., of 110 East 59th Street, New York, New York 10022, whose main activity is issuing and supervising mechanical licenses on behalf of the copyright owners that it represents. Its basic license calls for the record manufacturer to account and pay on a quarterly basis for all records manufactured and distributed.

Under the compulsory license provisions of Section 115 of the 1976 Copyright Act, there are established mechanical license fees for each record manufactured and distributed of 4 cents per composition or ¾ cent per minute or fraction thereof, whichever is larger. This formula is likely to serve as a ceiling on royalties in United States negotiated licenses for a previously recorded copyrighted musical composition.*

Some jazz compositions are of similar length to that of a common popular song and qualify for mechanical license fees of 4 cents per composition. Other jazz selections are considerably longer, and the applicable fee will be determined by the standard of ¾ cent per minute or fraction thereof, which is triggered for compositions which exceed 5 minutes in length.

* The rates will increase on January 1, 1983, to 4.25 cents (or 0.8 cents per minute of playing time or fraction thereof, whichever is larger); on July 1, 1984, to 4.5 cents (or 0.85 cents per minute of playing time or fraction thereof, whichever is larger); and on January 1, 1986, to five cents (or 0.95 cents per minute of playing time or fraction thereof, whichever is larger).

Publications

The music trade press in the United States—*Billboard, Record World,* and *Cashbox*—have limited coverage of jazz. Each contains a weekly listing of top-selling jazz LPs.

However, there are publications with more intensive coverage of jazz. In the United States, some of the leading jazz journals include *Down Beat,* which was established in 1934, *Jazz,* and the *Journal of Jazz Studies* (Rutgers University Transaction Press). There are also the *Jazz Echo,* the *World Jazz Calendar,* and the *Jazz Man's Reference Book,* which originate in New York City. There are sundry other jazz publications in the United States.

Numerous publications which stress jazz are released outside the United States. For example, there are *Coda* from Canada, and the *Melody Maker* and *Jazz Journal* from England. Japan has the *Swing Journal. Le Jazz Hot* and *Jazz Magazine* come out of Paris, France. *Jazz Forum* is published in Warsaw, Poland, and *Orkester Journalen* in Stockholm, Sweden. There are *Musica Jazz* from Milan, Italy, *Jazz/Press* from Holland, and *Jazz Podium* from Stuttgart, West Germany.

For a list of other publications around the world, refer to the *Jazzman's Reference Book,* Part 3, a publication of the International Jazz Federation, Inc., of P.O. Box 777, New York, New York 10108.

Jazz Organizations

Organizations and associations which are intensively interested in jazz abound in the United States. A listing which appears in the aforementioned *Jazzman's Reference Book,* Part 3, is set forth in Appendix 18.

The range of names includes the Afro-American Arts Institute, the American Federation of Musicians, the American Music Conference, the Boston Jazz Society, the Charlie Parker Memorial Jazz Foundation, the Dallas Jazz Society, the Duke Ellington Society, the Institute of Jazz Studies, the Jazzmobile, the National Association of Jazz Educators, The Santa Monica Jazz Club, and WPFW–FM Pacifica, Washington.

The International Jazz Federation, which publishes the *Jazzman's Reference Book,* is worthy of special note. It is a nonprofit organization with several thousand members, including leading personalities on the international jazz scene—composers, musicians, radio and television personalities, producers, photographers, journalists, festival organizers, agents, publishers, promoters, and collectors. An important purpose of the organization is to stimulate the worldwide development of jazz. It is the only body to represent jazz on the International Music Council of UNESCO. It operates independently of its parent organization, the European-based International Jazz Federation, which was founded in Venice, Italy in 1969. The United States federation publishes its own quarterly magazine, along with the *Jazz Echo* newspaper, the yearly directory, *Jazzman's Reference Book,* and the biannual World Jazz Calendar. The federation acts to stimulate live performances, tours, festivals, and concerts, and is a center for jazz references and information.

PART TWO
Other Aspects of the Music Industry

7

Production and Sale of

Printed Music

UPON the appointment of former Justice Abe Fortas to the U.S. Supreme Court, the press called attention to his musical habits. One evening a week he regularly joins with three other musicians in private performance as a string quartet. In doing so, he is one of 50 million Americans who are part of the category of amateur musicians. This is defined by the American Music Conference as that group of people who play nonprofessionally 6 or more times a year. There were, in 1979, over 18 million piano players, more than 15 million guitarists, over 6 million organists, and a vast number of woodwind instrumentalists.

The boom in instrument sales was recognized by the Columbia Broadcasting System at the time of its $13 million acquisition of the Fender Guitar and Amplifier Corporation, a manufacturer of electric guitars and amplifiers. Commenting on the purchase, the then president of Columbia Records said, "This is a fast-growing business tied into the expanding leisure time market."

The number of instrumentalists, and of instruments in the hands of the public, is reflected in the sales and uses of printed music. Retail sales volume of printed music reached a level of over $266 million a year in 1980.

Types of Printed Music

The same composition may be available for use in many different printed versions. There are numerous printed editions of the single selection "Rhapsody in Blue," ranging from a full symphonic orchestra score with a list price of $75 to an organ solo of the theme selling for $1.95. A piece that is available in a wide range of individual printed forms will appear in folios, which are soft-cover collections, and in song books or albums. These may have a list price as high as $25 for the hard-cover illustrated edition. Examples of the types of printed music available are shown in the following list:

BAND
Collections (Folios)
Concert Selections (Quarto Size)
Methods
Marching Band
Symphonic or Complete

BRASS
Solos, Duets, Trios, and Ensembles

CANTATAS AND CHORAL ARRANGEMENTS
Unison
Two Part
SSA (Soprano, Soprano, and Alto)
SSAA (Soprano, Soprano, Alto, and Alto)
SATB (Soprano, Alto, Tenor, and Bass)
Three Part Male
TTBB (Tenor, Tenor, Bass, and Bass)
Interchangeable Chorus (SA, SSA, and SAB)
Choral Collections
Choral Selections
Festival Choral Works

STAGE BANDS
Collections (Folios)
Stage Band Series
Original Transcriptions

FRETTED INSTRUMENTS
Collections and Methods
Solos

HARMONICA
Methods
Collections

METHODS AND STUDIES
Instrumental
Strings
Band and Orchestra

ORCHESTRA
Collections (Folios)
Concert Selections
Major Orchestral Works
Miniature Scores (Full)
String Orchestra
String Orchestra Collections

ORGAN
Methods
Collections
Solos

PIANO
Methods and Studies
Collections (Folios)
Teaching and Recital Pieces
Piano Duets
Two Pianos—Four Hands
Solos (Easy Piano, Regular Piano, and Intermediate)

STRINGS
Violin
Viola
Cello
String Bass
Methods
Solos and Duets
Trios and Quartets

VOCAL
Collections (Song) (Folios)
Community Song Books (with
  booklets)
Duets, Secular, and Sacred
Duet Collections (Folios)
Folk Collections (Folios)
Methods

Pocket-size Song Books
Scores
Selections
Songs, Standard, Sacred, and
  Popular
Song Books (Cloth Bound,
  with Music)

"Educational music" is music intended to be sold to schools, colleges, institutions, or industrial plants for performances by amateur musical groups. Included are solo or group arrangements of classical, semiclassical, and popular music deemed suitable for vocal or instrumental renditions.

For example, there are educational versions of "You Light Up My Life" and "Smoke Gets in Your Eyes." To meet the demand for multiple voice and instrument combinations, the number of different publications of the same song may exceed 40 or more. Arrangements of popular music are often revised to satisfy the most recent taste of the public. Classical and semiclassical music arrangements are modified from time to time to include different instrumentation and voices.

Indexes to Printed Music

Some of the indexes available for printed music are listed in Appendix Q in *This Business of Music.** There is a tremendous amount of printed music available in various categories, such as band music, choral music, etc.

Fake Books

A major problem in the field of printed music is the illegal publication of popular song collections, which are in large demand, especially by professional musicians. An illegal fake book is an unauthorized compilation of the melody line and chord symbols of as many as 1,000 top songs. It is sold for varying prices ranging as high as $35.00. It flouts the Copyright Act, which gives to the copyright proprietor the exclusive right to make and print copies of compositions.

The illegal printer and distributor pay no royalties to the legal composers and publishers of songs contained in the fake book. In effect, the fake book replaces and substitutes for folios and sheet music, on the sales of which writers would earn royalties and publishers would derive profits.

* Sidney Shemel and M. William Krasilovsky, rev. ed. (New York: 1979), p. 516.

Assuming a retail price of $1.95 for a copy of sheet music of a popular song, the sheet music for 1,000 such songs in a fake book would sell for an aggregate of $1,950. Instead the fake book may sell for $35.

The bargain price to the user and the profit to the illicit printer and distributor make fake books difficult to control. Substantial awards of damages under the Copyright Act have been made by courts against fake book printers and distributors, and the dealer of such books is also liable.

Moreover, criminal penalties under Section 506 of the Copyright Act are available. These are sought by the National Music Publishers' Association, Inc., of 110 East 59th Street, New York, New York, against people who willfully and for profit engage in the printing or selling of fake books or knowingly and willfully aid or abet such infringement. The practice is punishable by imprisonment of up to 1 year, or by a fine of up to $10,000, or both, for the first offense, and by imprisonment of up to 2 years, or by a fine of up to $50,000, or both, for any subsequent offense. A copy of Sections 506 (a) and (b) of the Copyright Act is included in Appendix 19.

Acting under the criminal provisions of the Copyright Act, a federal jury in New York has convicted a Long Island band leader for publishing fake books without paying royalties to the copyright owners. He allegedly published more than 46,000 plastic-bound books that included songs by George Gershwin, Lorenz Hart, and Oscar Hammerstein, among others. According to the United States Attorney the $35 book was to return $1.6 million on an investment of $81,535.

A former Staten Island music teacher was sentenced to a year in prison and fined $1,000 for the unauthorized printing and selling of fake books.

Acting to combat fake books, a number of larger publishers and some of the independent licensee distributors of printed editions have published legitimate compilations of numerous songs in the same form as fake books. These are sold for prices ranging up to about $25. An example is a folio entitled, "Legit Professional Fake Book," which contains 1,010 songs.

Preparation for Printing

Rarely in any field of music does a composer submit a manuscript that is ready for printing. Popular songs accepted by a publisher from a writer are usually in lead sheet form that requires arrangement and copying in preparation for printing. For folk and rock and roll music, lead sheets are often not submitted, and it is necessary for the publisher to engage a skilled copyist who can write a lead sheet while listening to a phonograph recording or tape.

Arrangements are made by staff arrangers in the case of many major publishers or by free-lance arrangers who are paid fees for their services. Computer engraving, which is available and common, is on the ascendancy. A combination of music typewriter and/or music typography machines, together with photo-offset may also be employed. However, there is still the need for limited handwork by skilled inserters who draw in such items as musical ties and slurs.

In the serious music field, the composer's basic manuscript requires substantial copying services, and costs to ready the many orchestral parts for printing are expensive.

Attractive packaging has become a significant factor in the sales of printed editions. Folios and current hit sheet music copies require appealing cover artwork and color printing in order to compete in the impulse-buying market. Color is often essential to make a folio or other publication stand out on a music store rack, and some covers are printed in four colors.

Most publishers use independent printers who can offer the speed, efficiency, and economies of modern giant presses, as well as color printing. For example, in the New York area, major contract printers of music include G. Schirmer, Inc., Hampshire Press, Inc., and Vicks Lithograph and Printing Corp.

The writer contracts in the popular music field include royalties payable for various categories of printed editions. The rate for sheet music usually ranges between 6 and 8 cents. Publishers may pay 10 cents for show tunes or, in contracts negotiated for the renewal period of the United States copyright, for established standards. Slightly less is paid for motion picture themes, and the lowest royalty is applied to new popular songs.

Some royalty contracts, including the 1978 Popular Songwriters Contract used by the American Guild of Authors and Composers, contain sliding scales of a songwriter's sheet music royalties. In that contract, the royalties range from a minimum of 10 percent of the wholesale price for the first 200,000 copies, to 15 percent of the wholesale price on copies sold in excess of 500,000. However, sliding scale provisions are rarely used. They involve cumbersome bookkeeping, and usually an unrealistic idea of anticipated sales.

While there are exceptions for top hits, sheet music sales of most popular compositions are small. For many songs, the sales are less than the minimum printing order of 1,000 copies. Many songs, especially rock and roll, are never printed.

Individual popular songs are rarely printed in any form other than piano-vocal sheet music or in folios until they become accepted as standard hits.

As a rule, the writer royalty for orchestrations, band arrangements, octavos, quartets, combinations of voices and instruments, and other copies of songs is 10 percent of the wholesale selling price. As noted previously, in the AGAC contract there is a sliding scale of royalties, commencing with 10 percent of the wholesale selling price for the first 200,000 copies and increasing to 15 percent for copies in excess of 500,000. Oddly enough, many popular publisher-songwriter contracts inadvertently base royalties on the retail price rather than on the wholesale price that is the standard for even the writer-oriented contract form of AGAC.

When a song is included in a folio or other collection, the AGAC and many other contracts provide that the aggregate royalty of 10 percent of the wholesale selling price is prorated among all the copyrighted songs in the compilation. Thus, in a folio of 10 copyrighted songs, 1 percent is applied to each song. If additional public domain songs are included in the folio, there is no diminution of the royalty for each copyrighted composition.

In the contract forms of some publishers no distinction is made between copyrighted and public domain songs in determining the prorated writer royalty. This results in a lower percentage royalty for each copyrighted song. However, the wholesale selling price on which the percentage is computed may be increased by the inclusion of the public domain songs in the compilation. When more than 25 songs are included in a folio, the overall rate is increased under the AGAC and certain other contracts by an additional ½ percent for each composition over the first 25.

Independent Folio Licensees and Selling Agents

In today's popular market, a large percentage of folios are not prepared and issued by the publishers of the compositions. Many publishers, especially the smaller ones without extensive catalogs, utilize the services of independent folio publishers and distributors, such as Charles Hansen Music & Books Ltd., Warner Bros. Music, Columbia Pictures Publications, The Big 3 Music Corporation, Cherry Lane Music Co., Inc., Plymouth Music Co., Inc., and Hal Leonard Publishing Corporation. These arrangements may be either exclusive or nonexclusive.

Operating from a Miami Beach base is Charles Hanson Music & Books Ltd. Columbia Pictures Publications, which is owned by Columbia Pictures Industries, is located in Hialeah, Florida. Plymouth Music Co., Inc., is a smaller firm in the Fort Lauderdale, Florida, area.

Warner Bros. Music and The Big 3 Music Corporation are old, established companies with facilities in the New York area, that have enlarged the scope of their activities to include licensed songs. They have the advantage of access to their own huge basic catalogs of compositions for interlarding in folios. Cherry Lane

Music Co., Inc., is a smaller firm in Greenwich, Connecticut, close to the New York area. Hal Leonard Publications Corporation, which handles the extensive catalog of Chappell & Co., Inc., as well as other publications, has its headquarters in Milwaukee, Wisconsin.

In the relationship between the music publisher and the folio publisher, the latter is usually either a licensee or a selling agent. Generally, a licensee arrangement provides for payment to the music publisher of a stated royalty. The folio publisher bears all costs of preparation and printing, as well as the risks of unsold inventory.

Under the less prevalent selling agency arrangement, the music publisher pays the expense of preparation and printing and is entitled to the sales receipts less a commission to the agent. There are elements common to both licensees and selling agents. The folio distributor, in both instances, handles the production and printing for the music publisher, and the sales organization of the folio distributor is utilized. Billing to dealers is usually similar.

The variance in the arrangements can result in a difference in the royalties payable to songwriters. In the case of a folio license, under many songwriter agreements, the publisher's United States and Canadian royalties are shared with songwriters on a pro rata basis. The AGAC form of agreement fixes the writer's share at 50 percent.

In the event of a selling agency, the songwriter royalty under the AGAC contract and under many agreements would be the same as that for folios handled directly in the United States and Canada by the music publisher, namely, a pro rata portion of 10 percent of the wholesale selling price.

Most popular music folios are issued by independent folio distributors acting as licensees. The licensee method has proved to be most adaptable to combining the songs of diverse publishers in one publication. Such compilations have generally the greatest appeal to the retail buying public.

Folio Licensee Royalties

What royalties are paid by independent folio distributor-licensees to music publishers? Typical rates are as follows for folios and for individual editions other than regular sheet music:

10 percent of the retail selling price for organ solos, band arrangements, choral arrangements, and all other separately printed copies except piano-vocal (regular sheet music).

A pro rata portion of 12½ percent of the retail selling price for folios.

Royalties to the licensor-publisher on the above editions are customarily paid on net sales. A typical contract form of license for folio and other editions is in Appendix 20.

Folio Selling-Agent Commissions

As previously noted, folios are also issued through selling agents. They are paid a commission for their services, with the costs of printing and preparation of editions borne by the music publisher. The commissions charged are about 20 to 30 percent of the amounts received from sales. A typical form of contract for selling-agent arrangements for folio and other editions is in Appendix 21.

Sheet Music Licensees

The same independent folio distributors, in addition, serve music publishers in the more volatile business of printing and selling regular piano-vocal copies. As many as a hundred thousand copies of a top hit can be sold in a year. Most songs do not even sell their minimum printing orders. Here, too, there are licensee and selling-agency arrangements made with music publishers.

Under a usual form of licensee agreement the distributor pays all expenses of preparation and production of copies. However, instead of the percentage royalties payable on folio editions, such as 12½ percent of the retail price on sales, there is a payment to the music publisher of 40 or 50 cents per copy sold. In some instances the royalty may be stated as 20 percent of the suggested retail list price, which gives the advantage to the publisher of an increased royalty when the suggested list price becomes greater.

Sometimes the distributor will pay an advance to the publisher, recoupable out of the royalties on sales.

Selling Agency

Some distributors also offer to act as selling agents, as an alternative to being licensees, for sheet music distribution. As noted previously, the receipts from sales are paid to the music publisher less the agent's commissions that, as in the case of folio editions, are about 20 to 30 percent of receipts. The form of selling-agent contract shown in Appendix 21 also applies to sheet music.

Emphasizing its role as agent rather than licensee, one firm offers special procedures for exclusive selling-agent rights to an entire catalog for a period of years. All bills for printing by outside printers are rendered, and all sales invoices are issued, in the name of the song publisher at the address of the sales agent. Checks from jobbers and dealers in payment for printed editions are drawn directly to the order of the song publisher, and these checks are transmitted monthly to the song publisher with statements showing the number of copies sold. The agent's commission is billed monthly to the song publisher.

These procedures give added assurance to the song publisher that bills for printing and receipts from sales are proper. They also help to establish and preserve customer relations between the song publisher and the jobber or dealer. A form of contract for this type of selling-agent arrangement is in Appendix 22.

Term of Licensee or Selling-Agent Agreements

The minimum terms of the nonexclusive or exclusive licensee or sales agent agreements range from 1 to 5 years. The contracts frequently provide for automatic extensions from year to year, unless either party gives a written notice of termination prior to the anniversary date. A licensee-distributor will often be granted the right to sell off accumulated inventory on hand at the termination date, subject to its rendering statements and paying royalties in accordance with the agreement between the parties. For protection the publisher will limit the sell-off period, e.g., 6 months. Sell-off periods may vary with the particular product. For example, sheet music and personality folios may be limited to from 6 to 12 months, mixed folios may be restricted to 12 to 18 months, or there may be unlimited rights provided that the royalty has been prepaid on all inventory.

Joint Ventures

In addition to independent folio licensees and selling agents, there is the possibility of a joint venture between music publishers and independent folio distributor-licensees. This is not common and would ordinarily be reserved for large music publisher licensors. In a joint venture, the music publisher makes his catalog available to the folio distributor-licensee on a profit-sharing basis. The costs of preparation and printing, royalties to writers, and other stipulated costs would be deducted from the receipts of the venture. Typically there is also deducted an administration fee of the folio distributor-licensee amounting to approximately 10 to 15 percent of the gross receipts. The remainder is then shared by the joint venturers in agreed proportions.

Personality Folios

The usual personality folio is published in conjunction with a best-selling record of a recording artist or a group. The folio will include all the compositions on the record, whether or not they were written by the artist, together with likenesses or photographs and a biography of the artist. The title of the folio is often the name of the recording artist and the title of the album, for example, "Rod Stewart, Foolish Behavior."

There may be personality folios featuring one artist where the contents cover selections from several LPs; a folio may also include compositions that are written by the artist but not recorded by him.

A folio may contain only the songs in a successful musical show (e.g., "Annie" or "Barnum") or in a best-selling motion picture soundtrack album. The cover and contents may reproduce the logo and artwork from the show or film, photographs of the scenes and performers, and comments concerning the show or film and its performers.

Personality folios ordinarily require the written permission of the artist for the use of his or her photographs and biography. Where a musical show or motion picture is involved, permission to utilize artwork, photographs, and biographies is needed.

The distributor-licensee of such folios will pay customary royalties of about 12½ percent of the suggested retail selling price, pro rata, to the licensing music publishers whose compositions are in the folios. It is common to pay an additional royalty of 5 percent to the featured personality in personality folios. An extra royalty of 5 percent for folios which correspond to shows or films is subject to negotiation.

Lyric Licenses

Song lyric publications seek licenses from publishers to print and vend the lyrics of hit popular songs. Licenses are sought for the United States and Canada, generally for a period of 1 year. Flat payments are made for the licenses, rather than royalties. For the usual song hit, the payment will approximate $75. Often there is the provision that if the song achieves one of the top 10 positions in the *Billboard* chart of top hits, an additional sum of, say, $50 will be paid. Appendix 23 is a form of license agreement for lyric reprint rights. Publishers who license the words and music of their songs to a licensee-distributor should be careful to retain the right to license the lyrics alone to song lyric publications and others.

Copyright Notice

Publication of a work must be accompanied by a notice of copyright on each copy published in the United States and elsewhere. Otherwise, unless the omission is excused under the 1976 Copyright Act, the work will be deemed dedicated to the public and all claims to copyright will have been permanently abandoned. The statute defines "publication" as "the distribution of copies . . . of a work to the public by sale or other transfer of ownership, or by rental, lease, or lending." Publication also includes an offer to distribute copies "to a group of persons for purposes of further distribution. . . ."

It is, therefore, imperative that a provision requiring a notice of copyright be inserted in licensee and selling-agent agreements. A common clause states that the licensee or selling agent will include a notice of copyright on each copy of the printed edition. The same provision sets forth the exact form of notice, or a model form of notice, or stipulates that the copyright owner will prescribe the form of notice to be followed.

Under Paragraph 401 of the Copyright Act of the United States, a notice of copyright shall consist of the symbol © or the word "Copyright," or the abbreviation "Copr.," together with the proprietor's name, or an abbreviation by which the name can be recognized, or a generally known alternative designation with respect to printed literary, musical, or dramatic works; the year of first publication is also stated.

A typical form of notice is

© 1982 John Doe or Copyright 1982 by John Doe

or frequently a combination of the two prior forms.

Copyright © 1982 John Doe

For musical works, the Copyright Act provides that the notice must appear on "copies in such manner and location as to give reasonable notice of the claim of copyright." It is also specified that the Register of Copyrights may prescribe by regulation, as examples, specific notice positions to satisfy this requirement, although these specifications are not exhaustive of what may be otherwise "reasonable" notices.

The United States and over 50 other countries adhere to the Universal Copyright Convention. For reciprocal international protection of a work in these countries pursuant to the convention, the required notice of copyright consists of the symbol ©, accompanied by the name of the copyright owner and the year date of publication. An example is

© 1982 John Doe

This form of notice, as indicated previously, also qualifies under Paragraph 401 of the United States Copyright Act. Since the 1976

Copyright Act, the United States standard for the placement of notice is the same as under the Universal Copyright Convention.

Many publishers will also attempt to obtain reciprocal international copyright protection in the many countries that adhere to the Berne Convention and in the Western Hemisphere nations that are parties to the Buenos Aires Convention of 1910. The United States is a signatory to the latter, but not the former, convention.

A work originating in a non-Berne Convention country such as the United States will be afforded protection under that convention if published first or simultaneously in a country that has signed the convention. Many American publishers who seek Berne Convention protection will usually arrange for first or simultaneous publication in Canada or England which adhere to the convention.

The Buenos Aires Convention calls for each work to carry a notice that property rights in a copyright are reserved. While the United States form of copyright notice seems sufficient for this purpose, it appears advisable to add the words "All Rights Reserved" to the copyright notice to ensure protection under the Buenos Aires Convention.

Independent licensee-distributors or selling agents for printed editions can usually be helpful in advising and arranging for proper copyright notices and for simultaneous publication in a Berne Convention country.

For a further discussion of notices and other formalities, including registration and deposit, involved in copyright protection in the United States and elsewhere, see the chapters entitled "The Nature of Copyright in the United States" and "International Copyright Protection" in *This Business of Music.**

Return Privileges

Return privileges to jobbers or dealers mean that they may return unsold copies to the seller. Such privileges are a means of encouraging them to stock copies without risk until they have a full opportunity to promote and sell the copies.

Often a song will be on the popular hit charts for only a limited period, and sheet music of the song will not sell thereafter. Return privileges may ensure that the jobber or dealer will stock sufficient copies to satisfy the public demand during the peak popularity of the song.

The short span and the volatility of the popular piano-vocal sheet music market make the risk of returnable jobber or dealer inventory a matter of considerable concern to the distributors.

* Sidney Shemel and M. William Krasilovsky, rev. ed. (New York: 1979), pp. 109, 271.

Distributors reduce their risk by giving special discounts to jobbers or dealers who accept large quantities of printed copies without return privileges.

Popular song copies are usually sold with a full return privilege unless a special discount deal has been arranged. Show tune sheet music is in some cases fully returnable and in others nonreturnable from the start.

Due to returns and bad debts, licensees commonly maintain reserves to avoid overpayment. This means that they treat the quantity covered by the reserve as if it is not sold, and therefore royalties on such quantity are not payable. Typical reserves are 50 percent for the first quarter-annual period of sales, diminishing to 25 percent for the second quarter, 15 percent for the third quarter, and no reserves for the fourth quarter.

Discounts

The basic discount structure for sales on daily orders rather than by stock orders provides for a jobber to receive discounts from 33⅓ to 50 percent of the retail price, with the average discount being just under 50 percent. For sales on daily orders the discounts to dealers range from 25 to 50 percent of the retail price, with an average dealer discount of about 40 percent on noneducational material and 33⅓ percent on educational editions. The lowest discount rates are for symphonic scores.

Stock order discounts are higher, ranging from 55 percent to, in unusual cases, 60 percent to jobbers, and from 45 percent to 55 percent to dealers.

A stock order purchase means that the dealer, using the individual publisher's or distributor's catalog or stock order bulletin, forwards very large semiannual orders rather than on a daily hit-or-miss basis. Stock orders are gauged to meet the store's 6-month requirements. A few publishers allow more frequent stock orders but set minimum dollar limits per order.

As noted previously, there is a variation in dealer discounts. While some publishers determine a retail store's daily order discount standing by the volume of daily orders in particular categories of music (such as show, popular, band, folk, concert, etc.), it is also common for a store's discount status to depend on the volume and regularity of its stock order purchases in the specific music categories.

Discount ratings sometimes depend as well on the dealer's willingness to buy and display "new issues" in the categories involved. A new issue is a new printed edition, for which special incentive discounts are offered in return for the dealer's purchasing copies without viewing a sample. The new issue discount may be as much as an extra 10 percent off the normal discounted figure. Frequently, the dealer may be allowed one reorder within a limited time at the same new issue discount.

Whereas most publishers may offer no discount on direct sales of educational music to institutions or schools, some may offer discounts from 10 to 15 percent depending on the potential buying capacity of the institution. Jobbers and dealers selling educational music may grant varying discounts to encourage sales.

For certain very large customers a special form of discount is given sometimes by the seller's prepayment of shipping or freight charges.

Prices of Printed Music

A copy of piano-vocal sheet music usually sells at retail from $1.95 to $2.50, and it costs the publisher 10 to 15 cents to print in quantities of 2,000 to 5,000 copies. A folio of 15 songs can be printed in quantity for about 40 cents. Folios containing 40 or 100 songs entail usual printing costs of 60 or 90 cents, respectively. A marching band edition may sell for about $20, and a full symphonic orchestration of a major piece for as much as $50. For the limited quantities expected to be sold, the printing costs may be as much as 20 percent of the retail selling price.

The publisher's operating expenses generally exceed his printing costs. Apart from being subject to overhead costs, the expenses of preparing and producing the printed edition, distribution and advertising costs, and royalty charges, the seller will also be affected by various other factors in determining the prices of printed music. One consideration is the potential market that determines the size and, in turn, the costs of the initial print order. Another factor is competition in the particular area of music. For example, one piano methods course cannot be priced considerably out of line with others.

Publishers use a formula of about 10 times the print costs to arrive at retail list prices. Thus, a printing cost of 80 cents for folios would lead to a $7.95 retail price.

A further factor in pricing printed music is whether the edition is part of a series in the serious music and educational fields. The cost of preparing a later issue may be reduced by the series' uniformity of style. Also, the advertising and promotion costs may be lessened by prior exploitation efforts. In addition, there may be an assurance of sales of a later issue. Prior purchasers, such as guitar teachers buying a methods series, are likely to be interested in acquiring later editions in the series.

Finally, because of the impact of inflation, prices are often raised for reprints of printed music despite the fact that the initial costs of preparation have been recouped. Reprints are of special importance in sales to educational institutions that may continue to reorder once the edition is a part of the curriculum.

Foreign Sales

Usually, popular printed music is not exported. Instead, it is licensed for printing and sales to foreign licensees or agents. These are generally referred to as subpublishers.

In some instances folio licensees will obtain worldwide printing rights and will produce folios that can be sold throughout the world. One prominent licensee prints for the world in the United States and exports quantities of folios for foreign distribution to international distributors.

Under the terms of the licensee printing arrangement with subpublishers, the foreign subpublisher agrees to pay the American publisher a royalty that is commonly a minimum of 10 percent, but may increase up to about 15 percent, of the foreign retail selling price. The receipts by the American publisher from the subpublisher are usually divided equally between the American writer and the American publisher.

If a foreign subpublisher administers the collection of mechanical license fees and performance fees, this, as a rule, will be more lucrative than the handling of printed editions. Some American publishers encourage printing in a foreign country. This is done by providing, in contracts with subpublishers, that the subpublisher's share of mechanical license fees and performance fees will be less for unprinted songs than for those that are printed. The question of whether folio publication, as distinguished from sheet music, satisfies this printing provision should be covered in the agreement with the subpublisher.

Printing may be especially important in the case of motion picture songs originating in films scored by members of the British Performing Right Society. Under the rules of the society, in the absence of special waivers from the composer, unless the music has been commercially recorded, the publisher who fails to print will not participate in motion picture performance fees collected from theaters outside the United States. In that case, the writer will receive the so-called publisher's share, as well as the writer's share of fees.

Due to contractual or society printing requirements, it is not unusual for inexpensive editions of music to be issued to fulfill the requirements.

Mailing Privileges

The music publishing, as well as the phonograph record, industry is the beneficiary of a favorable postage policy of the United

States government. Special fourth-class rates can be used to mail the basic materials produced by the enterprises. Postage charges are 63 cents for the first pound, 23 cents for each additional pound or fraction thereof through 7 pounds, and 14 cents for each additional pound or fraction thereof. The policy reason for this favored treatment is to encourage the widespread dissemination of educational and cultural materials and thereby to foster a national cultural life.

Included in the fourth-class rate category are printed music, whether in bound or sheet music form, and music manuscripts. The rate applies regardless of the number of copies, provided that maximum size and weight of containers are observed. The rates can also be used for sound recordings, as well as scripts and guides prepared solely for use with the recordings.

The size of the package is limited to a combined length and girth of 100 inches. The weight of the package is restricted to 70 pounds.

Although many companies still use the outdated phrase "Educational Materials," the proper notation should be "Special Fourth-Class Rate" followed by "Printed Music," or "Sound Recordings," or "Manuscripts," depending on the contents.

Enclosures with mailings of printed editions of music or music manuscripts may include any loose printed matter which would be mailable as third class mail, such as circulars, reply envelopes, and cards.

8

Background Music and

Transcriptions

THE growing field of background music should be distinguished from foreground music. The latter has goals of "show-stoppers" and million-record hit singles that, in the words of former Muzak executive Don O'Neill, attempt to "catch your ear and start you whistling." Background music, on the other hand, avoids being the center of attention. Whether it serves as background to dinner table conversation at a restaurant or as underscoring to a feature motion picture, it is a mood-setting accompaniment.

The music industry recognizes a division of the general field of background music into two parts. One part, sometimes referred to here as "background music services," is generally identified with Muzak and its competitors. The other part is the background music, sometimes referred to here as "film music," used in sound tracks for motion picture and television films. There is also the additional minor area of transcribed music for radio broadcasting.

Muzak describes its programming as ". . . functional music with a mission of relieving fatigue or boredom, dampening machine clatter, or simply relaxing people."

The field of background music for films was described by the late Judge John E. McGeehan, formerly a Justice of the Supreme Court of the State of New York. He was appointed under the 1960 ASCAP consent decree to periodically examine the design and conduct of the ASCAP survey of performances. In his 1963 report on ASCAP he stated:

> . . . with the voracious consumption of background music by television, more people have heard music composed by any

one of the many active background composers within a very short period than have listened to the symphonic works of any one of the great composers in the whole history of the latter works. It is also true, however, that the works of the great symphonic composers have been listened to, whereas background music, however important it may be to the dramatic action, is heard and in most instances the hearers are not consciously aware of the music itself.

Muzak officials have said: "Muzak isn't music to listen to. It's music to hear. We don't play hard rock because it's a little too obvious." In 1980 during one of the last interviews before his death, John Lennon mused on his changes as he reached the age of 40. He said, "You know what I listened to for the last five years? Muzak! For the kind of chores I was doing around the house, it was perfect."

Both major areas of background music, namely, background music services and film music, require special consideration of both business and legal aspects. Accordingly, the discussion in this chapter will, for the most part, deal separately with each type of background music.

Background Music Services

Background music services are increasingly found in locations such as hotels, restaurants, bars, taverns, factories, offices, banking institutions, stores, professional offices, ships, trains, and airplanes. As in the case of Muzak, the music may be transmitted to locations by means of central studio facilities using FM multiplex broadcasting or leased telephone wires. Distribution in the 1980s from central Muzak offices to distributors has tended toward utilizing satellite facilities for all major United States markets and tape for remote or foreign markets. Another method is the use of on-location equipment, such as the tape playback apparatus sold by Minnesota Mining and Manufacturing (3M). In addition to Muzak and 3M, there are a number of other companies in the field, including Canteen Corporation and Seeburg, a division of Capitol Broadcasting of Roanoke, Virginia.

Each of these background music services offers what is described in the applicable BMI public performance license as "... unobtrusive accompaniment to work, shopping, conversation, dining, and relaxation."

The special problems relating to public performance and mechanical reproduction licenses for background music services are discussed later. Each will be better understood after a review of business practices in the field.

Muzak

Since its organization in 1934, Muzak has been the acknowledged leader in the field of functional music services. It estimates its present general audience in its 24 hours of programming to be over 80 million people. Muzak was an independent company from its inception until its sale to the Wrather Corporation in 1957. It was subsequently resold and has been, since 1972, a division (and trademark) of Teleprompter Corporation, which, in 1981, was merged into the Westinghouse Broadcasting Company.

In 1980 Muzak revenues were $19.59 million, an increase from the previous year's $16.65 million. A similar increase was predicted for 1981, with a 10 percent growth in the number of its subscribers. These revenues represent central home office receipts and not distributors' at-source revenues.

The central offices of Muzak are in New York City, from which the following activities are supervised:

Programming: Muzak maintains a library of about 30,000 individual selections, indexed on automated punchcards for programming needs. In the 2-year period of 1979 through 1981, over 3,500 selections were added to the working library.

Licensing copyrighted works: Muzak central offices, in consultation with their franchisees, negotiate public performance licenses with ASCAP and BMI and allocate these licenses to franchised dealers who make license fee payments to ASCAP and BMI. The central offices also obtain reproduction licenses from music publishers for each song used and pay the license fees centrally. A limited number of copyrights are owned by Muzak.

Arranging of Music: Muzak central offices engage free-lance arrangers and conductors.

Recording activities: Until recently all Muzak records were made in United States studios by members of the American Federation of Musicians. Recordings have, in recent years, been produced all over the world, with the intention of recording wherever Muzak is supplied. Recordings are done in 15-minute segments. Each session is recorded in both stereo and monaural, but tapes are utilized, in almost all cases, in monaural only.

Manufacturing and shipping of tapes: Eight-hour tapes are centrally manufactured, shipped under strict control to foreign franchise holders, and reshipped after use to a further-designated franchise holder.

Broadcast transmission: Muzak's investment in special equipment is indicated by its 7-year, $2.8 million contract with Western Union, signed in 1980, for transmission by satellite. It is planned that by the end of 1981 all United States franchisees will be serviced by the satellite system and its 200 earth station receptors. Foreign transmission still uses the former system of 8-hour tapes. Advantages of the Westar I Western Union satellite system to Muzak include better and more direct signals to franchisees. Whereas a series of retapings to make sufficient duplicate masters were required under the former system, Muzak signals can now be broadcast and received directly 24 hours a day; they do not require the retapings, with their inherent loss of quality, as in the past. The satellite system also reduces circuit installations for remote franchises and enables the expansion of available markets at lower costs. Franchisees pay supplementary fees for the satellite service.

Equipment approval: All subscribers must use approved audio equipment.

Franchise issuance: Franchises are issued to the nearly 218 franchise holders throughout the world, including 21 foreign outlets. The foreign outlets include Argentina, Australia, Belgium, Canada, Colombia, Denmark, Finland, France, Germany, Great Britain, Israel, Japan, Mexico, New Zealand, Norway, Panama, Peru, Spain, Switzerland, and Uruguay.

Advertising and promotion: Muzak central offices handle the general advertising and promotion programs. These are aimed at subscribing locations rather than individual listeners. The central offices also conduct a number of psychological personnel and management studies geared to show industrial and office efficiency and savings through the use of background music.

Franchises are issued on a 10-year basis, and the local dealers perform the following functions:

Sales: Three- to five-year subscriptions are sold in four different categories: (1) industrial programs (2) office programs (3) public area programs (restaurants, hotels, etc.), and the relatively new and less important (4) travel programs (planes, ships, trains, etc.) Prices go up to four figures for monthly rates to some major accounts, in addition to initial basic charges for labor and installed equipment.

Service: Franchise holders send Muzak music to subscribers either by leased telephone lines or through special FM multiplex broadcast facilities. The tapes themselves are run through centrally located automated transmitters, specially cued to change programs as well as to deliver regular intervals of silence that are part of the industrial and office programs. Equipment maintenance is also a franchisee duty.

License fee payments: Each franchise holder separately accounts and pays to ASCAP and BMI.

Muzak lays great stress upon its particular qualities to distinguish its service from that of the restaurant proprietor who merely plays regular LPs. It claims to have "scientifically programmed background music arranged ingeniously to be unobtrusive and to render a subtle, subliminal impetus to efficiency and an environmental well-being." Its management studies are alleged to show the achievement of better personnel relationships in difficult situations involving machine clatter and office routine monotony. It claims that the background music encourages better attendance records. In accomplishing these results it is alleged that a certain uniformity of style of performance and arrangement is required in conjunction with identifiable melodies.

A new Muzak on-location foreground music service, called "Tones," supplies recorded music in popular and ethnic formats to on-location devices pursuant to license of the recorded material from the record companies which record the material. Other purveyors of such services are Yesco and Audio Environments, both of Seattle, Washington.

3M

Under the background music project of the 3M company, sales are made of a tape cartridge playback machine and of tapes, most of which contain 700 compositions; there are also specialty tapes with a lesser number of compositions. The 3M equipment is alleged to be cheaper both to operate and maintain than other apparatus. It can be sold to users together with tapes rather than leased with a maintenance contract for the equipment.

In its earlier years all the material in 3M tapes had been recorded in Europe so as to take advantage of lower recording costs for musicians, arrangers, copyists, and studios. However, in the 1980s, recordings made in the United States have been added. The recording activities of 3M require functions similar to those of Muzak. There are problems of programming, licensing of copyrighted works, arranging of music, hiring of musicians, and manufacturing and shipping of tapes. 3M has announced that in 1982 it will introduce a music transmission program, to be communicated by FM, Side Band, and telephone lines, such as Muzak franchisees are utilizing. The service would be targeted at the free radio service market.

Licenses from Copyright Owners

The licenses obtained by background music service companies, such as Muzak and 3M, from copyright proprietors for the mechanical reproduction of music by tape or other means are known as "transcription licenses." Correspondingly, the resultant tapes are frequently called "transcription tapes."

The terms of a transcription license issued by a copyright proprietor are subject to negotiation. Frequently, as in most licenses to Muzak, they are for a fixed term of years with a single payment covering all copies made of a composition during the term. Some licenses to Muzak run for 3 years and call for payment to a publisher of $14 for each selection appearing on the transcription. An alternate license arrangement is $6 per year for each composition.

Any use of a transcription beyond the original transcription license period requires an extension or renewal of the transcription license. Sometimes an option is acquired to extend the license beyond the initial period. This is obtained at the time of the original license and is subject, in all instances, to an additional transcription license fee. The background music supplier, having made a substantial investment in arranging and producing the transcribed selection, may desire to extend the term of use beyond the initial term. The supplier's option to renew at a fixed price is good insurance that the product will be continually available.

The form of Muzak-type license used by The Harry Fox Agency, Inc., which represents many publishers, is Appendix 24. In the case of Muzak-type licensees, public performance licenses for the music are separately obtained from the performing rights organization (ASCAP or BMI). These licenses are discussed on page 48.

The form of license negotiated by the 3M company for its tape transcriptions, which are sold rather than leased to users, is substantially different from the traditional or Muzak form of transcription license. Instead of a fixed fee for a number of years regardless of the number of copies made, the 3M license calls for 5¾ cents a selection for each copy of a transcription tape that is sold. This represents 2¾ cents for a mechanical reproduction license and 3 cents for a performance rights license. The 3-cent performance payment covers a 3-year license period, and there is a further performance fee payment of 1 cent per year for each additional year granted by a licensor of music. It is expected that the mechanical reproduction fee under 3M licenses will increase from 2¾ cents (the old compulsory license rate) to the new mechanical rate of 4 cents, which became effective July 1, 1981, pursuant to compulsory license statutory provisions. Accordingly, the aggregate 3M license fee will become 7 cents instead of 5¾ cents.

The 3-cent-per-copy performing rights fee under the 3M license is paid directly to the music publisher/licensor for the users' right to perform the ASCAP or BMI music on 3M tapes.

The 3-year performance rights license begins on the date of initial delivery of a 3M tape to a customer. The publisher-licensors who are affiliated with ASCAP or BMI have the problem of policing the purchasers after the expiration of the 3-year period. The 3M company has agreed to have each customer sign an agreement acknowledging the rights of the copyright proprietors. 3M will also notify customers before the end of the 3-year period that their rights will expire and that for continued use of the tape, an additional license from the copyright proprietors must be arranged. The names and addresses of the customers will be transmitted by the 3M company to the copyright proprietors.

Compulsory Licenses and Transcriptions

Prior to the Copyright Act of 1976, there were questions as to whether transcriptions were excluded from the compulsory license provisions for mechanical reproductions under the Copyright Act of 1909. In practice, a transcription license was sought from the copyright owner and there was no reliance on compulsory licenses.

Any ambiguities were settled by Section 115 of the Copyright Act of 1976. Thereunder it is provided that "a person may obtain a compulsory license only if his or her primary purpose in making phonorecords is to distribute them to the public for private use." A transcription comes within the definition of a "phonorecord" under the Copyright Act. However, transcriptions are not distributed to the public at large in most instances, but rather to a limited group of commercial users who do not intend private use. Transcriptions are therefore not entitled to the benefits of a compulsory license.

1976 Copyright Act Changes

Muzak and 3M recordings are "phonorecords" and "sound recordings" as defined in the 1976 Copyright Act. Accordingly, they are within the copyright protection afforded such works. The act grants to the copyright owner exclusive rights to duplicate, to prepare derivative works, and to distribute to the public by sale or other transfer of ownership, or by rental, lease, or lending. There is no protection afforded against performance. Only the franchise contracts or customer contracts themselves can be used for safeguarding against unauthorized performances. Thus Muzak and 3M have carefully drafted contractual provisions covering restrictions on performances of their products.

Public Performance Licenses for Musical Compositions

Background music services to offices, factories, and public places entail public performances of the underlying music. These composition uses, as distinguished from sound recordings, are subject to the Copyright Act, and must be licensed by the copyright proprietors of the music or their agents. Licenses for such performances can be obtained from ASCAP, BMI, and SESAC.

As noted previously, 3M, in respect to ASCAP and BMI music, has acquired direct licenses from the copyright proprietors.

Forms of ASCAP and BMI background music service license agreements are included as Appendices 25 and 26, respectively. These licenses are issued to the supplier of the services and not to the ultimate user, such as a factory or restaurant. ASCAP's fees are in substance 3½ percent of the gross receipts charged by the background music supplier to most premises other than those establishments serving food and beverages and those selling or offering goods or services to the public. For the excepted premises the fee is usually $27 per establishment for a year. The fees of BMI are in essence 1 percent of the gross receipts charged by the background music supplier to industrial premises and 1½ percent of such gross receipts in the case of other users. BMI licenses specifically provide in certain instances for annual minimum charges for each location. The licenses should be read to ascertain the charges for a particular type of business.

SESAC generally licenses background music service on a fixed fee basis for each outlet, regardless of the type of business or the gross receipts involved.

Performing Rights Organization Distributions

ASCAP distributions to publishers and writers of collections for background music in stores, factories, etc., are aided by the submission to ASCAP of music cue sheets prepared by the background music supplier. These show the actual compositions used and the time involved in the performance. ASCAP makes special distribution of the funds received from this category of users. It accounts to its writer and publisher members on separate "wired music" distribution reports. These list the compositions involved and the amounts earned. BMI and most SESAC payments for this category are not segregated. Such funds received by BMI and SESAC have been distributed as a part of their regular performance fee distribution. For 3M, SESAC charges a combined fee for performance and transcription licenses and distributes the monies to affiliates as if received for mechanical licenses.

Film Music

As noted previously, a significant and separate area of background music is that used as accompaniment to motion picture and television films. An ASCAP definition of background music follows:

Background music shall mean mood, atmosphere, or thematic music performed as background to some nonmusical subject matter. . . . A vocal or a visual instrument rendition which is a principal focus of audience attention shall not be regarded as background music regardless of the context in which performed.

Background music may be specifically composed, arranged, and performed, as is prevalent in feature motion pictures produced in the United States. It may also consist of specially edited sound tracks originating in sound track libraries. This is frequently the case in industrial films and sometimes occurs in television films.

Music used in sound tracks requires copyright synchronization licenses from music publishers or other copyright proprietors, as well as public performance licenses.

Synchronization Licenses

When background music is recorded on the sound track of a theatrical or television film, the form of license from a copyright owner is called a "synchronization" license.

Synchronization is a word that does not appear in the Copyright Act, but it is recognized as covering the act of mechanical reproduction of music in a synchronized relationship to the dramatic action of the film.

Synchronization licenses, as well as transcription licenses, are most often handled through The Harry Fox Agency, Inc., on behalf of the many publishers associated with that organization. Some publishers issue such licenses either directly or through other agents. A copy of a publisher-television synchronization license is in Appendix 27. SESAC publishers issue both transcription and synchronization licenses through SESAC.

Background music synchronization licenses will usually be for a fixed fee. They will frequently specify the number and lengths of playings that the producer may utilize, the type of production authorized, the geographic area of such use, and a limited term of years during which the license will be effective.

In recent years, the rate of license fees for television has dropped substantially, to as low as $50 to $75 per use. This is due to several factors. The publishers take into consideration the additional ASCAP or BMI performance credits granted when the film is shown on television. There is also competition from other publishers and from sound track libraries. A copy of a sound track library synchronization license is in Appendix 28.

Only a relatively small amount of background music stems from publisher licenses, since original background music composers and, to a lesser extent, sound track libraries supply the bulk. Another source of music available for additional background music synchronization is music in earlier films. This is due to the free synchronization right that had been reserved by many producers on original music composed for their films.

Performing Rights Licenses

Television film producers do not usually request a performance license for the music in their films; the broadcasting stations are licensed by the performing rights organizations. Theatrical film producers need not necessarily obtain a performance license for exhibitions outside the United States, since the theaters and broadcasters in foreign countries are licensed by the local performing rights organizations. However, the producers will ordinarily acquire a performance license for United States theatrical performance.

This is because ASCAP, by a court decree, is prohibited from requiring licenses from theaters for ASCAP music in films. The performance license will be granted by original music composers when they assign synchronization rights. Publishers, either directly or through The Harry Fox Agency, license United States performance rights at the same time as synchronization rights.

Television stations in the United States are licensed in almost all cases under blanket licenses issued by ASCAP, BMI, and SESAC. Under licenses issued by ASCAP and BMI, the fees charged the stations are a percentage of their gross receipts. SESAC's fees are based on fixed amounts; these vary in accordance with such factors as market population and highest 30-second spot rate.

In rare instances, a television station in the United States may obtain a "per program" license from ASCAP. In its "per program" license, ASCAP charges a lesser rate for films that are originally produced for theaters without feature music than for similar films that include vocals or other feature music. In 1978, a group of local television stations, led by Buffalo Broadcasting Company, Inc., sued to enjoin ASCAP from licensing on the blanket and per program bases prescribed by the 1950 Amended Final Judgment in *United States* v. *ASCAP*. Instead, they sought a license limited to music in programs the stations themselves produce. The suit is against ASCAP and its members and is also against BMI and its affiliates on similar grounds. At this writing the suit is pending.

ASCAP and BMI Distributions for Background Music

There has been much controversy over the question of the relative weight of film background music as against film feature music. The standard generally applied by ASCAP and BMI is that payment on a pure durational basis would not fairly reflect the worth of each performance. They give greater weight to feature music in determining distributions of performance fees.

In general, BMI makes no distinction, for payment purposes, among equal segments of background music; all portions of the music are treated equally.

Under the ASCAP distribution format, well-established works with a specified minimum of past feature performances are deemed "qualifying" works. When these works are used for background music, they earn considerably more under the ASCAP distribution rules than other background music works that are not so qualified. For example, effective July 1, 1981, nonqualifying works performed as background, cue, or bridge music receive, for each 3 minute duration in the aggregate, 36 percent of a feature performance use credit, whereas a qualifying work receives 50 percent of a feature performance use credit for the first such performance on a single program, regardless of duration.

Separate and apart from the actual rates of payment applied, there are various other distinctions in the payment formulas of ASCAP and BMI for background music.

BMI lowers the payment rate by about 27 percent for network television broadcasts for nonprime time versus prime time. ASCAP reduces credit by 50 percent for all network showings from 2:00 A.M. to 12:59 P.M. and by 25 percent for weekday exhibitions from 1:00 P.M. to 6:59 P.M.; these lower credits do not apply to background music in network television or radio programs appearing 4 or more times a week for which special reductions, as noted below, apply.

BMI's payment for background music is based on the use of music up to one-half of the duration of the program and there is no additional payment for the extra music. There is an exception for feature films shown in motion picture theaters in the United States prior to television release or motion pictures made for television whose duration is not less than 90 minutes; in such instances the payment will be 22 cents per minute regardless of whether the broadcast is local or network. ASCAP's rates, based on duration, for background music are not reduced regardless of the extent of the background music in a program, although there are special maximum credit provisions applying to the repetition of themes, qualifying works, and a limited number of other printed or recorded works.

For background music in network television or radio programs appearing 4 or more times a week, ASCAP curtails credits to 25 percent of the otherwise applicable credit. This particularly limits the accumulation of credits for background music in soap operas and other programs that are frequently shown. BMI diminishes credits by 33⅓ percent for any programs on television 4 or more times a week, unless the music is performed on a single instrument, in which case it is computed at one-fourth the usual rate.

The payment distribution formulas of ASCAP and BMI are constantly subject to change and reference should be made to those organizations for the rules applicable at any given time.

Composers of Television Music

For years the applicable guild of background music composers has been the Composers and Lyricists Guild of America (CLGA), many of whose members in 1972 instituted a major law suit by composers against three major television networks and eight major motion picture studios. The suit charged restraint of trade in requiring the assignment by the composers to producers or their affiliates of the full copyright in the scores of films. The litigation has been settled on a basis which left the copyright ownership in essence undisturbed but gave the plaintiffs a limited right to exploit if the publishers failed to meet certain exploitation standards.

The last agreement between CLGA and the film producers expired in 1971 and at this writing had not been renewed. Under the terms of the expired agreement the guild did not require that any film, whether theatrical or television, contain original music. It set standards and general terms and conditions of employment to the extent that the producer chose to employ original music composers. The agreement provided for minimum weekly salary standards for composers, and there was no stipulated sum per minute of music.

It set forth minimum writer royalty payments if the original music was assigned for publication. A copy of the writer minimum compensation and royalty provisions in the expired CLGA agreement is in Appendix 29. The composer remained entitled to collect the writer's share of performance rights payments through his affiliated performing rights organization.

The CLGA agreement had been adhered to by most important television producers.

Sound Track Libraries

When not utilizing live musicians for underscoring, producers resort to various sound track libraries. Some of these are controlled by Chappell & Co., Inc., Emil Ascher, Inc., and Boosey & Hawkes, Inc. Libraries license directly and not through an agent such as The Harry Fox Agency. A library is a categorized, alphabetized collection of recordings available to fit background music needs. Thus one may request music suitable for Autumn and Zebras. A library usually adheres to published rate cards with rates depending on the type of film (e.g., industrial show or commercial television) and the number and duration of usages. A copy of a rate card is included as Appendix 31.

Heavy usage of sound track libraries occurs in travelogues and industrial film productions. In these instances, the combination of a restricted budget with limited sound requirements permits less reliance on original music.

A common sound track library rate system is based on the "needle drop" method of computing payments for recordings on tape or on disks used by television producers on a nonexclusive basis. Under this method, it is usual for a one-time fixed payment (e.g., $60) to be made by the user for each continuous portion of the recording employed. An incentive to the licensor for this form of arrangement is his reservation of the right to collect ASCAP or BMI performance fees.

Union Standards

Sound track libraries for film purposes are almost wholly derived from foreign recordings. The American Federation of Musicians has repeatedly appealed without success to Congress to ban the importation of foreign music tapes and tracks.

The use of sound track libraries for feature and television films, however, has been limited significantly by musician union agreements applicable to pictures produced in the United States and Canada. Signatories to agreements with the union have contracted that all such films must be scored in the United States and Canada. No sound track library music may appear in the theatrical films. Television films are required to employ music recorded live by union musicians except that, in respect to a television series, music recorded for any picture in the series may be reused to score other pictures in the series produced for the same broadcasting season. But there are union requirements for the minimum amount of fresh union-scored music for a given series.

The union agreement permits library music or "historical" music sound tracks to be combined with new union-made music in documentaries if the minimum live scoring standards for other films are complied with and if the scoring is done by an orchestra of a minimum size. There is no requirement for the size of an orchestra that scores the music for other films.

Radio Broadcast Transcriptions

In today's radio broadcasting, transcriptions are used for special programming introductions, themes, background music, and sports breaks. There are full programs such as public service programs presented by the Veterans Administration, Treasury Department, and Armed Forces. These transcriptions are distributed free of charge to stations. There is also full-time or substantially full-time programming of music, with blank spots for announcements, available from certain suppliers of tapes.

It is now common for publishers to license such transcription use through The Harry Fox Agency at a rate per song of $6 a year or $14 for 3 years, as in the case of the Muzak-type licenses.

An agreement in use by a modern transcription company provides for a lease to the broadcast user of the transcription library. The lease grants exclusive rights for the local broadcast area, at monthly rental rates varying with the size and location of the station. The transcription library consists of tapes and disks covering sound effects, time and weather announcements, tailored introductions of the local station's programs, backgrounds for commercials and public service announcements, and also full-time or substantially full-time music programs with blank spots for announcements. The music used on the transcriptions is subject to ASCAP or BMI licenses.

9

Live Performances:

Concerts and Festivals

HUNDREDS of millions of dollars are collected annually from live performances at concerts, cabarets, nightclubs, coffeehouses, discos, and other miscellaneous public places. There are large- and small-scale financial undertakings, with varying success.

A sample weekly report of concert grosses, as published by *Billboard* in May of 1981, showed a top figure of $307,053 paid by over 22,000 fans of the Doobie Brothers at Denver, Colorado, and a figure of $237,325 for an audience of 24,641 attending a concert of Rush at Seattle, Washington.

In the same general period, night clubs were paying as high as $350,000 a week for certain stars appearing in Las Vegas. The Riviera Hotel announced the signing of Dolly Parton in that price category. Such talent costs are consistent with top seat prices of $30 and, in rare instances, $50.

Artist fees are not the only concern of promoters and night club owners. Essential to any presentation are costly advertising and promotion; security; hall or concert ground rentals; labor costs; transportation; audio equipment; lighting; management, staff, and agency fees; and general overhead.

Illustrative of one aspect of artist touring expenses is the *Wall Street Journal* report in 1981 on the growing field of rental of customized buses by music stars. Entertainers such as James Taylor, Loretta Lynn, Barry Manilow, Donna Summer, Earth, Wind and Fire, and Jackson Browne have rented $3,000-per-week luxury buses. The buses include special facilities such as showers, beds, bars, and entertainment centers which help to alleviate the stress and strain of constant travel under pressure. The group The Village People has reported tours lasting as long as 11 months out of a year. The jazz fusion group Spyro Gyra doubles its six-man basic personnel with a road crew of six, which includes lighting and sound specialists.

Reacting to the high risk and costs of major concert promotion, rock promoter Ron Delsener established the 950-patron capacity Savoy Club in 1981. With scheduled acts including Cliff Richard, Don McLean, Count Basie, Santana, James Taylor, and Jimmy Cliff, he hoped to establish a new profit center with more regular patronage than occasional superstar, major audience events. Ticket prices were scheduled as low as $3 for special "Savoy Stomp" nights, with average ticket prices of $10 for regular performances reduced to $7.50 for after-midnight, dance-only patrons.

The high cost of talent, tickets, and gasoline and the resistance of record companies to touring subsidies have made the concert scene in the early 1980s one of flux and uncertainty. Madison Square Garden in 1979—its 100th anniversary year—was the site of 54 concerts grossing over $11 million. Attendance averaged over 18,000 people and gross receipts averaged more than $200,000 per show. In that year, more than 1 million patrons came to see concerts at Madison Square Garden. In the 1980–1981 period, a major new popular music and rock concert hall was successfully introduced—New Jersey's Brendan Byrne Arena. Named for the state's governor, the arena was inaugurated with a series of sold-out performances by Bruce Springsteen. On the other hand, in the same period lesser concert halls undoubtedly had much poorer results.

Engagement Contracts

Artists who perform before live audiences at popular concerts or festivals are musicians, vocalists, comedians, or performers possessing a combination of such varied talents. The basic contract for their services will be either the American Federation of Musicians form for musicians or the American Guild of Variety Artists (AGVA) form for vocalists.

There are numerous elements to be considered in an engagement contract. Among these are the following:

1   The time and place of performance.
2   The duration of the individual performance (e.g., 1 or 2 hours).
3   The stipulated capacity of the concert hall or auditorium.
4   The manner and amount of compensation.

5   The marquee and advertising billing.
6   Place and time of rehearsals.
7   Provisions for backup musicians.
8   Provisions for sound technicians.
9   Accommodations and dressing rooms.
10   Payment of travel costs.
11   Cancellation of engagements due to rain or other adverse elements.
12   Options for return engagements.
13   Whether or when the artist is restricted from appearing in the same geographic area.

Basic Terms

The engagement contract will normally be negotiated by the booking agent for the performer long in advance of the date of appearance. Its basic terms will specify the time and date of performance, the length of the performance, the capacity of the hall, and the manner and amount of payment. It is common to provide for a down payment, upon signing of the contract, of one-half the fixed or guaranteed sums, with the balance to be paid on the date of performance in the form of cash or a certified check.

Lesser artists may command relatively smaller fees. Under applicable union agreements, their compensation cannot fall below the minimum union scale for their services. It is common for so-called backup musicians to receive only union scale.

On the other hand, well-known artists may be compensated by a fixed overscale payment or a percentage of the gross receipts with a minimum that is an overscale amount.

Additional Terms

The additional terms, over and above the basic provisions, may be the subject of a rider or addendum to the engagement contract. These supplemental negotiated terms are significant in making concert appearances attractive to an artist, but they may make a concert promoter wring his hands in agony. An important provision is the "billing" for advertising and promotion wherein the parties agree on whether the artist is a headliner or a supporting act and on the manner in which the artist's name will be listed. Some performers will seek advertising commitments from the promoter. Certain promoters will obtain artist and record company financial assistance and cooperation for local ads on radio and in newspapers.

Rehearsal requirements and opportunities are of basic mutual interest to ensure that an act is sufficiently prepared, with appropriate musicians and under proper stage and audio conditions.

The supplying of backup musicians, at the cost of the promoter or artist, will be a negotiated clause. Sometimes, at his or her own cost, a star performer will travel with the lead members of an orchestra such as piano, guitar, and bass, but will require a certain number of local musicians to complete the orchestra.

Consideration is given in contracts as to whether sound technicians are to be provided by the promoter or artist, and there will be negotiations about the specific sound equipment to be rented for the artist's performance.

Accommodations and dressing room requirements should be specified in the contract, including whether it is the artist or promoter who pays for hotel costs. Travel charges are usually borne by the performer; in some instances the promoter will pay for travel costs and the contract will specify whether the airline seats will be first class or tourist and stipulate the number of seats required.

Promoters will seek protection in the event of cancellation for reasons such as inclement weather and will attempt to obtain options in some instances for return engagements. They will try to restrict the artist from appearing in the same local area for specified periods before and after an engagement so as not to water down the audience appeal by competitive engagements.

Feature Artists, Supporting Acts, and Package Shows

It is rare that a promoter will present an evening with only a single feature artist. Whether it is Dolly Parton, Styx, or REO Speedwagon that attract the ticket buyers, it is considered good business to spend the additional sums that are required for a supporting act.

Motivations for using a supporting act include warming up the audience, keeping the audience seated in the event the featured act is delayed, and relieving the featured act from the exhaustive burden of performing by itself during an entire evening. It is believed that the audience may increase if it is invited to review or discover new talent or if it is supplied with two acts for the price of one. The supporting act may be willing to take the second spot so as to obtain the exposure of an established star's audience or perhaps to fill in open performance dates.

Frequently the booking agent or manager of the primary featured act will have a financial incentive to introduce or popularize a second act and will induce or even compel the promoter to accept the supporting act as a condition to obtaining the featured act. The combination of acts is marketed to promoters as a "package show."

The featured artist with a strong bargaining position may insert into the contract the right to approve not only the supporting act but also its length of appearance on the show and its order of appearance. The preferred spot for the feature artist is the closing of the show and the natural spot for the supporting act is as an opener. However, where there are crowd control problems, the supporting act may be brought back for a closing number to allow an orderly departure of the star.

Combined use of backup musicians and equipment would seem to be sensible for any two or more acts on a single stage. When special instruments are rented and carted in for one act, it also seems desirable for supporting acts to share their use and to thereby alleviate moving problems and additional costs. Yet, the more normal situation is for each act to use its own audio equipment on stage, hooked into the concert hall audio equipment.

Where a featured solo singer, for example, comes to a date with only the nucleus of an orchestra such as a pianist, bass player, and drummer, the singer will require backup musicians. Sometimes the backup musicians can even double by themselves as the supporting act. Can the backup musicians be used by a supporting act soloist? If the featured performer does not object in advance or if he or she fails to specify otherwise in the contract, the backup musicians may serve the supporting act. However, the featured soloist may be unwilling to water down his or her appearance by allowing the backup musicians to be used for supporting acts and may forbid it.

Free or Reduced Price Concerts

There are a great variety of noncommercial or nonprofit concerts. Outdoor concerts are given at political rallies or voter registration drives to attract or entertain a crowd, and there are the old-fashioned "Music in the Park" performances on many small-town bandstands.

One type is exemplified by the concerts presented on a New York City pier with reduced ticket prices. These concerts are sponsored by the Dr. Pepper soft drink company. There are other free or reduced-price summer series of concerts, with various sponsors. Occasional blockbuster events, such as Elton John or Simon and Garfunkle's free New York concerts in Central Park, have drawn hundreds of thousands without major incident. These free concerts in Central Park are cosponsored by the New York City Department of Parks and Recreation. In some instances small subsidies are given by record companies and the artists appear free of charge. Part of the free concert concept is to minimize advance publicity so as to avoid competition with the act's paying audiences and to restrict crowds to manageable proportions. Thus, announcements may be limited to on-air radio notices a few days ahead of a particular concert.

In all instances, a significant motivation of the artist is public exposure to potential record buyers. Another incentive is the normal or near-normal fee payable by a civic or commercial sponsor that can often afford fairly large budgets. If the concert is free, a subsidy from the American Federation of Musicians' Music Performance Trust Fund can be applied to cover union scale. This has been described in more detail in Chapter 1.

Seating Patterns

A concert patron customarily expects a seat when buying a ticket to a musical event. Arrangements for the seating of ticket buyers include varied pricing for different locations, general admission at a fixed price with no reserved seats, or a mixture of both with special reserved sections for some ticket holders and general admission for others at a lesser price. The issues of nonreserved seating and inadequate supervision and security assumed tragic dimensions in the December 3, 1979, appearance of The Who in Cincinnati, Ohio. At that event, eleven deaths and numerous injuries resulted from a rush by patrons for good seats. Largely as a result of this tragedy, unreserved seating and general admission, sometimes referred to as "festival seating," are frequently frowned upon, or actively discouraged, by local authorities.

Sound Control

Rock concerts necessarily involve sound equipment of great technical sophistication, as well as cost. There may be medical and legal ramifications if the sound level exceeds 90 decibels, the recognized threshold of negative stress. Yet a 1981 survey of three dozen Los Angeles area concerts showed only two measuring under 125 decibels. It is generally recognized that rock concerts frequently reach sound levels of 110 decibels.

Some festival licenses require sound level limits while some concert hall leases contain clauses to control sound level excesses. The potential of litigation must always be considered. The wise promoter should consider sound level monitoring equipment, which is generally available. Further, artist contracts may be negotiated with provisions limiting excess sound delivery by the artist, who may be accustomed to performing at high decibel levels.

Where unusual sound limitations exist, it is important for all parties to make such restrictions clear in contracts and correspondence so as to avoid conflicts and refusal by an artist to play after an audience has been assembled.

Computer Ticketing Agencies

Ticketron and the several other computer ticketing agencies have revolutionized box office practices. The scope of this activity, which includes sports and theater, as well as music events, is indicated by Ticketron's estimate of 44,265,000 tickets sold in 1980 for a dollar volume of over $250 million.

Ticketron is a wholly owned division of Control Data Corporation and has over 1,000 locations in 16 major, and some 400 other, cities. It furnishes computer-assisted box office services at each location so that tickets are printed as sold, with sold seat locations immediately withdrawn from other location offices. The purchaser pays not only the official ticket price but a service charge of up to $1.50, depending on the type and location of event. The computer ticketing agency gets a further fee either from the facility (stadium, arena, concert hall, etc.) or from the individual concert promoter. Such an additional fee is an amount negotiated, based often on the past sales history for the facility, a possible initial computer programming input fee, volume rebates, special fees for interim computer read-outs, and other factors. Generally, however, there is a percentage charge on a sliding scale on the gross collections.

There are regional computer services available through Bay Area Seating (BAS) of San Francisco, California, and Selectaseat (a division of Globe Tickets) of Virginia.

In considering whether to use such services, the promoter must anticipate the effect of the necessary delay in the transmission of cash to the theater, auditorium, or arena. This may cause a problem since moneys must be paid in advance for artist fees, equipment, rental, bonds, and similar expenses.

Security

The business side of concert presentation requires early consideration of security. A Carnegie Hall concert of an eminent violinist can be handled with a modest complement of ticket takers at a single entrance, with a dozen or less ushers to direct patrons to their reserved seats. A popular music concert can require more than a hundred security personnel, including possibly horse-mounted police outside the arena, as well as hall or stadium bouncers to protect the stage. Fire marshals may also be part of the security line-up.

Security has three purposes in a large audience setting: protect the patron, protect the performer, and safeguard the hall and promoter. One prominent promoter uses security guards at ticket entrances to search for alcoholic beverages or fireworks and to eject recognized drug dealers. Cincinnati now requires minimum levels of off-duty police and fire security personnel at as much as $17 an hour.

Charges for security are assumed initially by the promoter or hall. Where an artist is on a profit participation basis, these charges are deducted from gross receipts before the computation of profit shares. The *Cincinnati Post* charged, in 1980, that certain promoters double bill for these services as a means of reducing artist payments.

College Concerts

Ever since the Kingston Trio discovered that college concert tours are profitable, the college concert market has been dominant in the rock and folk fields. Serious musicians have long traveled the college concert circuit with success. Whereas a Rudolf Serkin will arrive a few days ahead of time to rehearse for a concert, the intense pressures of a rock band arriving within minutes of (or slightly after) a scheduled performance will, for a 35-minute set, require business, promotional, and even psychological skills that can tax the abilities of the average college representative.

Despite the heavy reliance upon college students as prospective rock concert patrons, it should be noted that rock music represents only a small share of college music interests.

Some state universities or tax-exempt nonprofit institutions will, out of caution, prefer to avoid a profitable concert. Ways of accomplishing this end include free or low-priced tickets or rental of halls at cost to an independent promoter who assumes the risk of losses if the venture proves unprofitable.

The campus buyer of talent is not like the average promoter. First, many concerts are subsidized by student activity dues (or are even free to patrons) and intentionally nonprofit, and thus the bargaining for a percentage of the box office can be quite different from that for the more commercial concert. Second, the campus "promoter" who is booking an act is more concerned than an off-campus promoter with audience satisfaction and enrichment. He may also be less sophisticated about business aspects and more susceptible to a bad deal in his eagerness to obtain a popular act for fellow students. Options to return in the future and exclusives for the territory are less likely to be points of negotiation than in an average commercial deal for an artist's services.

An official college-sponsored concert is different from a fly-by-night promoter's concert. One college president wryly remarked about an agency's conventional demand for a financial guarantee and deposit, "We have been in this same location for 200 years. It's a sure bet we will be here for the concert. Perhaps the agency should pay us a guarantee that the artist will be here also."

Where student activity cards are being used instead of paid admissions, one alternative to a fixed artist fee is to deem each attending card holder the equivalent of a stated ticket charge for nonholders. Where tickets are not used, provision must be made for some official police or school estimate of the number who attend.

In addition to having the advantages of free use of halls or low rental costs, colleges and universities are currently the beneficiaries of very favorable music clearance licenses from ASCAP and BMI, and they thus have more to spend for talent. There are schools with substantial entertainment budgets, such as the University of Miami. There are various colleges within Yale or Harvard that offer to pay substantial fees for popular acts.

Concert artists, managers, agents, and promoters have a convenient means of meeting on a regular basis through national and regional conventions. The National Entertainment and Campus Activities Association (NECAA) and Association of College, University and Community Arts Administrators, Inc. (ACUCAA), have many members concerned with, respectively, the popular and serious fields of music. Showcase presentations of aspiring new, and some established, acts are a feature of both conventions. NECAA holds conventions in different cities each year but also has regional meetings throughout the year. College representatives can exchange views as to available acts, hold symposiums and workshops on current problems, and meet with concert representatives at convention center booths.

At these conventions, even acts with no commercial records have a chance to establish careers. They may generate a following that leads to a record contract, as well as regular bookings. For concert bookers at the college level, the interchange of views as to merits of particular acts may result in the avoidance of financial and professional problems that might accompany inexperience. A form of a NECAA artist/agency report is shown in Appendix 30.

Smaller colleges and high schools, instead of auditioning, may find it more convenient to use an independent booking agent to line up available talent and deliver a show within a particular budget. The independent booker may be charging the concert sponsor over and above the 15 percent booking agent fee, normal for one-nighters, that is deductible from the artist's compensation. However, the occasional buyer of talent will avoid such things as union bonds and welfare payments and other problems by paying a middleman who takes care of the details and often supplies the entire package. Larger schools will find that major agencies will perform many of the same functions without requiring a markup over and above talent costs.

A special promotional aspect of college towns is that the campus appearance can be tied in with college radio and newspapers for publicity. This direct access to a large potential audience of concert goers and record buyers is facilitated by the early transmittal of publicity material.

Road Managers

Artists are frequently accompanied by individuals working as road managers. They should be distinguished from personal managers, and generally receive a fixed salary. Their responsibilities include the supervision of the details of travel, shopping, and the concert itself. A reminder schedule of the duties of a typical road manager is as follows:

Ten Days before the Concert:
Call the promoter.
Check the setup time available.
Schedule a sound check.
Get the telephone number and name of the person to contact at the hall.
Give your local telephone number at the time of the call.
Give your telephone number where you will be the night before the concert.
Obtain descriptions of the type of stage and equipment.
Get the names of other accompanying acts.
Remind the promoter that no personal check is acceptable on the night of the concert and suggest a certified check be ready and, if on a percentage basis, that perhaps two alternate certified checks be held together with supplemental cash.
Make a list of alternate sound technicians in the local area in case the promoter fails to deliver an acceptable person.
One Day before the Concert:
Check all the above for any new developments, and see whether deposits have been received.
Check motel and transportation, and communicate time schedules to all personnel involved.
Arrival at Concert:
Find the promoter and get a ticket manifest (the ticket printing office gives a manifest describing the price, number, and color of tickets), and check whether the promoter or person who signed the contract is the same person for additional arrangements.
Check the physical layout of the hall, and confirm whether extra seats have been added, inconsistent with the ticket manifest.

Check the dressing rooms.

Check the lighting and sound.

Check the security with the police in charge, the stage manager, and stage hands, and obtain a copy of the guest list. Also arrange for exits for departure in the event of crowd problems. Check the stage entrance for the easiest mode of group arrival.

During the Concert:

Pick up some of the unsold tickets, and check the hall to see if the seats are occupied, as an indication of whether double sets of tickets are used; and if occupied, get the usher to obtain ticket stubs.

After the Concert:

Get the manifest signed by the promoter, together with a box office statement and payment. Handle hotel checkouts and bills. Equipment should be shipped so that it will be delivered to the airport 2 hours before the group arrives.

Selection of Hall or Festival Site

Experienced concert promoters recognize that the location, seating, and reputation of a hall or site is of great importance to the success of a concert. See *Audarena Stadium,* a directory compiled by *Amusement Business,* for a listing of arenas, auditoriums, stadiums, exhibit halls, sports facilities, concert halls, and convention sites available for public use and private rental or in which commercial events sponsored by a nonprofit sponsor may be held in the United States and Canada. There is also information on facilities in foreign countries. A typical page of this directory is included in Appendix 32.

The magazine *Performance* ("The International Touring Talent Weekly") provides regular box office reports for arenas, theaters, etc. It lists itineraries of touring acts and provides a comprehensive directory of booking agents, personal managers, promoters, facilities, clubs, and sound, lighting, and staging services.

The annually published *Billboard Talent Directory* lists artists, booking agents, promoters, and facilities on a regional basis. The weekly *Billboard* magazine regularly republishes from *Amusement Business* magazine current attendance data under the chart title, "Boxscore." It shows artist names, gross ticket receipts, the number of tickets sold, capacity of the hall, ticket prices, and geographic locations.

PART THREE
Appendixes

Appendix 1

ORCHESTRA CLASSIFICATIONS BY THE AMERICAN SYMPHONY ORCHESTRA LEAGUE

The American Symphony Orchestra League has identified approximately 1,500 orchestras in the United States and Canada as of 1980. Of these, over 720 hold membership in the League. In most cases, classification of these orchestras is based on the orchestra's annual operating income. Youth orchestras and college orchestras are categorized separately. Although the number of chamber orchestras has been noted, for membership purposes they are categorized by budget size.

MAJOR ORCHESTRAS

Number Identified: 35   Members: 35

For Major Orchestra status in December 1980, annual operating income of $2 million in 1978–1979 *and* $2.25 million in 1979–1980; currently ranging through $16 million. Musicians are engaged on a full-time basis for a contracted number of weeks per year, and the orchestra employment provides their major source of income.

REGIONAL ORCHESTRAS

Number Identified: 36   Members: 35

For Regional Orchestra status in June 1980, annual operating income of $500,000 in 1977–1978 *and* $600,000 in 1978–1979. Musicians may be employed on a per-service or weekly basis, and orchestra employment may provide up to one-half of their yearly income.

METROPOLITAN ORCHESTRAS

Number Identified: 111   Members: 90

For Metropolitan Orchestra status in June 1980, annual operating income of $100,000 in 1977–1978 *and* $150,000 in 1978–1979. Musicians do not earn their main source of income from the orchestra, although all are professionally trained.

URBAN ORCHESTRAS

Number Identified: 83   Members: 74

For Urban Orchestra status in June 1980, annual operating income of $50,000 in 1977–1978 *and* $60,000 in 1978–1979. The conductors and managers are generally engaged on a full-time basis. Most of the musicians are professionally trained; most are paid, but depend on other employment for their main source of income.

COMMUNITY ORCHESTRAS

Number Identified: 669   Members: 270

Orchestras with annual operating income of less than $50,000 in 1977–1978 *and* less than $60,000 in 1978–1979. The conductors and managers may be full-time or may work with the orchestras on an avocational basis. Musicians include professional musicians, avocational musicians, and students; most of whom depend primarily upon other sources of income.

CHAMBER ORCHESTRAS

Number Identified: 159   Members: 53

Orchestra size ranges from 15 to 30 musicians; musicians include professionals, avocational musicians, and students. (Chamber orchestras are listed within appropriate budget category.)

COLLEGE ORCHESTRAS

Number Identified: 392   Members: 71

Orchestras composed exclusively of faculty and students of a college or university.

YOUTH ORCHESTRAS

Number Identified: 237   Members: 147

Orchestras composed of junior high, high school, and/or college students; orchestras are not exclusively affiliated with a single educational institution.

Appendix 2

EMPLOYMENT OUTLOOK FOR MUSICIANS AND SINGERS
(Extracts from 1980–1981 Report by U.S. Department of Labor on Performing Arts and Entertainment Related Occupations)

MUSICIANS

NATURE OF THE WORK

The important role that music plays in most people's lives makes it difficult to imagine a world without musicians. Professional musicians are those whose livelihoods depend upon performing for the enjoyment of others. These professionals—whether they play in a symphony orchestra, dance band, rock group, or jazz combo—generally have behind them many years of formal or informal study and practice. As a rule, musicians specialize in either popular or classical music; only a few play both types professionally.

Musicians who specialize in popular music usually play the trumpet, trombone, clarinet, saxophone, organ, or one of the "rhythm" instruments—the piano, string bass, drums, or guitar. Dance bands play in nightclubs, restaurants, and at special parties. The best known bands, jazz groups, rock groups, and solo performers sometimes perform on television.

Classical musicians play in symphonies, opera, ballet, and theater orchestras, and for other groups that require orchestral accompaniments. These musicians play string, brass, woodwind, or percussion instruments. Some form small groups—usually a string quartet or a trio—to give concerts of chamber music. Many pianists accompany vocal or instrumental soloists, choral groups, or provide background music in restaurants or other places. Most organists play in churches; often they direct the choir.

A few exceptional musicians give their own concerts and appear as soloists with symphony orchestras. Both classical and popular musicians make individual and group recordings.

In addition to performing, many musicians teach instrumental and vocal music in schools and colleges, or give private lessons in their own studios or in pupils' homes. Others combine careers as performers with work as composers. Some work as arrangers, adapting musical compositions to different types of instruments or to styles for which they were not originally intended.

A few musicians specialize in library science for work in music libraries. Some receive training in music therapy to enable them to use music in treating persons with physical and mental disabilities. Others work as orchestra conductors or band directors, whose duties include selecting the music to be performed, auditioning and selecting members of the performing group, and directing the group at rehearsals and performances to achieve the desired musical effects.

WORKING CONDITIONS

Musicians generally work at night and on weekends, and they must spend considerable time in practice and rehearsal. These long and irregular hours can be very exhausting. Performances often require travel. Many people cannot obtain year-round work as musicians, and are forced to supplement their incomes by other types of work.

PLACES OF EMPLOYMENT

About 127,000 persons worked as performing musicians in 1978. Many thousands more taught in elementary and secondary schools and in colleges and universities. (See the statements on teachers elsewhere in the *Handbook.*) Almost every town and city has at least one private music teacher. Some musicians with training in music therapy work in psychiatric hospitals, centers for the mentally retarded, hospitals and schools, community mental health centers, day care centers, nursing homes, and special service agencies.

Most performing musicians work in cities where entertainment and recording activities are concentrated, such as New York City, Chicago, Los Angeles, Nashville, Miami Beach, and New Orleans. Many perform with one of the 31 major symphony groups, the 76 metropolitan orchestras, or the hundreds of community orchestras. Many communities have orchestras and dance bands which offer at least part-time work. The various branches of the Armed Forces also offer career opportunities in a number of different musical organizations.

TRAINING AND OTHER QUALIFICATIONS

Most people who become professional musicians begin studying an instrument at an early age. To acquire great technical skill, a thorough knowledge of music, and the ability to interpret music, young people need intensive training. This training may be obtained through private study with an accomplished musician, in a college or university which has a strong music program, or in a conservatory of music. For advanced study in one of these institutions, an audition frequently is necessary. Many teachers in these schools are accomplished artists who will train only promising young musicians.

About 540 colleges, universities, and music conservatories offer bachelor's and/or higher degrees in musical performance, composition, and theory. In addition, about 750 conservatories and colleges and universities offer a bachelor's degree in music education to qualify graduates for the State certificate for elementary and secondary school teaching positions. College teaching positions usually require advanced degrees, but exceptions may be made for well-qualified artists.

Musicians who play popular music must have an understanding of and feeling for that style of music, but classical training may expand their employment opportunities. As a rule, they take lessons with private teachers when young, and seize every opportunity to play in amateur or professional performances. Establishing a reputation with other musicians is very important in getting started in a career in popular music. Some young people form small dance bands or rock groups. As they gain experience and become known, they may audition for other local bands, and still later, for the better known bands and orchestras.

Young persons who consider careers in music should have musical talent, versatility, creative ability, and poise and stage presence to face large audiences. Since quality performance requires constant study and practice, self-discipline is vital. Moreover, musicians who do concert and nightclub engagements must have physical stamina because of frequent traveling and schedules that often include night performances.

EMPLOYMENT OUTLOOK

Employment of musicians is expected to grow faster than the average through the 1980's, but competition for jobs will be keen. Opportunities for concerts and recitals are not numerous enough to provide adequate employment for all the pianists, violinists, and other instrumentalists qualified as concert artists. Competition usually is keen for positions that offer stable employment, such as jobs with major orchestras, with the Armed Forces, and in teaching positions. Because of the ease with which a musician can enter private music teaching, the number of music teachers has been more than sufficient and probably will continue to be. Although many opportunities are expected for single and short-term engagements to play popular music in nightclubs and theaters, the supply of qualified musicians who seek such jobs is likely to exceed demand. On the other hand, first-class, experienced accompanists and outstanding players of stringed instruments are likely to remain relatively scarce.

EARNINGS

The amount received for a performance by either classical or popular musicians depends on their geographic location as well as on their professional reputation. Minimum salaries for musicians in the 31 major symphony orchestras in the United States in 1978 ranged from $232 to $490 a week, according to the American Symphony Orchestra League. Minimum salaries for musicians in the 28 regional symphony orchestras ranged from $90 to $270 a week. Minimum wages for musicians in metropolitan symphony orchestras were generally between $20 and $40 per concert. Some musicians earned substantially more than the minimums, however.

The major symphony orchestras have seasons ranging from 45 to 52 weeks. None of the metropolitan or community orchestras have seasons of 50 to 52 weeks, however.

Musicians in large metropolitan areas who had steady engagement contracts to play at dances, clubs, variety shows, ballets, musical comedies, concerts, and industrial shows generally earned minimums ranging from $6.50 to $10.50 per hour, depending on the length and type of engagement. Wages for the same types of engagements tended to be less in smaller cities and towns. Musicians employed in motion picture recording earned a minimum of about $108 for a 3-hour session; those employed in television commercials earned a minimum of $54 each for 2 to 5 musicians and $50 each for more than 5 musicians for a 1-hour session. Musicians employed by recording companies were paid a minimum of about $127 for a 3-hour session.

Music teachers in public schools earn salaries comparable to those of other teachers. (See statements on elementary and secondary school teachers elsewhere in the *Handbook*.) Many teachers give private music lessons to supplement their earnings. However, earnings often are uncertain and vary according to the musician's reputation, the number of teachers and students in the locality, and the economic status of the community.

Many musicians, primarily those employed by symphony orchestras, work under master wage agreements, which guarantee a season's work up to 52 weeks. Musicians in other areas, however, may face relatively long periods of unemployment between jobs. Thus, their earnings generally are lower than those in many other occupations. Moreover, since they may not work steadily for one employer, some performers cannot qualify for unemployment compensation, and few have either sick leave or vacations with pay. For these reasons, many musicians take other types of jobs to supplement their earnings as musicians.

Most professional musicians belong to the American Federation of Musicians (AFL-CIO). Concert soloists also belong to the American Guild of Musical Artists, Inc. (AFL-CIO).

RELATED OCCUPATIONS

Performing musicians express ideas and emotions through the music they play. Other occupations in the music field include arrangers, composers, copyists, music critics, music directors, music librarians, music teachers, music therapists, orchestra conductors, orchestrators, instrument repairers, music or instrument sales people, and radio music producers.

SOURCES OF ADDITIONAL INFORMATION

For information about wages, hours of work, and working conditions for professional musicians, contact:

American Federation of Musicians (AFL-CIO), 1500 Broadway, New York, N.Y. 10036.

The requirements for certification of organists and choir masters are available from:

American Guild of Organists, 630 Fifth Ave., New York, N.Y. 10020.

For information about a career in music therapy, contact:

National Association for Music Therapy, Inc., P.O. Box 610, Lawrence, Kans. 66044.

For programs in music teacher education, contact:

Music Educators National Conference, 1902 Association Dr., Reston, Va. 22091.

Information about certification of private music teachers is available from:

Music Teachers National Association, 2113 Carew Tower, Cincinnati, Ohio 45202.

A list of accredited schools of music is also available for $3.25 from:

National Association of Schools of Music, 11250 Roger Bacon Dr., Reston, Va. 22090.

A brochure entitled *Careers in Music* is available from any of the last three organizations listed above.

SINGERS

NATURE OF THE WORK

Singing is an age-old form of entertainment which, in one form or another, can be understood and appreciated by almost everyone. Professional singing often requires not only a fine voice but also a highly developed technique and a broad knowledge of music. A small number of singing stars make recordings or go on concert tours in the United States and abroad. Somewhat larger numbers of singers obtain leading or supporting roles in operas and popular music shows, or secure engagements as concert soloists in oratorios and other types of performances. Some singers also become members of opera and musical comedy choruses or other professional choral groups. Popular music singers perform in musical shows of all kinds—in the movies, on the stage, on radio and television, in concerts, and in nightclubs and other places of entertainment. The best known popular music singers make and sell many recordings.

Some singers combine their work as performers with related jobs. Many give private voice lessons. A number of singers teach and direct choruses in elementary and secondary schools. (See the statements on teachers elsewhere in the *Handbook.*) Others give voice training or direct choral groups in churches, synagogues, music conservatories, or colleges and universities.

WORKING CONDITIONS

Singers generally work at night and on weekends, and must spend much time in practice and rehearsals. Work in the entertainment field is seasonal and few performers have steady jobs. Except for a few well-known concert soloists, opera stars, and top recording artists of popular music, most professional singers experience difficulty in obtaining regular employment and have to supplement their incomes with other kinds of jobs. Moreover, a singing career sometimes is relatively short, since it depends on a good voice, physical stamina, and public acceptance of the artist, all of which may be affected by age.

PLACES OF EMPLOYMENT

About 22,000 persons worked as professional singers in 1978. Many others were employed as music teachers in elementary and secondary schools, colleges, universities, and conservatories throughout the country. Opportunities for singing engagements are concentrated mainly in New York City, Los Angeles, Las Vegas, San Francisco, Dallas, and Chicago—the Nation's chief entertainment centers. Nashville, Tenn., a major center for country and western music, is one of the most important places for employment of singers for "live" performances and recordings. Many singers work part time as singers and choirmasters for churches and synagogues. The various branches of the Armed Forces also offer career opportunities for vocalists.

TRAINING AND OTHER QUALIFICATIONS

Persons who want to sing professionally should acquire a broad background in music, including its theory and history. The ability to dance may be helpful, since singers sometimes are required to dance. In addition, those interested in a singing career should start piano lessons at an early age to become familiar with music theory and composition. As a rule, voice training should not begin until after the individual has matured physically, although young boys who sing in church choirs receive some training before their voices change. An audition often is required for advanced voice training. Since voice training often continues for years after the singer's professional career has started, a prospective singer must have great determination.

To prepare for careers as singers of classical music, young people can take private voice lessons or enroll in a music conservatory or a school or department of music in a college or university. These schools provide voice training and training in understanding and interpreting music, including music-related training in foreign languages and, sometimes, dramatic training. After completing 4 years of study, the graduate may receive the degree of bachelor of music, bachelor of science or arts (in music), or bachelor of fine arts.

Singers who plan to teach in public schools need at least a bachelor's degree in music and must meet the State certification requirements for teachers. About 750 conservatories and colleges and universities offer a degree program in music education. In addition, about 540 colleges and universities offer training in musical performance, composition, and theory, leading to a bachelor's degree. Most college teachers must have a master's or a doctor's degree, but exceptions may be made for well-qualified artists.

Although voice training is an asset for singers of popular music, many with untrained voices have had successful careers. The typical popular song does not demand that the voice be developed to cover as wide a range on the musical scale as does classical music, and the lack of voice projection may be overcome by use of a microphone.

Young singers of popular songs may become known by participating in local amateur and paid shows. These engagements may lead to employment with local dance bands or rock groups and possibly later with better known ones.

In addition to musical ability, a singing career requires an attractive appearance, poise and stage presence, and perseverance. Singers also must have physical stamina to adapt to frequent traveling and rigorous time schedules, which often include night performances.

EMPLOYMENT OUTLOOK

Employment of singers is expected to grow faster than the average through the 1980's, but competition for jobs will be keen. Many short-term jobs are expected in the opera and concert stage, movies, theater, nightclubs, and other areas. The demand is growing for popular singers who can do radio and television commercials. However, these short-term jobs are not enough to provide steady employment for all qualified singers.

EARNINGS

Concert singers who were part of a chorus earned a minimum daily rate of $35 in 1978, or $45 to $50 per performance. Members of an opera chorus earned a minimum daily rate of $40, or $45 per performance. A featured soloist received a minimum of $200 for each performance. A few opera soloists and popular singers, however, earned thousands of dollars per performance. Minimum wage rates for group singers on network or syndicated television ranged between $165 and $175 per singer for a 1-hour show. Solo or duo singers received per performance minimums of $350 each.

Professional singers usually belong to a branch of the AFL-CIO union, the Associated Actors and Artistes of America. Singers on the concert stage or in opera belong to the American Guild of Musical Artists, Inc.; those who sing on radio or television or make phonograph recordings are members of the American Federation of Television and Radio Artists; singers in the variety and nightclub field belong to the American Guild of Variety Artists; those who sing in musical comedy and operettas belong to the Actors' Equity Association; and those who sing in television or theatrical motion pictures belong to the Screen Actors Guild, Inc.

RELATED OCCUPATIONS

Singers express themselves and entertain others through song. Some related occupations include arrangers, choral directors, copyists, music therapists, orchestrators, songwriters, and voice teachers.

SOURCES OF ADDITIONAL INFORMATION

A directory of accredited schools and departments of music is available for $3.25 from:

National Association of Schools of Music, 11250 Roger Bacon Dr., Reston, Va. 22090.

For information regarding programs in music teacher education, contact:

Music Educators National Conference, 1902 Association Dr., Reston, Va. 22091.

Information about certification of private music teachers is available from:

Music Teachers National Association, 2113 Carew Tower, Cincinnati, Ohio 45202.

A brochure entitled *Careers in Music* is available from any of the three organizations listed above.

LIST OF MEMBERS OF THE MUSIC PUBLISHERS' ASSOCIATION OF THE UNITED STATES

ABINGDON PRESS
(Methodist Publishing House)
201 Eighth Avenue South
Nashville, Tennessee 37202

ALFRED PUBLISHING CO., INC.
15335 Morrison Street
Sherman Oaks, California 91403

ARSIS PRESS
1719 Bay Street Southeast
Washington, D.C. 20003

ASSOCIATED MUSIC PUBLISHER'S, INC.
866 Third Avenue
New York, New York 10022

C. L. BARNHOUSE COMPANY
110 B. Avenue East
Oskaloosa, Iowa 52577

BELWIN MILLS PUBLISHING CORP.
25 Deshon Drive
Melville, New York

THE BIG THREE MUSIC CORPORATION
729 Seventh Avenue
New York, New York 10019

BOOSEY & HAWKES, INC.
30 West 57th Street
New York, New York 10019

BOURNE COMPANY
1212 Avenue of the Americas
New York, New York 10036

THE BRASS PRESS
136 Eighth Avenue, North
Nashville, Tennessee 37203

BRECKENHORST PRESS
P.O. Box 14273
Columbus, Ohio 43214

MICHAEL BRENT PUBLICATIONS, INC.
70 Winding Wood Road
Port Chester, New York 10573

BRODT MUSIC COMPANY
Box 1207
Charlotte, North Carolina 28201

ALEXANDER BROUDE, INC.
225 West 57th Street
New York, New York 10019

CANYON PRESS, INC.
P.O. Box 447
Islamorada, Florida 33036

CHANTRY MUSIC PRESS, INC.
32-34 North Center Street
Springfield, Ohio 45501

CHERRY LANE MUSIC CO., INC.
50 Holly Hill Lane
Greenwich, Connecticut 06830

COLUMBIA PICTURES PUBLISHING
16333 N.W. 54th Street
Hialeah, Florida 33014

CONCORDIA MUSIC PUBLISHING HOUSE
3558 South Jefferson Avenue
St. Louis, Missouri 63118

EUROPEAN AMERICAN MUSIC CORP.
195 Allwood Road
Clifton, New Jersey 07012

CARL FISCHER, INC.
62 Cooper Square
New York, New York 10003

MARK FORSTER MUSIC CO.
Box 4012
Champaign, Illinois 61820

GALAXY MUSIC CORP.
2121 Broadway
New York, New York 10023

GENERAL MUSIC PUBLISHING CO., INC.
Box 267
Hastings-On-Hudson, New York 10709

HANSEN PUBLICATIONS
1860 Broadway
New York, New York 10023

HINSHAW MUSIC, INC.
P.O. Box 470
Chapel Hill, North Carolina 27514

HOPE PUBLISHING CO.
Carol Stream
Chicago, Illinois 60187

JENSON PUBLICATIONS, INC.
2880 South 171st Street
New Berlin, Wisconsin 53151

KELTON PUBLICATIONS
P.O. Box 49720
Los Angeles, California 90049

KENDOR MUSIC, INC.
Delevan, New York 14042

NEIL KJOS MUSIC COMPANY
525 Busse Highway
Park Ridge, Illinois 60068

HAL LEONARD PUBLISHING CORP.
8112 West Bluemond Road
Milwaukee, Wisconsin 53123

LORENZ INDUSTRIES
501 East Third Street
Dayton, Ohio 45401

LUDWIG MUSIC PUBLISHING CO.
557-67 E. 140th Street
Cleveland, Ohio 44110

MAGNA MUSIC-BATON, INC.
10370 Page Industrial Blvd.
St. Louis, Missouri 63132

MAGNAMUSIC DISTRIBUTORS, INC.
Sharon, Connecticut 06069

MARGUN MUSIC, INC.
167 Dudley Road
Newton Centre, Massachusetts

EDWARD B. MARKS MUSIC CORP.
1790 Broadway
New York, New York 10019

MCA MUSIC
445 Park Avenue
New York, New York 10022

MYKLAS PRESS
P.O. Box 929
Boulder, Colorado 80302

NOVELLO & COMPANY LIMITED
145 Palisade Street
Dobbs Ferry, New York 10522

OXFORD UNIVERSITY PRESS
Music Department
200 Madison Avenue
New York, New York 10016

J. W. PEPPER & SON, INC.
Valley Forge, Pennsylvania 19481

C. F. PETERS CORP.
373 Park Avenue South
New York, New York 10016

PLYMOUTH MUSIC CO., INC.
170 N.E. 43rd Street
Ft. Lauderdale, Florida 33334

THEODORE PRESSER COMPANY
Presser Place
Bryn Mawr, Pennsylvania 19010

RUBANK, INC.
16215 N.W. 15th Avenue
Miami, Florida 33169

E. C. SCHIRMER MUSIC COMPANY
112 South Street
Boston, Massachusetts 02111

G. SCHIRMER, INC.
866 Third Avenue
New York, New York 10022

SHAPIRO, BERNSTEIN & CO., INC.
10 East 53rd Street
New York, New York 10022

SHATTINGER INTERNATIONAL
MUSIC CORP.
A Division of Hansen Publications
1860 Broadway
New York, New York 10023

SHAWNEE PRESS, INC.
Delaware Water Gap, Pennsylvania 18327

SOUTHERN MUSIC COMPANY
1100 Broadway
San Antonio, Texas 78206

SOUTHERN MUSIC PUBLISHING,
INC.
1740 Broadway
New York, New York 10019

STANDARD MUSIC PUBLISHING,
INC.
P.O. Box 1043
Whitman Square
Turnersville, New Jersey 08012

SUMMY-BIRCHARD MUSIC
Box CN27
Princeton, New Jersey 08540

VOLKEIN BROTHERS, INC.
117 Sandusky Street
Pittsburgh, Pennsylvania 15212

WARNER BROTHERS, MUSIC
DIVISION
75 Rockefeller Plaza
New York, New York 10019

WINGERT-JONES PUBLICATIONS
2026 Broadway
Kansas City, Missouri 64141

WORD INCORPORATED
P.O. Box 1790
Waco, Texas 76703

LIST OF MEMBERS OF THE NATIONAL MUSIC COUNCIL

AMATEUR CHAMBER MUSIC
PLAYERS
Donald Spuehler, Chairman
P.O. Box 547
Vienna, VA 22180

AMERICAN ACADEMY OF
TEACHERS OF SINGING
Willard Young, Chairman
William Gephart, Secretary
75 Bank Street, New York, NY 10014

AMERICAN ACCORDIONISTS'
ASSOCIATION
Maddelena Belfiore Greco, President
580 Kearny Avenue
Kearny, NJ 07032

AMERICAN ASSOCIATION FOR
MUSIC THERAPY
Jerrold Ross, President
Education Building
35 West 4th Street, New York, NY 10003

AMERICAN COLLEGE OF
MUSICIANS; NATIONAL GUILD OF
PIANO TEACHERS
Irl Allison, Jr., President
Walter Merchant, Vice President
International Headquarters
P.O. Box 1807
Austin, Texas 78767

AMERICAN COMPOSERS ALLIANCE
Nicholas Roussakis, President
Francis Thorne, Executive Director
170 West 74th Street, New York, NY 10023

AMERICAN FEDERATION OF
MUSICIANS
Victor Fuentealba, President
1500 Broadway, New York, NY 10036

AMERICAN GUILD OF AUTHORS
AND COMPOSERS
Ervin Drake, President
Lewis M. Bachman, Executive Director
40 West 57th Street, New York, NY 10019

AMERICAN GUILD OF MUSICAL
ARTISTS
Gene Boucher, President
DeLloyd Tibbs, Executive Secretary
1841 Broadway, New York, NY 10023

AMERICAN GUILD OF ORGANISTS
Roberta Bitgood, President
Charles Dodley Walker, Interim Executive
Director
815 Second Avenue
New York, NY 10017

AMERICAN HARP SOCIETY
Ann Mason Stockton, President
10717 Wilshire Blvd. No. 701
Los Angeles, CA 90024

AMERICAN LISZT SOCIETY
Fernando Laires, President
David Z. Kushner, Chairman
Dept. of Music, University of Florida
Gainesville, Florida 32611

AMERICAN MATTHAY ASSOCIATION
Chandler Gregg, President
19 Hundred Circle
Wellesley Hills, MA 02181

AMERICAN MUSIC CENTER
Charles Dodge, President
Margaret Jory, Executive Director
250 West 54th Street Room 300
New York, NY 10019

AMERICAN MUSIC CONFERENCE
Gene Wenner, President
1000 Skokie Blvd.
Wilmette, IL 60091

AMERICAN ORFF-SCHULWERK
ASSOCIATION
Lillian Yaross, President
Department of Music
Cleveland State University
Cleveland, Ohio 44115

AMERICAN SOCIETY OF
COMPOSERS, AUTHORS AND
PUBLISHERS
Hal David, President
1 Lincoln Plaza, New York, NY 10023

AMERICAN SOCIETY OF
UNIVERSITY COMPOSERS
Edwin London, Chairman of National
Council
250 West 54th Street
New York, NY 10019

AMERICAN STRING TEACHERS
ASSOCIATION
Phyllis Young, President
Department of Music
University of Texas
Austin, Texas 78712

AMERICAN SYMPHONY ORCHESTRA
LEAGUE
Philip H. Yasinski, Chief Executive Officer
P.O. Box 669
Vienna, VA 22180

BROADCAST MUSIC, INC. (BMI)
Edward M. Cramer, President
320 West 57th Street
New York, NY 10019

CENTRAL OPERA SERVICE
Elihu M. Hyndman, National Chairman
Maria F. Rich, Administrative Director
Metropolitan Opera
Lincoln Center
New York, NY 10023

CHAMBER MUSIC AMERICA
Michael Jaffee, President
Benjamin Dunham, Executive Director
1372 Broadway
New York, NY 10018

CHOPIN FOUNDATION OF THE
UNITED STATES
F. Warren O'Reilly, President
1000 Brickell Avenue Suite 600
Miami, FL 33131

COLLEGE MUSIC SOCIETY
Chappell White, President
Craig Short, Executive Secretary
Regent Box 44
University of Colorado
Boulder, CO 80309

COUNTRY MUSIC ASSOCIATION
Dan McKinnon, President
Jo Walker, Executive Director
Seven Music Circle North
Nashville, Tennessee 37203

DELTA OMICRON
INTERNATIONAL MUSIC
FRATERNITY
Kay Calfee Wideman, President
Jane Wiley Kuckuk, Executive Secretary
1352 Redwood Court
Columbus, Ohio 43229

INTERLOCHEN ARTS ACADEMY
NATIONAL MUSIC CAMP
Roger E. Jacobi, President
Interlochen Center for the Arts
Interlochen, Michigan 49643

INTERNATIONAL ASSOCIATION OF
ORGAN TEACHERS
Dorothy S. Greig, President
Jack C. Greig, Administrative Director
7938 Bertram Avenue
Hammond, Indiana 46324

INTERNATIONAL BACH SOCIETY
Rosalyn Tureck, Director
165 West 57th Street
New York, NY 10019

INTERNATIONAL LEAGUE OF
WOMEN COMPOSERS
Nancy Van de Vate, Chairperson,
Executive Board
P.O. Box 23152
Honolulu, Hawaii 96822

INTERNATIONAL SOCIETY OF
BASSISTS
David Walter, President
Barry Green, Executive Director
University of Cincinnati
College-Conservatory of Music
Cincinnati, Ohio 45221

KAPPA KAPPA PSI
Richard Rodean, President
Thomas F. Siridge, Executive Secretary
112 Seretean Center, OSU
Stillwater, Oklahoma 74074

LEAGUE OF COMPOSERS—
INTERNATIONAL SOCIETY FOR
CONTEMPORARY MUSIC
Paul Alan Levi, President
250 West 54th Street
New York, NY 10019

LESCHETIZKY ASSOCIATION
Genia Robinor, President
105 West 72nd Street
New York, NY 10023

MORAVIAN MUSIC FOUNDATION
John Giesler, Chairman, Board of Trustees
Karl Kroeger, Director
Drawer Z, Salem Station
Winston-Salem, North Carolina 27108

MU PHI EPSILON
Marian B. Davidson, National President
7440 West 89th Street
Los Angeles, California 90045

MUSIC CRITICS ASSOCIATION, INC.
Patrick J. Smith, President
Richard D. Freed, Executive Secretary
6201 Tuckerman Lane
Rockville, Maryland 20852

MUSIC EDUCATORS NATIONAL
CONFERENCE
James A. Mason, President
Donald Dillon, Executive Director
1902 Association Drive
Reston, VA 22091

MUSIC PUBLISHER'S ASSOCIATION
OF THE U.S.
Arnold Broida, President
Arnold Rosen, Secretary
130 West 57th Street
New York, NY 10019

MUSIC TEACHERS NATIONAL
ASSOCIATION
Robert Sutton, President
Mariann H. Clinton, Executive Director
2113 Carew Tower
Cincinnati, OH 45202

NATIONAL ACADEMY OF POPULAR
MUSIC
Sammy Cahn, President
Abe Olman, Managing Director
One Times Square
New York, NY 10036

NATIONAL ASSOCIATION OF
COMPOSERS, U.S.A.
P.O. Box 49652, Barrington Station
Los Angeles, California 90049

NATIONAL ASSOCIATION OF JAZZ
EDUCATORS
Joel Leach, President
Matt Betton, Executive Secretary
Box 724
Manhattan, Kansas 66502

NATIONAL ASSOCIATION OF NEGRO
MUSICIANS
Betty Jackson King, President
Beatrice S. Cloud, Executive Secretary
1305 East 73rd Street
Chicago, Illinois 60619

NATIONAL ASSOCIATION OF
SCHOOLS OF MUSIC
Robert Bays, President
Samuel Hope, Executive Director
11250 Roger Bacon Drive No. 5
Reston, VA 22090

NATIONAL ASSOCIATION OF
TEACHERS OF SINGING, INC.
Irvin Bushman, President
James Browning, Executive Secretary
250 West 57th Street
New York, NY 10019

NATIONAL FEDERATION OF MUSIC
CLUBS
Lucile Ward, President
Mrs. John McDonald, Office Manager
Suite 234
3901 North Meridian Street
Indianapolis, IN 46208

NATIONAL FLUTE ASSOCIATION
Ronald L. Waln, President
Myrna Brown, Executive Secretary
805 Laguna Drive
Denton, TX 76201

NATIONAL GUILD OF COMMUNITY
SCHOOLS OF THE ARTS
Allen Sapp, President
Marcy Horwitz, Director
175 Fifth Avenue
New York, NY 10010

NATIONAL MUSIC PUBLISHERS
ASSOCIATION, INC.
Leonard Feist, President
110 East 59th Street
New York, NY 10022

NATIONAL OPERA ASSOCIATION
Natalie Limonick, President
Constance Eberhart, Secretary-Registrar
Hotel Wellington
Seventh Avenue at 55th Street
New York, NY 10019

NATIONAL ORATORIO SOCIETY
Thomas E. Wilson, President
6686 Brook Way
Paradise, CA 95969

NATIONAL PIANO
MANUFACTURERS ASSOCIATION
Luke Borger, Aeolian Corp., President
George M. Otto, Executive Director
435 North Michigan Avenue
Chicago, IL 60611

NATIONAL SCHOOL ORCHESTRA
ASSOCIATION
James Godfrey, President
330 Bellevue Drive
Bowling Green, KY 42101

PEOPLE-TO-PEOPLE MUSIC
COMMITTEE, INC.
Ann Schein, President
Ruth Sickafus, Executive Director
c/o John F. Kennedy Center for the
Performing Arts
Washington, D.C. 20566

PHI BETA
Carol M. Miller, President
Marilyn Dimond, Executive Secretary
Lawrence Drive
Fayette, MO 65248

PHI BETA MU
Richard C. Crain, Executive Secretary
221 East 21st Street
Belton, Texas 76513

PIANO TECHNICIANS GUILD, INC.
Bob Russell, President
1414 Lander Road
Mayfield Hts., OH 44124

PI KAPPA LAMBDA
Eugene Bonelli, President
Wilbur H. Rowland, Executive Secretary-
Treasurer
P.O. Box 6222
University, Alabama 35486

RECORDING INDUSTRY
ASSOCIATION OF AMERICA
Stanley M. Gortikov, President
Stephen Traiman, Executive Director
1633 Broadway
New York, NY 10019

SESAC INC.
A. H. Prager, Chairman
10 Columbus Circle
New York, NY 10019

SIGMA ALPHA IOTA
Patricia Stenberg, National President
431 Valencia Avenue
Oviedo, FL 32765

SOCIETY FOR THE PRESERVATION &
ENCOURAGEMENT OF BARBER
SHOP QUARTET SINGING IN
AMERICA
Roger Thomas, President
Hugh A. Ingraham, Executive Director
6315 Third Avenue
Kenosha, Wisconsin 53141

SONGWRITERS RESOURCES AND
SERVICES
Douglas Thiele, President
6318 Hollywood Boulevard
Hollywood, CA 90028

Appendix 5

CENTRAL OPERA SERVICE PUBLICATIONS

Directory of Operas and Publishers (Volume 18, Nos. 2 and 3)	$10.00
Directory of American Contemporary Operas (Volume 10, No. 2)	5.00
Directory of Foreign Contemporary Operas (Volume 12, No. 2)	5.00
Directory of American Operatic Premieres 1962–1968 (Volume 11, No. 2)	2.00
Directory of American and Foreign Contemporary Operas 1967–75 (Volume 17, No. 2)	8.00
Directory of American and Foreign Contemporary Operas 1975–80 (Volume 22, No. 2)	8.00
Directory of Children's and Christmas Operas (Volume 15, No. 2)	8.00
Directory of English Translations (Volume 16, No. 2)	6.00
Directory of Sets and Costumes for Rent (Volume 21, No. 2)	8.00
Career Guide for the Young American Singer (Volume 20, No. 3)	6.00
Directory of Opera/Musical Theatre Companies and Workshops in the U.S. and Canada	8.00
Directory of Selected Opera Films Available from American Distributors (Volume 19, No. 2)	6.00
Arts Administration Courses at Academic Institutions	2.00
Guide to Operatic Music Suitable for Performance in or by Religious Institutions	2.00
News Issues of the COS Bulletin beginning Volume 9, No. 1	each 2.00
Transcripts of COS National Conferences (1973, 1974, 1976, 1977, 1978, 1980)	each 8.00
Condensed speeches at COS National Conferences (1966, 1968 1970, 1972)	each 3.00

Appendix 6

LIST OF CONCERT MANAGEMENTS UNDER AGMA AGREEMENT

American Concert Management
Ansonia Station, P.O. Box 748
New York, New York 10023

Associated Concert Artists
Maria Irgen
120 W. 70 Street, New York 10023

Dina Bader Associates
444 E. 82 St., N.Y.C. 10028

Herbert Barrett
1860 Broadway, N.Y.C. 10023

Bellamente & Hammel Mgt., Inc.
309 Edgewood Ave., Teaneck, New
Jersey

Bernard and Rubin Management
255 West End Ave., N.Y.C. 10023

Wayne Bolton Agency
6347 Hillcrest Pl., Alexandria, Va. 22312

Joseph N. Catania Associates
215 West 78 St., N.Y.C. 10024

Colbert Artists Management
111 West 57 St., N.Y.C. 10019

Columbia Artists Management Inc.
(including Community Concerts)
165 West 57 Street, N.Y.C. 10019

Courtenay Artists, Inc.
411 E. 53 St., Suite 6F, N.Y.C. 10022

D. M. I. Talent Associates, Ltd.
250 West 57 Street, New York City 10019

Dubé Zakin Management, Inc.
1841 Broadway, New York 10023

Elwood Emerick
596 Crystal Lake Rd., Akron, OH 44313

William Felber Agency
2126 Cahuenga Blvd.
Los Angeles, Calif.

John B. Fisher
Dorchester Towers
155 W. 68 St., Suite 801, N.Y.C.

Lou Ann Francis
4231 So. 35 Street
Arlington, Virginia

Erica Gastelli
50 Riverside Drive, New York, N.Y.

Robert M. Gewald
Tower 58, 58 West 58th Street
New York, New York 10019

Reuben Guss Artists Mgmt.
120 W. 70 Street
New York, New York 10023

Tony Hartman Associates
250 West 57 Street Suite 1128-A
New York, New York 10019

Kazuko Hillyer International, Inc.
250 West 57 St., N.Y.C. 10019

Hans J. Hoffmann
200 West 58th Street, N.Y.C.

ICM Artists Ltd.
40 West 57th Street, New York 10019

Helen Jensen Artists Management
716 Joseph Vance Building
3rd and Union, Seattle, Wash.

Judd Concert Bureau
155 West 68 Street, Apt. 1003
New York, New York 10023

Paulina Kakides
170 W. 74 Street
New York, New York 10023

Katherine Dome Artists Representatives,
Inc.
23 West 73rd Street,
New York, New York 10023

Melvin Kaplan, Inc.
1860 Broadway
Suite 1010
New York, N.Y. 10023

Albert Kay Associates
58 West 58 Street (31E)
New York City 10019

Kolmar-Luth Entertainment, Inc.
1776 Broadway, N.Y.C. 10019

Richard Lescsak
60 West 68 St., New York City 10023

Lew/Benson
204 West 10th Street,
New York, New York 10014

Judith Liegner
1860 Broadway, New York City 10023

Ludwig Lustig and Florian, Ltd.
225 West 57th St., New York City 10019

Allan Lokos Enterprises, Inc.
250 W. 57 Street
New York, New York 10019

Matthew/Napal, Ltd.
270 West End Ave., New York City
10023

Mariedi Anders Artists Management, Inc.
535 El Camino Del Mar,
San Francisco, Calif. 94121

William Morris Agency
1350 Sixth Avenue
New York, New York 10019

Nutmeg Artists, Inc.
33 White Avenue
West Hartford, Conn.

Overland Talent Association, Inc.
210 East 52 Street
New York City 10022

Salmon & Stokes
280 Riverside Drive
New York, New York

. Sardos Artist Management Corporation
180 West End Ave., New York City

David Schiffman
60 West 68 St., N.Y.C. 10023

Jim Scovotti Associates
185 West End Avenue, N.Y. 10023

Joseph A. Scuro International
Artists Management
111 W. 57 Street
New York, New York 10019

Eric Semon Associates
111 West 57 Street, Suite 1412, N.Y.C.

Shaw Concerts, Inc.
1995 Broadway, New York City 10023

Sheldon Soffer Management, Inc.
130 West 56 Street, New York City 10019

Tornay Management
1995 Broadway, New York 10023

Unique Talent Association
(William H. Johnson)
297 Lenox Road, Brooklyn, N.Y. 11229

Vincent Attractions, Inc.
435 W. 57 Street
New York, New York 10019

Louise Williams
124 E. 91 St. Suite 4-B
New York, New York 10028

Appendix 7

FORM OF STANDARD AGMA ARTIST-MANAGER AGREEMENT

STANDARD ARTIST'S MANAGEMENT CONTRACT

This contract is between _____ (hereinafter

called "MANAGER), located at _____

and _____ (hereinafter called "ARTIST")

whose residence or usual place of business is _____

1. ARTIST hereby appoints MANAGER as his sole and exclusive manager and personal representative in all branches of the entertainment industry in the United States and Canada, except the legitimate stage, motion pictures, radio, television, lectures and the variety field, and MANAGER hereby accepts such appointment.

2. ARTIST warrants that he is a member of AGMA in good standing, or will become so pursuant to Rule "C" on the reverse side hereof, and agrees to remain in good standing throughout the term hereof.

3. The term of this contract shall commence the _____ day of _____

_____, and end the _____ day of _____

_____ ARTIST grants MANAGER an option to extend the term of this contract upon the same terms for an

additional _____ ( ) year, commencing upon the first day subsequent to the day that the term of this contract would otherwise expire. In the event that such option is exercised, ARTIST grants MANAGER an additional option further to extend

the term of this contract upon the same terms for an additional _____ ( ) year, commencing upon the first day subsequent to the day that the term of this contract, as theretofore extended, would otherwise expire. In the event that such additional option is exercised, ARTIST grants MANAGER a second additional option further to extend the term of this contract upon the same

terms for an additional _____ ( ) year, commencing upon the first day subsequent to the day that the term of this contract, as theretofore extended, would otherwise expire. In each instance that MANAGER shall elect to exercise any option contained in this paragraph, MANAGER shall give or mail to ARTIST notice not later than the December 1st next preceding the expiration of the then term of this contract, and upon such notice being given or mailed the term of this contract shall be so extended.

4. MANAGER is hereby appointed as the attorney-in-fact for ARTIST to execute in ARTIST's behalf contracts for the personal services of ARTIST in the branches of the entertainment field covered by this contract.

For Regular Concert Engagements, the Minimum fee shall be _____ $ _____
per engagement

For Symphony Orchestra Engagements, the Minimum Fee shall be _____ $ _____
per engagement

For Civic, Community and Similarly Organized Concert Engagements, the Net Minimum Fee (after deduction of "differential") shall be _____ $ _____
per engagement

5. (a) In consideration of the performance by MANAGER of the terms of this contract ARTIST agrees to pay MANAGER the following percentages of the gross earnings of ARTIST as herein defined.

Regular Concert Engagements Including Symphony Orchestra and Oratorio _____ %
(not more than 20%)

Civic, Community and Similarly Organized Concert Engagements _____ %
(not more than 15%)

Operatic Engagements and Ballet Engagements (other than concerts) _____ %
(not more than 10%)

(b) MANAGER shall use his best efforts to collect for ARTIST and in ARTIST's behalf all monies which may become due to ARTIST for engagements performed by ARTIST on which MANAGER shall be entitled to commissions hereunder. MANAGER shall pay to ARTIST net balances due to ARTIST from all funds received in ARTIST'S behalf, at thirty (30) day intervals, accompanied by a written statement showing how such net balances were arrived at, unless ARTIST shall request otherwise.

6. (a) ARTIST agrees that he will conscientiously fulfill all engagements contracted for by MANAGER in behalf of ARTIST, pursuant to this contract except as provided in Rule "H" on the reverse side hereof.

(b) ARTIST will promptly turn over to MANAGER all inquiries with reference to his services in all branches of the entertainment industry covered by the terms of this contract.

(c) ARTIST will be responsible for all traveling, hotel and all other non-booking expenses whatsoever of ARTIST and his accompanist as well as accompanist's salary.

(d) ARTIST shall pay for all of his normal promotional expenses incurred by himself or MANAGER.

7. ALL OF THE PROVISIONS ON THE REVERSE SIDE OF THIS CONTRACT SHALL BE DEEMED INCORPORATED HEREIN WITH THE SAME FORCE AND EFFECT AS THOUGH THEY PRECEDED THE SIGNATURES HERETO AFFIXED.

IN WITNESS WHEREOF, the parties hereto have executed this contract in triplicate as of the _____

day of _____, 19____

Manager _____

By: _____

_____
ARTIST

(Title) _____

3/66 form (AGMA copy)

RULES

A. ARTIST warrants that he has no contract for management and personal representation which is inconsistent with the terms of this contract.

B. MANAGER warrants that he has executed the AMERICAN GUILD OF MUSICAL ARTISTS, INC. (AGMA)—MANAGERS BASIC AGREEMENT. MANAGER represents and warrants that he is organized and equipped to render capable and efficient services to ARTIST in all branches of the entertainment industry covered by this contract and will continue to be so equipped throughout the balance of the term hereof; that he will use his best efforts in furthering the career of ARTIST and, incidentally, in assisting ARTIST in procuring engagements and that he will, at the request of ARTIST, counsel and advise ARTIST in matters which concern ARTIST'S professional interests in the fields covered by this contract; and that MANAGER will maintain an adequate organization to serve ARTIST during the term of this contract.

C. In the event that ARTIST is not presently a member of AGMA in good standing, ARTIST agrees either

I. to become a member of AGMA in good standing, immediately after his first public appearance in the United States or Canada after the date hereof, and to remain in good standing throughout the balance of the term hereof; or
II. if ARTIST is not within continental United States at the time of the execution of this contract, to become a member of AGMA in good standing within thirty (30) days after the arrival of ARTIST in continental United States or Canada or, in any event, immediately after the first public appearance of ARTIST in continental United States after the date hereof and to remain in good standing throughout the balance of the term hereof.

D. As used in Paragraph "3," the phrase "the same terms" shall mean that ARTIST grants MANAGER any additional options to extend the term of this contract, and no additional options shall be effective unless in writing signed by ARTIST.

E. In the event that ARTIST shall, for any reason whatsoever, breach any term set forth in Paragraph "2" of this contract subsequent to the execution hereof, and AGMA shall, by written notice, require Manager to terminate the term of this contract, MANAGER shall have the right to terminate the term of this contract immediately upon giving ARTIST notice thereof; provided, however, that MANAGER shall have the right, which shall be stated in said notice, to continue to represent ARTIST and to receive commissions with respect to such engagements as were secured prior to receipt by MANAGER of said written notice from AGMA.

F. In the case of the fields specifically enumerated in Paragraph "4," no contract shall provide for payment to ARTIST of a lesser fee than is therein set forth, unless ARTIST shall have approved such lesser fee in advance. In the case of the fields not specifically enumerated in Paragraph "4," no commitment shall be made by MANAGER until there has been mutual agreement between ARTIST and MANAGER as to fee, date, place of engagement, time of engagement.

G. "Gross earnings" of ARTIST as referred to in Paragraph shall consist of all money and other consideration (a) received by ARTIST directly or indirectly from engagements covered by contract performed during the term or extended term hereof, (b) received by ARTIST directly or indirectly from engagements covered by Paragraph VII (g) of AGMA-MANAGERS BASIC AGREEMENT performed subsequent to the expiration of the term or extended term hereof, (c) stipulated in contracts as and for ARTIST'S fee for engagements providing for performances during periods specified in (a) or (b) above but which ARTIST, without just cause, fails to perform, (d) accruing under engagements which are paid to creditors or assignees of ARTIST or are withheld pursuant to law, and (e) monies received in settlement less deductions as stipulated in Paragraph VII (h) of AGMA-MANAGERS BASIC AGREEMENT. Except as to (c) and (d) above, the foregoing shall be payable only when, as and if such monies are received by ARTIST or by anyone on ARTIST'S behalf.

H. The exceptions referred to in Paragraph "6 (a)" are as follows:

I. Engagements contracted for by MANAGER after ARTIST shall have given MANAGER ninety (90) days prior notice of ARTIST'S unavailability for the date of such engagement, provided, however, that no such notice shall be given during the period commencing January 15th and ending April 15th, in any year during the term or extended term of this contract.

II. Engagements which ARTIST is unable to fulfill due to physical disability, the acts or regulations of public authorities, civil tumult, epidemic, interruption or delay of transportation service, labor difficulties or strikes which are not in violation of Paragraph IX or III (c) of the AGMA-MANAGERS BASIC AGREEMENT, or any other cause beyond the control of ARTIST.

I. ARTIST grants to MANAGER the right to use and to license others to use the name, likeness and biography of ARTIST for informative purposes and to publicize and advertise ARTIST and ARTIST'S engagements. Such use may be in combination with advertising of products or services of any employer of ARTIST, but shall not amount to an endorsement thereof by ARTIST.

J. All membership dues of ARTIST which are payable to AGMA may, upon the written request of AGMA be deducted by MANAGER from the compensation or other monies of ARTIST received by MANAGER and paid by MANAGER directly to AGMA, but the authority granted by this Paragraph J may be revoked by ARTIST giving written notice to MANAGER at any time after one (1) year from the date hereof.

K. Where any contract for ARTIST'S services requires that all or any part of ARTIST'S fee shall be paid prior to the performance of ARTIST'S engagement, MANAGER shall have the right to direct ARTIST to collect such fee or part thereof prior to ARTIST'S performance of the engagement; provided, however, that if MANAGER so directs ARTIST and ARTIST fails to perform MANAGER'S directions, such failure by ARTIST shall not confer any right on MANAGER with respect to ARTIST nor shall it relieve MANAGER of any of his duties or obligations under this contract.

L. For the purposes of Paragraph 4 of this contract, a pair of symphony orchestral appearances is to be considered as one engagement hereunder, provided that such symphony pair takes place with the same orchestra within three (3) days, it being understood, however, that the symphony pair need not necessarily take place in the same city, provided that one city is the home city of the orchestra, and the other a nearby city.

M. Any and all notices herein provided for shall be in writing, addressed to MANAGER or ARTIST at the address set forth for each of them in this contract, or at such other address as either of them may for himself hereafter in writing designate. Such notices shall be personally delivered, mailed or telegraphed, and if mailed shall be deemed given when enclosed in a properly addressed, postpaid, sealed envelope deposited in a U.S. Post Office or mail box or mail chute maintained by the United States. If telegraphed, such notice shall be deemed to have been given when delivered to the telegraph company.

N. MANAGER agrees that the following persons, and the following persons only:

(here the parties may, but need not, insert the names of not more than four (4) persons in MANAGER'S employ) shall personally supervise ARTIST'S business during the term of this contract. One of such persons shall be available at all reasonable times for consultation with ARTIST in the City in which the office of MANAGER is located as hereinabove set forth. Employees of MANAGER who are not named herein may aid any of the named persons in handling managerial matters for ARTIST. In the event that all the persons above named sever their connections with MANAGER, ARTIST shall have the right within a period of thirty (30) days after the receipt of notice thereof, to terminate the term of this contract.

O. ARTIST shall be or become, and remain during the term of this contract, a member in good standing of all labor organizations having jurisdiction over the services scheduled by MANAGER for ARTIST pursuant to the terms of this contract.

P. ALL OF THE PROVISIONS OF THE AGMA-MANAGERS BASIC AGREEMENT SHALL BE DEEMED INCORPORATED HEREIN WITH THE SAME FORCE AND EFFECT AS THOUGH HEREIN SET FORTH IN FULL. No written or oral waiver by ARTIST of any of the provisions of the said BASIC AGREEMENT or of this contract shall be valid or binding unless the written consent of AGMA with respect to the making of such a waiver is first obtained.

Q. If any provision of this contract or the application of such provision to any person or circumstance, is or shall be or become illegal or invalid, the remainder of this contract, or the application of such provision to persons or circumstances other than those as to which it is held invalid, shall not be affected thereby.

R. This contract cannot be changed orally, and shall be construed, governed and interpreted pursuant to the laws of the State of New York.

S. NOTE: At no time shall ARTIST be bound to MANAGER for a period extending more than four (4) years in the future including all options and rights or renewals exercisable by MANAGER.

T. Further terms not set forth above in this contract may be set forth under Schedule "A" annexed hereto, and any terms so set forth are hereby made a part of this contract. If any such terms are contrary to the terms of the printed portions of this contract or to the terms of the AGMA-MANAGERS BASIC AGREEMENT or are less favorable to ARTIST than the said AGMA-MANAGERS BASIC AGREEMENT, such contrary or less favorable terms shall be void and of no effect.

Appendix 8

FORM OF STANDARD AGMA EMPLOYMENT AGREEMENT

AMERICAN GUILD OF MUSICAL ARTISTS

(BRANCH OF ASSOCIATED ACTORS AND ARTISTES OF AMERICA)
AFFILIATED WITH A.F.L. — C.I.O.

1841 BROADWAY • NEW YORK, NEW YORK 10023
COlumbus 5-3687

STANDARD ARTIST'S CONTRACT FOR EMPLOYMENT

FOR USE FOR EMPLOYMENT IN OPERA, CONCERT, RECITAL, BALLET AND DANCE, CHORUS
AND CHOIR, AND FOR OTHER TYPES OF EMPLOYMENT UNDER THE JURISDICTION OF AGMA

Agreement made this...day of..., 19..............,

by and between.., a corporation organized and existing

under and by virtue of the laws of ....hereinafter referred to as the

"EMPLOYER", and... of..
(Artist's usual place of business or residence must be inserted here), hereinafter referred to as "ARTIST", a member in good
standing of the AMERICAN GUILD OF MUSICAL ARTISTS, (hereinafter referred to as "AGMA".)

I.   AGREEMENT OF EMPLOYMENT AND COMPENSATION. The EMPLOYER hereby engages the ARTIST to

render services as ....
(Singer, dancer, chorister, stage director, or in other capacity under the jurisdiction of AGMA)

in the company or production known as...
(Name of Opera Company, Ballet Company, Concert Attraction, etc.)

A.   REHEARSALS
The maximum number of rehearsal-hours, days and/or weeks, the maximum number of hours of rehearsal per day and/or
per week, and all other regulations and restrictions in connection with rehearsals for employment of the type agreed to
hereunder which are set forth in AGMA RULES and/or in any BASIC AGREEMENT governing this contract, shall govern
rehearsal hereunder and the rate of payment for rehearsals and for any and all overtime rehearsal-hours, days or weeks.
For and in consideration of the employment agreed to above, and in connection therewith, it is agreed that the ARTIST

will rehearse for..commencing with the.......................day of................................, 19............,
(number of days, hours, weeks, etc.)

and the EMPLOYER agrees to pay the ARTIST the sum of $ .... per............................as compensation
therefor.   (hour, day, week, etc.)

Cross out Inapplicable Paragraphs B or C.
B.   ENGAGEMENT ON A PERFORMANCE BASIS
The EMPLOYER hereby engages the ARTIST to render services in the following productions and roles, on the following
dates and for the following compensations:

PRODUCTION	ROLE	DATE OF PERFORMANCE	COMPENSATION	PER DIEM	TRANSPORTATION AMOUNT

and the ARTIST hereby accepts such employment upon the terms set forth herein. The employment of the ARTIST under this
Paragraph B shall be non-cancellable.

C.   ENGAGEMENT ON A WEEKLY BASIS
The EMPLOYER hereby engages the ARTIST to render services for a PERIOD OF ....WEEK(S), commencing

with the.......................day of....................., 19............, and ending the.......................day of........................, 19............,
and the EMPLOYER hereby guarantees that the ARTIST will receive the compensation hereinafter set forth for the period of
time hereinabove set forth.

D.   List below the roles and operas for which the ARTIST is engaged:

PRODUCTION	ROLE	TRANSPORTATION (AMOUNT)

E.   The EMPLOYER agrees to pay the ARTIST the sum of $ .... per week during the above stated period
for rendering the services stated above. The ARTIST hereby agrees to accept this employment upon the terms stated
herein. The employment of the ARTIST under paragraph C above shall be non-cancellable and continuous without a lay-off or
interruption.
F.   The compensation under paragraphs B and C above shall be "PAY OR PLAY" and all compensation shall be paid in
United States currency (a) prior to the commencement of each single performance or (b) before 6 P.M. on the last day of each
performance week.
G.   TRANSPORTATION. It is understood and agreed that the ARTIST'S first-class railroad transportation from
.... to .... and return, which must be paid for by the EMPLOYER, is not to be
included in the amount of the ARTIST'S compensation, but must be separately stated in this contract by the EMPLOYER.

2.   **SECURITY DEPOSIT OR BOND.** The EMPLOYER MUST, simultaneously with the filing with AGMA of this contract, but in no event less than one week prior to the 1st rehearsal of the company or production hereinabove described in paragraph 1 hereof, deposit with AGMA a bond, cash or other security as provided in the Basic Agreement.

The EMPLOYER agrees that this contract is not binding upon the ARTIST until such time as the EMPLOYER deposits a bond, cash or other security as hereinabove provided and the same has been approved by AGMA.

3.   **DEDUCTIONS.** The actual net compensation of the ARTIST shall be set forth herein and there shall be no remissions, rebates, discounts, booking fees, commissions or other payments or deductions whatsoever from the ARTIST'S compensation except such taxes or withholdings as are required by statute, and except further that initiation fees, and delinquent dues payable to AGMA shall be deducted from the compensation of the ARTIST and paid by the EMPLOYER to AGMA, and the ARTIST hereby authorizes the EMPLOYER to make such deductions and payments as AGMA directs. The EMPLOYER warrants that this clause will be fully and faithfully observed by himself and by any and all of his agents, representatives and employees. Artist may revoke above authority at any time after 1 year from date hereof.

4.   **AGMA RULES– ARTIST'S OBLIGATIONS TO AGMA.** The ARTIST hereby warrants that he is a member of AGMA in good standing and that he will remain so for the duration of this contract and the ARTIST and the EMPLOYER hereby jointly and severally agree that the ARTIST'S obligations hereunder are subject (1) to the ARTIST'S prior obligations to AGMA as a member thereof, and (2) to AGMA's Constitution, By-Laws, and Rules and Regulations as they now exist or as they may hereafter be amended. The EMPLOYER agrees that its obligations under this contract with the ARTIST are subject to the provisions of AGMA's Constitution, By-Laws, and Rules and Regulations as they now exist or as they may hereafter be amended.

The EMPLOYER represents that a Collective Bargaining Agreement (hereinafter referred to as "BASIC AGREEMENT") exists between AGMA and the EMPLOYER. All the provisions of such Basic Agreement and all AGMA Rules as they now exist or as they may hereafter be amended shall be deemed to be included in this contract as an integral part hereof, except to the extent that any provision of this contract which is more favorable to the ARTIST than any conflicting or inconsistent provision of such Basic Agreement or AGMA Rules, in which event such provision in this contract shall prevail. If no such BASIC AGREEMENT exists between the EMPLOYER and AGMA, then this contract shall not be binding upon the ARTIST but shall nevertheless be enforceable against the EMPLOYER at the option of AGMA or the ARTIST.

The EMPLOYER further agrees (1) that he has notice that the ARTIST is a member of AGMA and must obey AGMA RULES, (2) that he will require the ARTIST to remain a member of AGMA in good standing throughout the duration of this contract, and (3) that he will not require the ARTIST to work in any company under his direction, management or control unless every ARTIST under the jurisdiction of AGMA employed in such company is a member of AGMA in good standing and remains so for the duration of his employment and only so long as the EMPLOYER has fully performed and is fully performing the covenants in each and every employment contract entered into, or hereafter during the term hereof entered into, with each and every AGMA member in each and every company operated and/or owned and/or controlled by him or with which he may be in any way connected.

5.   **NO WAIVERS OR CHANGES ALLOWED SCHEDULE "A":** The EMPLOYER and the ARTIST hereby mutually agree that no riders, changes or alterations of this printed form, and no addition to this printed form under Schedule "A" below, shall be made or agreed to by either the EMPLOYER or the ARTIST without the written consent of AGMA, and the EMPLOYER further agrees that no such rider, change, or alteration shall be required of or deemed binding upon the ARTIST unless approved by AGMA as provided in the Basic Agreement.

Further provisions and agreements not set forth above in the printed portion of this contract may be set forth under Schedule "A" below, subject, however, to the provisions of the preceding paragraph.

The acceptance by the ARTIST of cash, checks, or other forms of payment, or the deposit or retaining of cash, checks or other forms of payment shall in no way affect the right of the ARTIST or of AGMA to insist upon full payment under this contract. The signing by the ARTIST of waivers or releases, or the deposit of checks or money orders under stipulations, letters or other writings that such deposit is in full payment or the like, shall be of no force or effect.

6.   **BENEFITS.** The EMPLOYER shall not request an ARTIST directly or indirectly to appear in or attend any benefit without first receiving written approval from Theatre Authority, Inc., 485 Fifth Avenue, New York, New York 10017 and the AGMA National Office, 1841 Broadway, New York, New York 10023.

7.   **DISCRIMINATION FORBIDDEN.** The EMPLOYER agrees that it will not discriminate against any ARTIST in compensation, performances, engagements or in its general relationship with any ARTIST, because of any such ARTIST'S activities in behalf of AGMA, nor shall EMPLOYER discriminate against any ARTIST because of his race, color or creed.

8.   **SEGREGATION.** No ARTIST will be required to appear in any theatre or place of performance where discrimination is practiced because of race, color or creed against any: (1) ARTIST or (2) patron, as to admission or seating arrangements.

9.   **ARBITRATION.** The EMPLOYER and the ARTIST hereby jointly and severally agree that any controversy or claim arising out of or relating to this contract or the breach thereof, or any controversy whatsoever between the EMPLOYER and the ARTIST, shall be settled by Arbitration, in accordance with the provisions of the BASIC AGREEMENT and the rules, then obtaining, of the American Arbitration Association (except as may otherwise be provided in AGMA RULES), and judgment upon the award rendered may be entered in the highest Court of the Forum, State or Federal, having jurisdiction.

10.   **LAWS GOVERNING.** This agreement shall be subject to, be construed by, and the right of all parties thereto shall be determined by the Laws of the State of New York, except as may otherwise be provided.

11.   **LIABILITY.** This contract shall be executed by the ARTIST and by the EMPLOYER. If the EMPLOYER or EMPLOYERS or any of them is a corporation, this agreement must be signed by the corporation and by an individual as an individual and not as a corporate officer; and in any event a person signing as an officer, agent or representative of a corporation agrees that his signature hereto binds him as an individual as well as such officer, agent or representative.

IN WITNESS WHEREOF we have executed this agreement as of the date first above set forth.

IMPORTANT	
All AGMA RULES which are in force at the time this contract is entered into are part hereof.	....
	EMPLOYER(s)
The EMPLOYER and the ARTIST should keep themselves advised of AGMA RULES posted on the bulletin board in the AGMA office.	Employer(s) Unemployment Insurance Number _____
The Basic Agreement between AGMA and the above Employer may contain modifications of the Standard Agreement.	....
	ARTIST
Check with AGMA before you sign this contract.	....
	ADDRESS
"SCHEDULE "A"	Social Security No. ☐☐☐ ☐☐ ☐☐☐☐

Appendix 9

FORM OF PUBLISHER-COMPOSER SERIOUS MUSIC CONTRACT

AGREEMENT made this_____day of _____, 19_____ , between

_____of_____(hereinafter called "Publisher")

and _____jointly and severally (hereinafter called "Composer").

WITNESSETH:

1. Composer hereby sells, assigns, transfers and delivers to Publisher, its successors and assigns, a certain heretofore unpublished original musical composition, and the manuscript and performance materials (if any) thereof, written and composed by Composer, now entitled:

(hereinafter called the "composition"), including the common law property therein, the title words and music thereof, and the right to secure copyright and all extensions and renewals of copyright therein throughout the entire world and to have and to hold the said copyright and all rights of whatsoever nature thereunder.

2. Composer warrants that the composition is his sole, exclusive and original work; that he has full right and power to make this agreement; that there exists no adverse claim to or in the composition; that valid copyright can be secured therein by Publisher; and that neither the composition nor any part thereof infringes upon the title or the literary, musical, personal or property rights of any person, firm or corporation anywhere in the world.

3. Publisher agrees to use reasonable efforts to exploit the composition in accordance with its business judgment and to pay to Composer, in respect of the composition, sums equal to:

(a) Ten percent (10%) of the retail list prices established by Publisher on all copies of all versions of the composition published by it and sold and paid for in the United States and Canada, and one-half (½) of such amount on all such copies sold outside of the United States and Canada and paid for; provided that if the composition is published in a book with other works, such sums shall be prorated according to the number of compositions in such book.

(b) Fifty percent (50%) of all net sums received by Publisher in respect of any and all licenses issued authorizing the manufacture in the United States and Canada of parts of instruments serving to reproduce the composition, or any parts, arrangements, versions, or adaptations thereof mechanically on phonograph records, tapes and similar devices, or authorizing such usage in synchronization with motion pictures.

(c) Fifty percent (50%) of all net sums received by Publisher for the rental in the United States and Canada of materials furnished to Publisher by Composer, and twenty-five percent (25%) of all net sums received by Publisher for the rental in the United States and Canada of materials produced and paid for by Publisher.

(d) Fifty percent (50%) of all net sums received by Publisher from the licensing of public performance of the composition directly by Publisher to the user.

(e) Fifty percent (50%) of all net sums received by Publisher for any grant to another publisher of the right to publish the composition in a book with other works.

(f) Fifty percent (50%) of all net sums received by Publisher in respect of foreign exploitation of the composition by any means, except as hereinabove otherwise provided.

(g) Fifty percent (50%) of all other net sums received by Publisher in the United States and Canada (except as specifically provided for herein).

Composer shall not share in any sum or sums received by Publisher from ASCAP or BMI or any public performing rights organization which pays performance fees directly to composers.

Except as specifically provided in this paragraph 3, no other royalties or payments of any kind shall be due from Publisher to Composer.

4. It is agreed that all sums payable hereunder to the parties named as Composer shall be divided among them as follows:

NAME	SHARE

5. Publisher agrees to render statements and make payments to Composer annually for the period ending December 31 of each year within ninety (90) days after such date, but no statement need oe rendered or payment made with respect to any year in which less than the sum of Five Dollars ($5.00) shall be due to Composer.

6. (Delete inapplicable section)

If Publisher has not published the composition two years after the date of this agreement, then at the option of either party this agreement may be cancelled, in which event the composition shall be returned to Composer and Publisher shall be relieved of all duty, liability and responsibility hereunder. Such option may not be exercised by Composer unless he shall have requested Publisher in writing to publish the composition and the Publisher shall have failed to do so within ninety (90) days after receipt of such request.

Publisher shall have the right but not the obligation at any time to publish or have published the composition. Composer shall have the option to cancel this agreement at the expiration of   years from the date hereof unless within such period of   years (a) Publisher has published the composition, or (b) a commercial phonograph recording thereof has been issued, or (c) Publisher has produced and paid for rental materials for the performance of the composition, or (d) Publisher has paid to Composer at least the sum of   Dollars ($) under this agreement and/or any other agreement between the parties relating wholly or in part to the composition. Such option may be exercised by written notice to Publisher given at least ninety days prior to the expiration of such period of   years, and if it is exercised, the composition shall be returned to Composer and Publisher shall be relieved of all duty, liability and responsibility hereunder.

7. Composer agrees to secure and deliver to Publisher an assignment of copyright or other instrument of authorization relating to the text (if any) for the composition in the form and to the extent required by Publisher. Publisher shall have the right to expend such sums as may be necessary to obtain such instrument from the owner of the copyright in such text (if any), in which event all sums so expended by Publisher shall be for the account of Composer and shall be charged to Composer and may be deducted by Publisher from any moneys due to Composer under this or any other agreement between the parties.

8. Anything to the contrary notwithstanding, nothing in this agreement contained shall prevent Publisher from authorizing publishers, agents and representatives in countries outside of the United States and Canada (and in Canada if said composition is printed by a party other than Publisher in Canada) from exercising exclusive publication and all other rights in said foreign countries in said composition, on the customary royalty basis; and nothing in this agreement shall prevent Publisher from authorizing publishers in the United States from exercising exclusive publication rights and other rights in the United States in said composition, provided Publisher shall pay Composer the royalties herein stipulated.

9. Composer may appoint a certified public accountant who shall, at any time during usual business hours, have access to all records of Publisher and of the United States publisher whom Publisher causes to publish said composition, relating to said composition, for the purpose of verifying royalty statements rendered, or which are delinquent under the terms hereof.

10 In the event that Publisher shall fail or refuse, within sixty days after written demand to furnish, or cause to be furnished, royalty statements described in paragraph 5, or to give Composer access to the records as set forth in paragraph 10, or in the event that Publisher shall fail to make payment of any royalty due, within thirty days after written demand therefor, then Composer shall have the option, to be exercised upon ten days' written notice, to cancel this agreement. Upon such cancellation, all rights of Publisher of any and every nature, in and to said composition, shall cease and come to an end and the said rights, including, but not limited to, the right to secure copyright and/or any copyright theretofore secured by Publisher, shall revert to, and become the property of, and shall be reassigned to Composer. Publisher agrees that it will thereupon execute any and all assignments or other documents which may be necessary or proper to vest the said rights in Composer.

11. Composer agrees that Publisher may make or have made any versions, arrangements, adaptations, interpolations, and translations of the composition, and the setting of words to music and of music to the words, and changes of the title, as Publisher may deem desirable.

12. If, after submission of a manuscript approved by Composer and after production has been commenced on the basis thereof, Composer suggests any alterations or revisions and such alterations or revisions are made by Publisher, the cost thereof shall be borne by Composer.

13. Composer consents to the use of Composer's name and likeness on and in connection with published copies and recordings of the composition, and in publicity, promotional material and advertising concerning the composition and Publisher.

14. Written demands and notices other than royalty statements provided for herein shall be sent by registered mail.

15. Any legal action brought by Publisher against any alleged infringer of said composition shall be initiated and prosecuted at its sole expense, and of any recovery made by it as a result thereof, after deduction of the expense of the litigation, a sum equal to fifty percent (50%) shall be paid to Composer.

(a) If a claim is presented against Publisher alleging that the said composition is an infringement upon some other composition, and because thereof Publisher is jeopardized, it shall thereupon serve written notice upon Composer containing the full details of such claim and thereafter, until the claim has been adjudicated or settled, shall withhold any moneys coming due Composer pending the outcome of such claim; provided, however, if no suit be filed in twelve months after written notice to Composer by Publisher of the adverse claim, the said moneys shall be released and paid to Composer. Such payment shall be without prejudice to the rights of Publisher in the event of a subsequent adverse adjudication.

(b) From and after the service of a summons in a suit for infringement filed against Publisher in respect of said composition, any and all payments hereunder thereafter coming due Composer shall be retained by Publisher until the suit has been finally adjudicated and then be disbursed accordingly, unless Composer shall elect to file an acceptable bond in the sum of such payments, in which event the sums due shall be paid to Composer.

16. Composer agrees to indemnify, save and hold harmless Publisher and its licensees, successors and assigns, from and against all claims, actions, proceedings, liabilities and costs, including attorneys' fees, which may be asserted against or incurred by any of them, arising out of or connected with any claim by a third party which is inconsistent with any of the warranties or representations made by Composer in this agreement or by reason of the exercise of any of the rights granted or purported to be granted by this agreement. Composer authorizes Publisher in its sole discretion and at Composer's expense to employ attorneys and to defend any action or proceedings and/or to take any other steps proper to protect the right, title and interest of Publisher in the composition and, in that connection, to settle, or in any other manner dispose of, any claim, action or proooceeding and to satisfy any judgment. Composer agrees to reimburse Publisher for any such expenses on demand and authorizes Publisher to withhold any and all sums which may be or become due to Composer under this or any other agreement between the parties until such claim, action or proceeding shall have been disposed of or the breach of any warranty hereunder repaired.

17. Any controversy or claim relating or arising out of this agreement, or the breach thereof, shall be settled by arbitration in New York City in accordance with the Rules of the American Arbitration Association, and judgment upon the award rendered by the Arbitrator may be entered in any Court having jurisdiction thereof.

18. This agreement is binding upon the parties hereto and their respective successors and assigns.

19. This agreement represents the entire understanding between the parties. It may not be changed orally. It shall be construed according to the laws of the State of New York.

IN WITNESS WHEREOF, the parties hereto have caused the agreement to be duly executed the day and year first above written.

Witness: PUBLISHER

_____   By _____
                                                              President

Witness: COMPOSER_____

_____   Address _____

Witness: COMPOSER_____

_____   Address _____

Appendix 10

RIDER TO AGAC FORM OF CONTRACT

RIDER APPLICABLE TO STANDARD WORKS

(Whenever any part of this contract is inconsistent with this rider, the latter shall prevail)

Initial Paragraph 24 or 25 or 26, whichever are applicable.

Initial:

. . . .

The following shall replace Paragraph 6 of this contract.

24. Publisher shall, within one year after the date of this contract, publish the Composition as a . . . . (orchestral version, piano version, etc.).

Initial:

. . . .

25. Publisher shall within one year after date of this contract, publish a score of the Composition as a . . . . (orchestral version, piano version, etc.) and maintain the orchestral and/or choral parts (as the case may be) for rental in accordance with paragraph 26 hereof.

Initial:

. . . .

26. (a) Publisher shall prepare customary rental material of the Composition as delivered by Writer to Publisher, and offer the composition for rental, within six months after the date of this contract and thereafter throughout the term of this agreement. Publisher shall maintain such material in good condition. Royalties to Writer on rentals shall be 50% of Publisher's gross receipts therefrom.

(b) If Publisher fails to prepare and offer the Composition for rental, rental material, as provided in (a) above, this contract shall terminate. If Publisher prepares and offers for rental, rental material, in accordance with (a) above, but does not maintain such material in good condition, and does not prepare new rental material and offer same for rental within three (3) months of receipt of notice by registered mail from Writer, this contract shall terminate.

27. The date when any publication takes place hereunder shall be deemed to be the date when Publisher delivers a copy of such publication to Writer. If such publication does not take place within such time, then this contract shall terminate.

28. (a) Wherever in this contract, "wholesale" price is referred to, there shall be substituted therefor, "Publisher's marked or suggested retail price".

(b) If the Composition or a score thereof is published hereunder and goes out of print, and Publisher does not reprint and offer same for sale within three (3) months of receipt of notice by registered mail from Writer, this contract shall terminate.

29. If this contract terminates in accordance with any provision of this rider, the following shall prevail: This contract shall terminate and all copyrights and rights received by Publisher under this contract or under this rider shall revest in Writer, immediately and automatically and without the necessity of further notice or procedure. Publisher shall promptly deliver to Writer a reassignment of such copyrights and rights, as evidence of such termination and revesting, but any failure to deliver such reassignment shall not affect such termination and revesting. Subparagraphs (a)-(f) of Paragraph 13 shall apply. For a period beginning on the date of such automatic termination and continuing until 60 days after Publisher shall have delivered such reassignment to Writer, Writer shall have the right to purchase from Publisher the plates and/or other materials from which copies of the published version(s) can be reproduced, at Publisher's actual cost of manufacture thereof.

Writer . . . .   Publisher . . . .

By . . . .

AMERICAN GUILD OF AUTHORS AND COMPOSERS

Countersigned by: . . . .

EXTRACTS FROM ASCAP WEIGHTING FORMULA
RELATING TO CREDITS FOR SERIOUS WORKS

(E) SERIOUS WORKS FOUR MINUTES OR LONGER IN DURATION

Works which require four minutes or more for a single, complete rendition thereof, and which in their original form were composed for a choral, symphonic, or similar concert performance (including chamber music), shall receive credit on the following basis when performed for the respective designated periods of time:

Minutes of Actual Performance	The Otherwise Applicable Credit Is Multiplied By:
4:00 to 5:30	2
5:31 to 10:30	6
10:31 to 15:30	12
15:31 to 20:30	20
20:31 to 25:30	30
25:31 to 30:30	40
30:31 to 35:30	50
35:31 to 40:30	60
40:31 to 45:30	70
45:31 to 50:30	80
50:31 to 55:30	90
55:31 to 60:30	100
Each additional 5 minutes or part thereof	10

(F) CONCERT AND SYMPHONY PERFORMANCES

The license fees which the Society receives from concert and symphony halls shall be multiplied by five in determining the credit to be awarded for performances of works in concert and symphony halls. For performances in concert and symphony halls, points shall be awarded as follows:

	POINT AWARD MINUTES						
	Up to 5	6 to 10	11 to 15	16 to 20	21 to 30	31 to 45	46 to 60
A) ENTERTAINMENT MUSIC—i.e. Light or Standard Instrumental and Choral Music ALL CATEGORIES	1	2	3	4	5	6	7
B) SERIOUS MUSIC IN THE ORIGINAL FORM							
a. Works for 1 or 2 instruments with or without voice	2	4	6	8	10	12	14
b. Works for 3 to 9 instruments with or without voice	3	6	9	12	15	20	25
c. Works for small orchestra with or without voice	4	9	18	24	30	40	50
d. Works for full orchestra with or without voice	8	18	36	48	60	80	100

For works in excess of 60 minutes, pro rata on the basis of the 60 minute points. The percentage of credit for arrangements of works in the Public Domain will be determined in accordance with Section (G).

(H) CONCERT AND SYMPHONY PERFORMANCES—ADDITIONAL CREDIT

In the case of any work which qualifies for credit under subdivision (B) of paragraph (F) above, and for which the Society holds the right to license such work from a writer member of the Society, or holds the right to license such work from the writer under Section I of the Order, such work shall receive for performances under paragraph (F) above, additional credit under this section. The additional credit shall be determined by multiplying the credit such work received under paragraph (F) above by twice the ratio of (i) the license fees which the Society received from concert and symphony halls in the survey year October 1, 1963 through September 30, 1964 to (ii) the license fees which the Society received from concert and symphony halls in the year of the performance. Such additional credit shall in no event be more than twice the credits awarded under paragraph (F) above. Distribution based on the additional credits awarded under this paragraph shall be in addition to the distribution based upon credits awarded under paragraph (F) above.

(I) RELIGIOUS WORKS FOUR MINUTES OR LONGER IN ORIGINAL DURATION

Religious works which in their original form require four minutes or more for a single complete rendition thereof shall, for four quarters commencing with the fourth quarter of 1981 receive *two* (2) times the otherwise applicable credit when performed in any form on a religious program sponsored or produced by a religious organization, or on a religious program of an exclusively devotional nature such as a program of hymns or other religious works. A work shall be deemed to be a religious work if it is a work of a devotional nature composed in a religious idiom for use in a church or other religious service or program, or for other similar use. A work qualifying for credit under paragraph (E) and paragraph (I) shall be entitled to receive credit under whichever paragraph provides the higher credit for such performance. In no event shall it receive credit under both paragraphs (E) and (I) for the same performance. Commencing with the fourth quarter of 1982, this paragraph (I) shall not apply.

Appendix 12

EXTRACT FROM ASCAP WRITERS' DISTRIBUTION FORMULA RELATING TO SPECIAL AWARDS

Notwithstanding any of the foregoing provisions, in calculating the total distributable revenues to be placed in the four funds referred to in Sections I through IV above or distributed pursuant to Section VII below, there may first be deducted an amount not exceeding 5% of such revenues prior to such deduction, for the purpose of making special awards to writers whose works have a unique prestige value for which adequate compensation would not otherwise be received by such writers, and to writers whose works are performed substantially in media not surveyed by the Society. The distribution of such awards shall be determined by an independent panel appointed for that purpose by the writer members of the Board of Directors, and the Society shall maintain a list of all awards recipients together with the amount awarded to each and shall send copies of the lists to any writer upon request.

Appendix 13

ASCAP SYMPHONY LICENSE

𝕸𝖊𝖒𝖔𝖗𝖆𝖓𝖉𝖚𝖒 𝖔𝖋 𝕬𝖌𝖗𝖊𝖊𝖒𝖊𝖓𝖙 between AMERICAN SOCIETY OF COMPOSERS, AUTHORS AND PUBLISHERS (hereinafter called "SOCIETY") and

(hereinafter called "LICENSEE"), as follows:

1. SOCIETY grants and LICENSEE accepts for a period of three years commencing October 1, 1973 and terminating September 30, 1976, a license to perform publicly in concerts given by
(hereinafter called "orchestra") at

and at other auditoriums in which LICENSEE shall give performances while on tour in the United States, its territories and possessions, and in any other place not within the territorial jurisdiction of another performing right society to which SOCIETY has granted the right to license public performances of works in SOCIETY's repertory, non-dramatic renditions of the separate musical compositions including symphonic and other concert works heretofore copyrighted or composed by members of SOCIETY and now or hereafter during the term hereof in the repertory of SOCIETY, or hereafter during the term hereof copyrighted or composed by members of SOCIETY, or of which SOCIETY shall have the right to license such performing rights.

2. This license is not assignable nor transferable by operation of law, devolution or otherwise, and is limited strictly to the LICENSEE and to the premises referred to in Paragraph "1" of this agreement. The license fee herein provided to be paid is based upon the performance of such non-dramatic renditions for the entertainment solely of such persons as may be physically present on or in the premises described, and does not authorize the broadcasting, or transmission by wire or otherwise, of such performances or renditions to persons outside of such premises, and no license is hereby granted for any such broadcasting or transmission.

3. This license shall not extend to or be deemed to include:

(a) Operatic or dramatico-musical works (including plays with music, revues and ballets) as such, in whole or in part, or songs or other excerpts from operas or musical plays accompanied either by pantomime, dance or visual representation of the work from which the music is taken; but fragments or instrumental selections from such works may be instrumentally rendered without dialogue, costume, accompanying dramatic action or scenic accessory, and unaccompanied by any stage action or visual representation of the work of which such music forms a part.

(b) The right to perform any special orchestral arrangements or transcriptions of the musical compositions licensed hereunder unless such arrangements or transcriptions have been copyrighted by members of SOCIETY or by members of foreign societies which have granted to SOCIETY the right to license such performances.

4. SOCIETY reserves the right at any time to restrict the first American performance of any composition in its repertory and further reserves the right at any time to withdraw from its repertory and from operation of this license, any musical work as to which any suit has been brought or threatened on a claim that such composition infringes a composition not contained in SOCIETY's repertory, or on a claim that SOCIETY does not have the right to license the performing rights in such composition.

5. LICENSEE agrees to furnish to SOCIETY each week a program containing a list of all musical compositions performed by LICENSEE in each of its performances during the previous week at the premises mentioned in Paragraph "1" as well as on tour, including all encores.

6. In consideration of the license herein granted, LICENSEE agrees to pay to SOCIETY on the first day of October 1973 and on the first day of October of each succeeding year during the term hereof a sum equal to one half of one percent (.005) of the total expenditure for conductors and orchestra personnel for the preceding year ending on the 30th day of September 1973 and on the 30th day of each succeeding September during the term hereof, or the sum of fifty dollars ($50.00), whichever is greater.

The term "total expenditure for conductors and orchestra personnel", as used in this agreement, shall be deemed to mean all payments made (in money or any other form) to conductors, associate conductors, assistant conductors, guest conductors engaged for an entire season in place of the regular conductor, and all playing personnel provided, however, that the following shall not be included: (a) payments for vacations for the foregoing personnel and (b) additional payments to such personnel made solely in connection with concerts to which the public is admitted free and no charge is made by way of admission fee, contribution or otherwise, and for which LICENSEE receives no money or other consideration.

The payments specified in this Paragraph "6" shall be accompanied by certified statements, on forms to be supplied by SOCIETY, showing the total expenditure for conductors and orchestra personnel for the preceding year.

7. SOCIETY shall have the right to require such reasonable data or information in addition to that furnished under Paragraph "6" of this agreement as may be deemed necessary in order to ascertain the annual expenditure for conductors and orchestra players, as provided by this agreement. SOCIETY shall have the further right, by its duly authorized representatives, at any time during customary business hours, to examine the books and records of account of LICENSEE only to such extent as may be necessary to verify such statement or statements as may be rendered pursuant to this agreement. SOCIETY shall consider all data and information coming to its attention as the result of any such examination of books and records as completely and entirely confidential.

8. (a) Upon any breach or default of any term or condition herein contained by either party, the other party may give the party in default thirty (30) days' notice in writing, to cure such breach or default, and in the event that such breach or default has not been cured within said thirty (30) days, the party giving such notice may then promptly terminate this license.

(b) SOCIETY shall have the right to terminate this agreement on thirty (30) days' notice in writing in the event that LICENSEE's budget for any year during the term hereof shall be $100,000 or more. In the event of such termination, LICENSEE shall have the right to enter into the then current form of agreement between SOCIETY and Metropolitan Orchestras or Major Orchestras, as the case may be depending on LICENSEE's then current budget.

9. (a) SOCIETY agrees to indemnify, save and hold LICENSEE and its artists and the proprietors of the premises mentioned in Paragraph "1", harmless, and defend LICENSEE and its artists and the proprietors of said premises from and against any claim, demand or suit that may be made or brought against them or any of them with respect to renditions given by LICENSEE during the term hereof in accordance with this license of "cleared compositions," or of musical compositions heretofore copyrighted or composed by members of SOCIETY and now or hereafter during the term hereof in SOCIETY's repertory, or hereafter during the term hereof copyrighted or composed by present members of SOCIETY or by future members of SOCIETY so long as such future members shall be members of SOCIETY. In the event of the service upon LICENSEE of any notice, process, paper or pleading under which a claim, demand or action is made or begun against LICENSEE on account of any such matter as is hereinabove referred to, LICENSEE shall promptly give SOCIETY written notice thereof and simultaneously therewith deliver to SOCIETY any such notice, process, paper or pleading, or a copy thereof, and SOCIETY at its own expense shall have sole charge of the defense of any such action or proceeding. LICENSEE, however, shall have the right to engage counsel of its own, at its own expense, who may participate in the defense of any such action or proceeding and with whom counsel for SOCIETY shall cooperate. LICENSEE shall cooperate with SOCIETY in every way in the defense of any such action or proceeding, and in any appeals that may be taken from any judgments or orders entered therein, and shall execute all pleadings, bonds or other instruments, but at the sole expense of SOCIETY, that may be required in order properly to defend and resist any such action or proceeding, and prosecute any appeals taken therein. In the event of the service upon LICENSEE of any notice, process, paper or pleading under which a claim, demand or action is made, or begun against LICENSEE on account of the rendition by LICENSEE of any musical composition (other than a "cleared composition") contained in SOCIETY's repertory but not heretofore or hereafter during the term hereof copyrighted or composed by members of SOCIETY, SOCIETY agrees at the request of LICENSEE to cooperate with and assist LICENSEE in the defense of any such action or proceeding, and in any appeals that LICENSEE may elect to take from any judgments or orders entered therein.

(b) As used in this Paragraph "9" a "cleared composition" shall mean any composition which SOCIETY shall have notified LICENSEE is a composition with respect to which SOCIETY is willing to indemnify LICENSEE, provided that the SOCIETY may limit such indemnity to a specific program of LICENSEE for which a clearance shall have been given by SOCIETY.

10. All notices required or permitted to be given by either of the parties to the other hereunder shall be duly and properly given if mailed to such other party by certified or registered United States mail addressed to such other party at its main office for the transaction of business.

IN WITNESS WHEREOF, this agreement has been duly subscribed and sealed by SOCIETY and LICENSEE

this   day of   , 197

AMERICAN SOCIETY OF COMPOSERS,
AUTHORS AND PUBLISHERS

By ....

....
LICENSEE

By ....

Appendix 14

ASCAP COLLEGES AND UNIVERSITIES EXPERIMENTAL LICENSE AGREEMENT (Two Tier)*

THIS AGREEMENT made and entered into this _____ day of _____ , 19____ , by and between AMERICAN SOCIETY OF COMPOSERS, AUTHORS AND PUBLISHERS, with its principal offices located at One Lincoln Plaza, New York, New York 10023, hereinafter referred to as SOCIETY, and

_____ , a College or University with its principal offices located at

_____ hereinafter referred to as LICENSEE:

WITNESSETH:

WHEREAS, SOCIETY's writer and publisher members have authorized SOCIETY to license, on a non-exclusive basis, nondramatic public performances of their copyrighted musical compositions; and

WHEREAS, LICENSEE is an institution of higher education and desires to perform publicly and nondramatically the copyrighted musical compositions in SOCIETY's repertory during the period hereof; and

WHEREAS, the parties hereto agree that this Agreement is being entered into on an experimental and nonprejudicial basis, shall apply for the term of this Agreement only, and shall not be binding upon or prejudicial to any position taken by either of the parties for any period subsequent to the termination of this Agreement.

NOW, THEREFORE, the parties hereto mutually agree as follows:

1. Definitions

(a) The term "LICENSEE" as used herein shall include the named institution and any of its constituent bodies, agencies or organizations.

(b) The term "premises" as used herein shall include LICENSEE's campus(es) and any site located off LICENSEE's campus which has been engaged for use by an organization referred to in Paragraph 1(a) above.

(c) The term "full-time student" as used herein shall include all graduate and undergraduate "full-time equivalent students" as such term is used in the Higher Education General Information Survey as conducted annually by the Department of Health, Education, and Welfare or the Department of Education.

(d) The term "musical attractions" shall mean concerts, shows, recitals, dances and other similar performances.

(e) The term "school year" shall mean the twelve month period commencing September 1 of any calendar year during the term hereof.

2. Term of License

The term of this Agreement shall be for three and one-half (3½) years commencing on the first day of January 1980 and terminating on the last day of June, 1983.

3. Grant of License

SOCIETY hereby grants to LICENSEE for the term of this Agreement a non-exclusive license to perform publicly, or cause the public performance, on LICENSEE's premises, of nondramatic musical compositions now or hereafter during the term hereof in the repertory of SOCIETY, and of which SOCIETY shall have the right to license such performing rights. Such performances shall include performances presented under the auspices of LICENSEE, including performances by faculty, staff, students or alumni of LICENSEE while performing under the auspices of LICENSEE.

4. Limitations on License

(a) This license is not assignable or transferable by operation of law or otherwise, and is limited to the LICENSEE and to the premises.

(b) This license does not authorize the broadcasting, telecasting or transmission by wire or otherwise, of renditions of musical compositions in SOCIETY's repertory to persons outside of the premises.

(c) This license does not authorize any performance by means of a coin-operated phonorecord player (jukebox) otherwise covered by the compulsory license provisions of 17 U.S.C. §116.

(d) This license is limited to nondramatic performances, and does not authorize any dramatic performances. For purposes of this Agreement, a dramatic performance shall include, but not be limited to, the following:

(i) performance of a "dramatico-musical work" (as hereinafter defined) in its entirety;

(ii) performance of one or more musical compositions from a "dramatico-musical work" (as hereinafter defined) accompanied by dialogue, pantomime, dance, stage action, or visual representation of the work from which the music is taken;

* There is also a One Tier License.

(iii) performance of one or more musical compositions as part of a story or plot, whether accompanied or unaccompanied by dialogue, pantomime, dance, stage action, or visual representation;

(iv) performance of a concert version of a "dramatico-musical work" (as hereinafter defined).

The term "dramatico-musical work" as used in this Agreement, shall include, but not be limited to, a musical comedy, oratorio, opera, play with music, revue, or ballet.

(e) SOCIETY reserves the right at any time to restrict the first American performance of any composition in its repertory and further reserves the right at any time to withdraw from its repertory and from operation of this license, any musical work as to which any suit has been brought or threatened on a claim that such composition infringes a composition not contained in SOCIETY's repertory, or on a claim that SOCIETY does not have the right to license the performing rights in such composition.

5. License Fees, Reports and Payments

(a) In consideration of the license granted herein, LICENSEE agrees to pay SOCIETY the following license fees:

(i) For the period January 1—June 30, 1980, 3 cents per full-time student or $25, whichever is greater, based upon the number of full-time students during the previous fall, payable upon execution of this Agreement (the "per student license fee");

(ii) For the period July 1, 1980—June 30, 1981, a per student license fee of 7 cents per full-time student or $58, whichever is greater, based upon the number of full-time students during the fall of 1980, payable on the first day of February, 1981;

(iii) For the period July 1, 1981—June 30, 1982, a per student license fee of 8 cents per full-time student or $67, whichever is greater, based upon the number of full-time students during the fall of 1981, payable on the first day of February, 1982;

(iv) For the period July 1, 1982—June 30, 1983, a per student license fee of 9 cents per full-time student or $75, whichever is greater, based upon the number of full-time students during the fall of 1982, payable on the first day of February, 1983; and

(v) For the full term of this Agreement, a fee for each musical attraction on LICENSEE's premises for which admission is charged and for which the performer or performers are paid a total of $1,300 or more, in accordance with the SOCIETY's "Concert Rate Schedule" a copy of which is attached hereto and made a part hereof, (the "concert license fees"). In cases where musical attractions are presented on LICENSEE's premises by LICENSEE and another licensee of SOCIETY, LICENSEE shall pay the appropriate license fee unless such other licensee has paid the appropriate license fee under its license agreement with SOCIETY. Said concert license fees shall be due and payable by the tenth day following the end of each calendar quarter for all performances for which payment is due during the previous quarter.

(b) LICENSEE agrees to report to SOCIETY, on forms supplied free of charge by SOCIETY, simultaneously with payment of per student and concert license fees, respectively, the following:

(i) LICENSEE's total full-time student enrollment; and

(ii) For each musical attraction presented during the previous quarter for which concert license fees are due, the date, name, address and seating capacity of the location, and highest price of admission (exclusive of tax), or a statement that no such musical attraction was presented.

(c) LICENSEE agrees to furnish to SOCIETY, simultaneously with the quarterly reports and payments of concert license fees, copies of all programs of musical works performed by LICENSEE in each of its musical attractions presented during the previous calendar quarter, which are prepared for distribution to the audience or for the use or information of LICENSEE or any department thereof. Such copies of programs shall include all encores to the extent possible. LICENSEE shall be under no obligation to furnish such programs when they have not been otherwise prepared.

6. Reservation of Rights

The parties hereto expressly reserve all rights and privileges accorded by the Copyright Act of 1976, decisions of the Copyright Royalty Tribunal and other applicable laws.

7. Breach or Default

Upon any breach or default of the terms and conditions of this Agreement, SOCIETY may terminate this Agreement by giving LICENSEE thirty days notice in writing to cure such breach or default, and in the event such breach or default has not been cured within said thirty days, this Agreement shall terminate on the expiration of such thirty-day period without further notice from SOCIETY. The right to terminate shall be in addition to any and all other remedies which SOCIETY may have. In the event of such termination, SOCIETY shall refund to LICENSEE any unearned license fees paid in advance.

8. Interference in Society's Operations

In the event of:

(a) Any major interference with the operations of SOCIETY in the state, territory, dependency, possession or political subdivision in which LICENSEE is located, by reason of any law of such state, territory, dependency, possession or political subdivision; or

(b) Any substantial increase in the cost to the SOCIETY of operating in such state, territory, dependency, possession or political subdivision, by reason of any law of such state, territory, dependency, possession or political subdivision, which is applicable to the licensing of performing rights,

SOCIETY shall have the right to terminate this Agreement forthwith by written notice, and, in the event of such termination, shall refund to LICENSEE any unearned license fees paid in advance.

9. Indemnity Clause

SOCIETY agrees to indemnify, save and hold harmless and to defend LICENSEE from and against all claims, demands and suits that may be made or brought against it with respect to the non-dramatic performance under this Agreement of any compositions in SOCIETY's repertory which are written or copyrighted by members of SOCIETY. LICENSEE agrees to give SOCIETY immediate notice of any such claim, demand or suit and agrees immediately to deliver to SOCIETY all papers pertaining thereto. SOCIETY shall have full charge of the defense of any such claim, demand or suit and LICENSEE shall cooperate fully with SOCIETY in such defense. LICENSEE however shall have the right to engage counsel of its own at its own expense who may participate in the defense of any such action. SOCIETY agrees at the request of LICENSEE to cooperate with and assist LICENSEE in the defense of any action or proceeding brought against it with respect to the performance of any musical compositions contained in the SOCIETY's repertory, but not copyrighted or written by members of SOCIETY. This Paragraph 9 shall not apply to performances of any works that may be restricted under Paragraph 4(e) of this Agreement.

10. Availability of Other License Agreements

In the event SOCIETY offers any other type of license agreement to colleges or universities, LICENSEE may elect to enter into such other type of license agreement. Such election shall be prospective only, shall be effective at the beginning of the school year, and shall be accomplished by serving written notice on SOCIETY of such election at least thirty days prior to the commencement of said school year.

11. Notices

All notices shall be given in writing by United States certified mail sent to either party at the address stated above. Each party agrees to inform the other of any change of address.

12. Modification of Agreement

This Agreement constitutes the entire understanding between the parties with respect to the subject matter hereof. This Agreement cannot be waived or added to or modified orally, and no waiver, addition or modification shall be valid unless in writing and signed by the parties. LICENSEE recognizes that SOCIETY must license all similarly situated users on a nondiscriminatory basis. LICENSEE agrees that any modifications of this Agreement by SOCIETY, which are required by local, state or federal law for other colleges or universities, shall not constitute discrimination between similarly situated users. Examples of such modifications are statements of equal employment opportunity or nondiscrimination on the basis of race, creed, color, sex, or national origin.

IN WITNESS WHEREOF, this Agreement has been executed in duplicate original by the duly authorized representatives of SOCIETY and LICENSEE all as of the date first above written.

AMERICAN SOCIETY OF COMPOSERS,
AUTHORS AND PUBLISHERS

LICENSEE:

BY _____

_____

Title

BY _____

Title

CONCERT RATE SCHEDULE

Seating Capacity*	Up to $3.00	$3.01 to $6.00	$6.01 to $9.00	$9.01 to $12.00	$12.01 to $15.00	$15.01 to $18.00	$18.01 to $21.00	Over $21.00
Up to 750	$ 15	$ 22	$ 31	$ 44	$ 57	$ 70	$ 85	$100
751-1500	21	29	41	55	70	85	100	125
1501-2500	29	41	53	70	85	100	125	150
2501-4000	41	53	65	85	100	125	150	180
4001-5500	53	65	80	100	125	150	180	210
5501-7500	65	80	100	125	150	180	210	240
7501-10,000	80	100	125	150	180	210	240	270
10,001-15,000	100	125	150	180	210	240	270	300
15,001-20,000	125	150	180	210	240	270	300	330
20,001-25,000	150	180	210	240	270	300	330	360
25,001-40,000	180	210	240	270	300	330	360	400
Over 40,001	210	240	270	300	330	360	400	450

DISCOUNTS:

1. Twenty-Five or more Concerts: A discount of 20% may be deducted from the above fees for payment for each concert in excess of twenty-five performed by LICENSEE during a school year.

2. Advance Payment for One Hundred or more Concerts: A discount of 5% may be deducted from the above fees for payment in advance by LICENSEE to SOCIETY for one hundred or more separate concerts.

*Where a concert occurs at a location whose total seating capacity has been altered to accommodate a particular performance, the term "seating capacity" shall mean the total number of seats made available for that particular performance.

Appendix 15

HIRE OF MATERIALS FOR THE PERFORMANCE OF MUSICAL COMPOSITIONS
(Prepared by the Music Publishers' Association
of the United States)

Publishers are often asked for guidance in renting performance materials for musical works (usually orchestral) that are not available for outright sale. This leaflet has been prepared by the Music Publishers' Association, in conjunction with the American Symphony Orchestra League, principally for use by the non-professional orchestral librarian.

The suggested standard form reproduced on page 159 is intended to present as clearly as possible the information needed by the publisher before he can quote the appropriate fees. Please feel free to reproduce and use this form when ordering music on rental. It should be understood that the form is not intended to be used in connection with ''grand rights'' performances—*i.e.*, opera, ballet, and the like, in respect of which further details will be needed by the publisher.

THE RENTAL CONTRACT

The information asked for by most publishers includes the following:

> The name of the orchestra
> The place of performance
> The dates of performances
> Whether there will be public rehearsals
> Whether there will be a radio broadcast or telecast
> Whether the work will be recorded, either for subsequent
>   radio transmission, or for a commercial company
> How long before the first concert the material will be
>   needed
> What complement of strings the orchestra has

The publisher will then set his fee. In Europe, these fees are for the most part fixed by general agreement throughout the industry. In the U.S. this is illegal, and the customs of the various publishers will be found to vary widely.

SOME POINTS TO BEAR IN MIND

Remember that the number of rental sets available is limited. Sometimes it is necessary to have a new set manufactured in order to meet a rental reservation; a publisher acting as agent for a foreign publisher may have to send abroad for additional material. For these and other reasons you should remember to order as far in advance as possible. Most major orchestras have made their reservations for future concerts at least a year in advance; anything less than six months invites disappointment. Sometimes last-minute orders can be met, but the chances of disaster are of course far greater.

The usual practice is for the orchestra to pay postage both ways. Immediately after the last use of the music the score and all parts should be checked and collated, cleaned up if necessary, and packed as carefully as they were found on arrival. If the return of the music is delayed more than a few days, most publishers will make an additional charge. And if the delay has caused the publisher to miss his obligation for the next reservation, the orchestra responsible will usually be asked to pay not only the rental fee, but also the performing fees that have been lost.

CLEARANCE OF RIGHTS

The general question of the clearance of performing rights, as distinct from rental fees, is dealt with in a separate booklet, "Clearance of Rights in Musical Compositions," available from the Music Publishers' Association of the United States, 609 Fifth Avenue, New York, N.Y. 10017.

SOME COMMON QUESTIONS

Why not just one standard rental fee?

Most contracts with union musicians specify additional fees when a performance is being broadcast or recorded, or in certain other special circumstances. Similarly, the fees for the various uses of the orchestral material are intended to secure an income for the composer which relates to the various uses made of his music, *i.e.*, to the size of the potential audience. If, for example, a concert is broadcast live over a local FM station, the potential audience is enlarged many times, though the chances are the composer will receive no additional performing fee as such. The additional materials fee is intended to go part of the way to allow for this. Similarly, the use of the material for a commercial record also enlarges the audience. So in respect of a recording session a special charge is usually made to make up for this.

Why should one orchestra pay more than another for the use of the same work?

Performance fees for dramatic works (plays, operas, and ballets) are usually fixed at an agreed percentage (say 10 per cent) of the box-office "take," so that the larger the house and the more expensive the individual ticket, the greater the potential income for the writer. Similarly, many publishers divide orchestras in a rough-and-ready way into categories corresponding to their annual budgets, using the ASOL categories. A major orchestra is accustomed to pay on a slightly higher tariff than a metropolitan orchestra, which again pays more than a college group. Rates differ also according to the length of the work, and may be lower for chamber works. For a first performance in a given country or city, from which the performing organization can expect to gain valuable publicity, additional premiums may also be asked. The general thought behind all this is that the composer shares in the importance of the occasion. Whether this occasion is "for profit" or not is for the most part irrelevant: scarcely any musical function can be said to make a "profit" in this sense.

Why can't I just buy a set of materials and have done with it?

For a time, during the nineteenth century, publishers did indeed find it possible to print and put on sale orchestral parts for the works of the great composers whose music is constantly in the repertory. But this is possible only when we are dealing in hundreds of sets of parts. Few contemporary works are in this category. Therefore, to make them available at all, they have to be put on rental. When to the cost of duplicating a set of parts is added a share of the initial cost of preparing the score and extracting the parts (which for a twenty-minute work may run anywhere from $1,500 to $5,000—or even $10,000)—it will be seen that the price for an out-right sale today would be prohibitive.

As for the income from rental transactions, this is divided between writer and publisher according to the terms of their contract.

Music Publishers' Association of the United States
May 1974

This part to be
signed by the active
and responsible
manager or librarian

Rental Music Reservation Request: Order Form

From: (Performing Organization)_____

To: (Publisher) _____

Kindly quote fees for the rental and performance of the following: Date:_____

Composer/Title _____

Delivery date:_____Public rehearsal:_____

Preferred Method of Shipment: _____

Performance dates: Place:

_____   _____

_____   _____

_____   _____

_____   _____

Conductor:_____Soloist(s):_____

_____

_____

If the music is to be used in any of the following ways, give details on separate sheet:

The work will be: ☐ broadcast live   ☐ taped for single delayed broadcast

☐ used with choreographic or   ☐ recorded for mechanical reproduction
other dramatic treatment

String parts required:____Vn 1____Vn2____Vla____Vcl____Dbl Bass

Extra scores/parts: _____

Other special requirements: _____

Performing fees: We are licensed by   ☐ ASCAP   ☐ BMI   ☐ SESAC   ☐ not licensed

Admission will be charged: ☐ Yes   ☐ No

Order reference no.:_____

Address for music and related correspondence: _____

_____

_____

Address for billing:

_____

_____

_____   Signed:_____

                                         Manager or Librarian

This part to be
filled in by the
publisher

Date: _____

Performing Organization: _____

Publisher: _____

Composer/Title: _____

String parts required: ____Vn1____Vn2____Vla ____Vcl____Dbl Bass

Extra scores/parts: _____

Other special requirements: _____

Rental fee:

For one month's rental and use in one performance $_____

Additional_____months rental $_____

Additional performance uses,_____at $_____ $_____

Public rehearsals,_____at $_____ $_____

Rental for live braodcast $_____

Rental for taping for delayed broadcast/telecast $_____

Rental for recording session $_____

Performing fees:

_____This work is covered by your ☐ ASCAP   ☐ BMI   ☐ SESAC license

The performing fee for each performance will be $_____ $_____

(Shipping costs
will be added to
the above)

Total fees:

Contingent upon receipt of confirmation from the performing organization, the materials will be dispatched on or

about_____.

Signed: _____
(For the Publisher)

Material must be returned within three days following final performance, or an additional fee will be charged.

A service charge of all or part of the rental fee will be made if notice of cancellation reaches us after the materials have been shipped.

Appendix 16

THE MSS MARKET
SOME SUGGESTIONS FOR GETTING YOUR MUSIC PUBLISHED
(Prepared by the Music Publishers' Association
and the National Music Publishers' Association)

So you've written some music! Even if you've been published before, there may be some thoughts here which will provide assistance and guidance to you in getting your new work published. If these suggestions are followed (where they apply) manuscripts will be more effectively submitted and they might be more cordially received by publishers' offices. The work of publishers would be made easier, their consideration of manuscripts would be expedited, and some simplification in the marketplace for music might result. In short, everyone concerned might have things just a little easier. Publishers, like composers, have personal and individual attitudes and objectives. These may be influenced by tradition, company policy or changing market conditions. Nevertheless, this paper represents a consensus of attitudes and experience for those publishers whose essential market is so-called *standard music*.

Although the line of demarcation becomes less and less clearly defined, all music can be divided into two parts and its publishers so classified. Hjwever, for our present purposes standard music covers all areas of educational, concert and sacred music in all media while popular music means, of course, popular songs. If popular songs are your *only thing*, you may want to stop reading now.

TO WHOM SHOULD YOU SUBMIT YOUR MANUSCRIPTS?

As a broad general guidline, it is a good idea to study publishers' catalogues to determine those which have major activity in the field in which you are writing. Obviously, it would be pointless to submit a choral manuscript to a band publisher or a woodwind quintet to a house which specializes in church music. This advice may seem rudimentary, but it is amazing how often manuscripts are sent without any concept of the interests of the publisher to whom they are submitted.

If circumstances make it possible to visit publishers' exhibits at the various conferences and conventions which take place throughout the country, an examination of the music issued by the publisher should be most helpful in determining where your manuscript will be most likely to find its market. If visiting conferences is impractical, then examination of publications at your music store is the next best thing.

While by no means a certainty, it seems rather likely that the publishers who issue music you like might like your music.

HOW TO APPROACH A PUBLISHER

Publishers' attitudes toward unsolicited manuscripts vary. Some return them unopened; others consider them routinely. However, it is politic and courteous to write to publishers with whom you would like to establish a relationship *before submitting any manuscripts*. Ask if they are interested in reviewing material at that time and state what you have to offer. Most publishers are polite and will reply to your letter candidly.

HOW TO SUBMIT A MANUSCRIPT

If you're an acknowledged genius, publishers will beat a path to your door. Let's face it. Probably you're not. At least, not yet. So let us concern ourselves with the *best* way for you to get the *best* and most favorable reception from a publisher.

1. Send a preliminary letter (enclosing a stamped self-addressed envelope) describing what you have written and the market it is intended for. Address this inquiry to the attention of the editor or department (choral, instrumental, keyboard, etc.) you would like to have consider your work. Although some houses have a single Director of Publications, addressing your initial inquiry in the manner described should bring it to the attention of the proper party.

2. Assuming an encouraging response to your preliminary inquiry, send your manuscript together with a self-addressed envelope stamped with sufficient return postage. Music manuscripts may be mailed at the special "fourth class educational materials" rate. However, letters enclosed should be covered by first class postage. If your manuscript is not bulky you may prefer to send the entire package via first class mail as it will travel faster.

3. Enclose a letter outlining the merits of your composition, the market for which you feel your work is most interesting together with some professionally oriented biographical information about yourself. If you have had

works published elsewhere, list them together with their publication date and publisher. While the editors who review manuscripts for music publishers are perceptive and knowledgeable in their work, they might overlook a potential of your music which could lead to a favorable decision.

4. NEVER SEND YOUR ONLY COPY.

5. Never submit the same piece for consideration by more than one publisher at the same time. Few things are more aggravating to an editor than to spend time evaluating a work and giving thought to how it can best be presented than to receive word subsequently that "Publisher X to whom I also sent the work has decided to accept it."

6. Put your best foot forward. Whether in pencil or ink, send a neat legible manuscript in which there is no doubt as to whether a note is on a line or space. If there is something unusual about your notation or intentions, show your ms. to a knowledgeable colleague before sending it off and see if he has any problems in deciphering it. Choral and keyboard music is easier to evaluate and edit if it is written on only one side of the ms. paper. Also, if four or more voice staffs are used in choral music, provide a keyboard reduction of the voice parts. Sad to say, many composers do not fully grasp or follow the basic grammar of music writing. Grammatically correct, literate manuscripts *do* make a better impression. Should you feel at all unsure of the basic rules concerning music writing, several publications may be helpful to you. The first is "Standards of Music Engraving" published jointly by the Music Publishers' Association of the United States and the Music Educators National Conference. It can be procured from the latter organization for 60¢. Other and more comprehensive presentations are "Practical Guide to Music Notation" by Carl Rosenthal published by MCA Music and "Music Notation—A Manual of Modern Practice" by Gardner Read published by Allyn & Bacon, Inc.

7. If a tape or recording is available, send it. It's easier and quicker for the editor to listen rather than to read. Even if the performance isn't entirely to your satisfaction, listening to a recording with the manuscript before him will enable the editor to make his best evaluation.

8. If it is a vocal work and the text is copyrighted, indicate in your accompanying letter whether or not you have secured permission for the use of the text and, if so, on what terms. Better still, save yourself and your prospective publisher possible disappointment and frustration by obtaining permission of the owner of the text prior to setting it.

9. If you are arranging a copyrighted musical work, under ordinary circumstances, it can be published only by the owner of the copyright or with his permission. You would therefore be saving yourself the work of making the arrangement if you ask the publisher who owns the copyright whether he might be interested in an arrangement such as you contemplate.

These are broad general suggestions which will be of benefit to you and helpful to the publisher. Obviously, submission of a simple choral work or a piano teaching piece is a different matter from submitting a number of large concert works. In the former case, the result may be the placement of a single composition. In the latter, the result may be the development of a continuing relationship with the publisher over a period of years with a substantial investment on your part of all your creativity and on his of very large sums of money and a very great expenditure of energy and enthusiasm.

In either case, evaluation procedures vary depending on the publisher and the works under consideration. Despite your understandable enthusiasm for your brain child, be patient. And if—praise be!—your work is accepted for publication, it is important for you to realize that it is not unusual for publishers to operate with a 12—24 months' "lead time" from date of acceptance to print in view of their existing obligations to other contributors to their catalog.

Perhaps the best advice is not really banal. Market your music and know your market. Even if you have written to the publisher and he has indicated an interest in seeing your work, don't send too much the first time. Be critical of your own work and send a small representative group. Don't impose your work on a publisher in unreasonable quantities. It should be evident that the process of reviewing music critically, carefully and thoughtfully (as most publishers do) is a time consuming and therefore expensive process.

If your music is rejected, don't be discouraged. There can be many varied reasons for the decision which have nothing to do with the quality of the compositions. The publisher is probably telling the truth when he says that his publication schedule for the type of music you've submitted is committed for the immediate future. Reading and interpreting rejection letters, most of which are couched in courteous terms, can become an art.

Also publishers have a special instinct for manuscripts which have made the rounds and been constantly rejected. After a reasonable effort, retire the rejects for a time, at least.

Just as writers need good energetic publishers, so do publishers need new talented writers. Don't for one moment think that the publisher is any less interested in finding useful, new material than you are in finding a publisher.

Good Luck!

Appendix 17

TYPICAL PAGE FROM MUSICAL AMERICA INTERNATIONAL DIRECTORY OF THE PERFORMING ARTS RELATING TO CONTESTS AND AWARDS FOR SERIOUS MUSIC COMPOSERS

Canada Council Grants to Artists & Arts Organizations
Charles Lussier, Dir.
Barbara Klante, Information Officer
PO Box 1047   (613) 237-3400
Ottawa, Ont., Canada   K1P 5V8
The Canada Council provides financial assistance and special services to individuals and organizations working in the arts (theatre, music, dance, visual arts and creative writing). Eligibility: Individual artists must have completed basic training and have some claim to professional status; applicants must be Canadian citizens or landed immigrants five years resident in Canada. Applications from organizations are assessed on the basis of professionalism, excellence, community acceptance, stability and sound financial management. Deadlines: Vary, depending on type of grant.

Robert Casadesus International Piano Competition
(Sponsored by the Cleveland Institute of Music & the Robert Casadesus Society)
Grant Johannesen, Cleveland Institute of Music Pres.
11021 East Blvd.   (216) 791-5165 x 228
Cleveland, Ohio   44106
Biennial. Eligibility: 17-32 years old. Prizes: (1st) $4000 & appearance with Cleveland Orchestra; (2nd) $2000; (3rd) $1000; (4th) $500; (5th) $250; (6th) $150. Competition: Aug. 15-23, 1981. Entrance fee: $25.

Il Cenacolo Award   (see San Francisco Opera Auditions/Merola Opera Program)

Chopin Piano Competition   (see Kosciuszko Foundation Music Competitions)

Van Cliburn International Piano Competition (6th)
Anthony Phillips, Exec. Dir.
3505 W. Lancaster   (817) 738-6536
Fort Worth, Tex.   76107
Quadrennial. Eligibility: 18-30 years old. Prizes: (1st) $12,000 plus Carnegie Hall recital & orchestral debuts, two American recital & orchestral tours, London & European debuts and two European orchestral & recital tours; (2nd) $8000 plus New York debut & American tour; (3rd) $6000 & US concert tour; (4th) $4000; (5th) $3000; (6th) $1500; other prizes totalling $3000 cash, a recording contract & a gold watch. Competition: May 17-31, 1981. Entrance fee: $35 (non-refundable).

Coleman Chamber Music Auditions (35th)
Mrs. Clarendon B. Eyer, Pres.
George Heussenstamm, Mgr.
202 S. Lake Ave., Suite 201
(213) 793-4191
Pasadena, Calif.   91101
For chamber ensembles, annual. Eligibility: Non-professional chamber ensembles under the direction of a coach; senior division under age 26, intermediate division under age 20, junior division under age 16. Prizes: Senior—$2000, $1000, $500; intermediate—$600; junior—$300; $50 for coach of every winning group. Deadline: Mar. 6, 1981. Competition: Apr. 24-26, 1981. Registration fee: $10 for each member of the ensemble.

Concert Artists Guild Annual Auditions
Dr. Jerome Bunke, Dir.
154 W. 57 St.   (212) 757-8344
New York, N.Y.   10019
For instrumentalists, chamber groups & singers, annual. Eligibility: Instrumentalists under 32 years old; singers under 35 years old. Prizes: Fully sponsored Carnegie Recital Hall debut concert, cash awards of $500 to $750, preview community concerts, plus radio & television appearances. Deadline: Feb. 1, 1981. Competition: Apr. 1981. Entrance fee: $20.

Concerto Competition of the Rome Festival Orchestra
Ernest Ferrell, Pres., Linda Owen, Admin. Ass't.
(212) 349-1980
170 Broadway, Suite 201
New York, N.Y.   10038
Annual. Purpose: To aid North American artists in the development of careers through performances in Rome, Italy. Eligibility: North American players of violin, viola, cello, bass, oboe, or French horn. Prizes: Five scholarships of $500 each & solo appearance in Rome. Competition: Jan. 15 each year.

Concours OSM
Denise Beique, Chm.
200 W. de Maisonneuve Blvd.   (514) 842-3402.
Montreal, P.Q., Canada
For voice & piano (1981), strings & winds (1982), rotating annually. 1981 Eligibility: Piano—18-25 years old for Class A; 17 years old and younger for Class B; Voice—18-30 years old. Prizes: 3 prizes in each category—$1500, $1000, $500. Deadline: Oct. 18, 1981. Competition: Early Nov. 1981. Entrance fee: $10.

Congress of Strings
(Sponsored by American Federation of Musicians)
J. Martin Emerson, Sec'y-Treas. & Project Chm.
1500 Broadway   (212) 869-1330
New York, N.Y.   10036
For string instrumentalists, annual. Eligibility: 16-23 years old; aspirant must win a contest sponsored by the participating AFM Local in student's jurisdiction in the spring. Prizes: Eight week scholarship program during the summer at an eastern & western university; scholarship covers transportation, room & board, lessons, rehearsals & performances. Entrance fee: None.

Contemporary Music Festival Composition Competition
Neal Fluegel, Festival Chm.
Indiana State Univ., Mus. Dept.
(812) 232-6311 x 2276
Terre Haute, Ind.   47809
No restrictions. Prizes: Attendance & expenses paid at festival & performance by Indianapolis Symphony. Deadline: Apr. 1, 1981. Competition: Sept. 1981.

Dallas News G.B. Dealey Awards Competitions
Diana Clark, Co-ord.
PO Box 2977   (214) 528-8242
Dallas, Tex.   75221
Two competitions—One for voice & one for piano,

violin & cello, annual. Eligibility: Students who are US citizens or foreign students studying in USA; instrumentalists 17-28 years old, singers 20-30 years old. Prizes: Instrumental—$1500 plus concert with Dallas Symphony, $750, $500; vocal: $1500 plus appearance with Dallas Civic Opera, $750, $500. Deadline: Feb. 2, 1981. Competition: Mar. 12-15, 1981. Entrance fee: $10.

D'Angelo Young Artist Competition
Louis Mennini, Art. Dir.
c/o Mercyhurst Coll., 501 E. 38 St.
(814) 864-0681
Erie, Pa.   16501
For voice (1981), strings (1982), piano (1983), rotating annually. Eligibility: Under 31 years old. Prizes: (1st) $2000 & performance with the Erie Philharmonic; (2nd) $1000; (3rd) $500. Deadline: Mar. 31, 1981. Competition: July 16-18, 1981. Entrance fee: $10.

G. B. Dealey Awards Competitions   (see Dallas News G.B. Dealey Awards Competitions)

Delius Composition Contest
William McNeiland, Chm.
c/o Jacksonville Univ.   (904) 744-3950 x 270
Jacksonville, Fla.   32211
Annual. Categories: Vocal, piano, instrumental, band & orchestra. Eligibility: No restrictions. Prizes: (1st) $200; plus $50 for each of four best-in-category winners. Deadline: Nov. 1 each year. Competition: Mar. each year. Entrance fee: None.

Delta Omicron International Music Fraternity's Composition Competition
Jo S. Holt, Pres.
115 Lawrence   (205) 365-4335
Prattville, Ala.   36067
Triennial. For music for a brass ensemble, not to exceed a quintet. Eligibility: Women composers college age or over; composition submitted may not have been previously performed in public or published. Prizes: $500 and premiere at the International Conference in Aug. 1983 (jury not obliged to award prize). Deadline: Aug. 1, 1982. Entrance fee: $5.

Denver Symphony Guild Annual North American Young Artist Competition
1245 Champa St.   (303) 292-1580
Denver, Colo.   80204
For piano (1981-82). Eligibility: Resident of or student in USA, Canada or Mexico under 29 years old by Jan. 1.

Alice M. Ditson Fund of Columbia Univ.
Jack Beeson, Sec'y
703 Dodge, Columbia Univ.   (212) 280-3825
New York, N.Y.   10027
Aids & encourages musicians, particularly American composers.

East & West Artists Auditions for Young Performers
East & West Artists Competition for Composers
Adolovni P. Acosta, Dir.-Founder
310 Riverside Dr., No. 313
(212) 222-2433
New York, N.Y.   10025
1) Auditions for Young Performers: Biennial. Eligibility: Instrumentalists & ensembles to 32 years old, singers to 35 years old, who have not given a New York City debut recital. Prize: Solo debut in Carnegie Recital Hall. Deadline: Feb. 11, 1982.
2) Competition for Composers: Annual. Purpose: For the promotion & encouragement of composers, the promotion of the performance & appreciation of contemporary music & the training of young artists in the performance of modern music. Eligibility: No age restrictions; unpublished & un-recorded compositions for one to five players; electronic tapes accepted; works

must not have won any contests. Prize: Performance in Carnegie Recital Hall plus $150 to the 1st prize winner. Deadline: May 20, 1981. Entrance fee: $12.

S. C. Eckhardt-Gramatte Annual Competition for the Performance of Canadian Music
Lorne Watson, Nat'l Chm.
Brandon Univ., School of Music
(204) 728-9520
Brandon, Man., Canada   R7A 6A9
For piano (1981), rotating annually. Eligibility: Canadian citizens or residents of Canada since Sept. 1979, born after Jan. 1, 1951. Prizes: (1st) $2500 & concert appearances; (2nd) $1500; (3rd) $1000 (Jury is not obligated to award 1st prize). Deadline: Oct. 1, 1980. Competition: May 14-16, 1981. Entrance fee: $20.

Alfred Einstein Award   (see American Musicological Society Inc.)

Fargo-Moorhead Symphony's Sigvald Thompson Composition Competition
Evelyn Nelson, Mgr.
PO Box 1753   (218) 233-8397
Fargo, N.D.   58107
For a medium length orchestral composition completed during the past two years which has not been performed publicly. Eligibility: Any American citizen, except previous competition winners. Prize: $1500 & premiere performance (special 50th anniversary prize). Deadline: Aug. 15, 1981. Competition: Aug. 15, 1981. Entrance fee: None.

Philip M. Faucett Prize   (see Young Concert Artists International Auditions)

Kathleen Ferrier Memorial Prize   (see Young Concert Artists International Auditions)

Avery Fisher Artist Program
Paula Kahn, Admin'r
Lincoln Center, 140 W. 65 St.
(212) 877-1800
New York, N.Y.   10023
Annual. Eligibility: Instrumental soloist who is a US citizen. Nominations made by a recommendation board. No applications will be accepted. Prizes: Avery Fisher Prize—$5000 cash award and appearances with Lincoln Center performing organizations, including New York Philharmonic and Chamber Music Society; Recital Awards—$1000 cash award and one recital.

Ford Foundation
320 E. 43 St.   (212) 573-5096
New York, N.Y.   10017
Supports experiments, demonstrations & studies that promise to be of national significance; grants-in-aid to individuals only through nationally conducted programs based upon nomination.

Friedheim Awards   (see Kennedy Center Friedheim Awards)

Fromm Music Foundation at Harvard Univ.
Christoph Wolff, Paul Fromm, Gunther Schuller, Dirs.
Harvard Univ., Mus. Bldg.   (617) 495-2791
Cambridge, Mass.   02138
Encourages & commissions contemporary compositions; awards prizes for existing works & sponsors the study, performance, publication & recording of contemporary music.

Fulbright Graduate Study Scholarships   (see Institute of International Education/Fulbright Graduate Study Scholarships)

LIST OF U.S.A. ORGANIZATIONS AND ASSOCIATIONS INTERESTED IN JAZZ

AFRO-AMERICAN ARTS INSTITUTE
Dr. Herman Hudson, Dir.
109 N. Jordan
Bloomington, Ind. 47401
Tel. (812) 337-3675

AFRO-AMERICAN MUSIC
OPPORTUNITIES ASSOCIATION INC.
2801 Wayzata Blvd.
Minneapolis, Minn. 55405
Tel. (612) 337-3730
C. Edward Thomas, Exec. Dir.

AMERICAN COLLEGE OF
MUSICIANS
P.O. Box 1807
808 Rio Grande
Austin, Tex. 78767
Tel. (512) 478-5775
Prl Allison, Jr., Pres.

AMERICAN COUNCIL FOR THE ARTS
570 Seventh Ave.
New York, N.Y. 10018
Tel. (212) 354-6655
Michael K. Newton, Pres.

AMERICAN FEDERATION OF
MUSICIANS
1500 Broadway
New York, N.Y. 10036
Tel. (212) 869-1330
Victor W. Fuentealba, Pres.

AMERICAN GUILD OF MUSIC
P.O. Box 3
Downers Grove, Ill. 60515
Tel. (312) 968-0173
Myrtle Robertson, Pres.

AMERICAN MUSIC CENTER INC.
250 W. 57 St., Suite 626-7
New York, N.Y. 10019
Tel. (212) 247-3121
Leo Kraft, Pres.

AMERICAN MUSIC CONFERENCE
1000 Skokie Blvd.
Wilmette, Ill. 60091
Tel. (312) 649-0050
Leslie B. Propp, Pres.

AKRON JAZZ WORKSHOP
590 Weber Avenue
Akron, Ohio 44303

AMERICAN BLACK ARTIST, INC.
Georgian Bldg. - Suite A-3
1981 S. McNichols Rd.
Detroit, Mich. 48203

ARKANSAS ARTS CENTER
MacArthur Park
Little Rock, Ark. 72203

ASSOCIATION FOR JAZZ
PERFORMANCE
39 Edward Street
Buffalo, N.Y. 14202

THE ART OF JAZZ
P.O. Box 400
Red Bank, N.J. 07701

ASSOCIATION FOR THE
ADVANCEMENT OF CREATIVE
MUSIC
c/o Richard Abrams
9119 S. Paxton St.
Chicago, Ill. 60617

ASSOCIATION FOR RECORDED
SOUND COLLECTIONS INC.
Univ. of New Mexico
Fine Arts Library
Albuquerque, N.M. 87131
Tel. (505) 277-2901
Gerald B. Gibson, Pres.

ASSOCIATION OF COLLEGE
UNIV. & COMMUNITY ARTS
ADMIN'RS INC.
P.O. Box 2137
Madison, Wisc. 53701
Tel. (608) 262-0004
William M. Dawson, Exec. Dir.

BATTLE CREEK SYMPHONY JAZZ
ENSEMBLE
P.O. Box 1319
Battle Creek, Mich. 49016

BOSTON JAZZ SOCIETY
24 Sahron Street
West Medrod, Mass. 02159

BLACK MUSIC ASSOCIATION
1500 Locust St., Suite 1905
Philadelphia, Pa. 19102
Tel. (215) 545-9600

LOUIS BRAILLE FOUNDATION FOR
BLIND MUSICIANS
215 Park Ave. S.
New York, N.Y. 10003
Tel. (212) 982-7290
Shel Freund, Exec. Dir.

BROADCASTING FOUNDATION OF
AMERICA
52 Vanderbilt Ave.
New York, N.Y. 10017
Tel. (212) 986-6448
Cable: BRODFOUNAM
Seymour N. Siegel, Pres.

CAPITAL DISTRICT JAZZ SOCIETY
INC.
P.O. Box 891
Albany, N.Y. 12201

CENTRAL MISSOURI STATE UNIV.
Music Dept.
Warrensburg, Mo. 64093

CHARLIE PARKER MEMORIAL JAZZ
FOUNDATION
4605 The Paseo
Kansas City, Mo. 64110

CENTER OF NEW ORLEANS MUSIC
P.O. Box 13977
New Orleans, La. 70185
Tel. (504) 482-4211

CLASSIC JAZZ SOCIETY OF
SOUTHWESTERN OHIO
P.O. Box 653
Cincinnati, Ohio 45201

COLLECTIVE BLACK ARTISTS, INC.
156 Fifth Avenue
New York, N.Y. 10013

COLLEGE BAND DIRECTORS
NATIONAL ASSOCIATION
c/o Univ. of California Bands
Berkeley, Calif. 94720

COLLEGE MUSIC SOCIETY, INC.
c/o SUNY, Music Dept.
Binghamton, N.Y. 13901
Tel. (607) 798-2433
Robert J. Werner, Pres.

THE COLORED MUSICIANS CLUB
145 Broadway
Buffalo, N.Y. 14202

COUNCIL OF AMERICAN MUSIC
786 Chapel Street
New Haven, Conn. 06520

CONCERT JAZZ, INC.
243 Rambling Way
Spring, Penn. 19064

CREATIVE MUSICIANS
ASSOCIATION
P.O. Box 671
Woodstock, N.Y. 12498

DALLAS JAZZ SOCIETY
P.O. Box 35023
Dallas, Tx. 75235

DETROIT BLUES CLUB
12653 Stoepel Street
Detroit, Mich. 48238

DUKE ELLINGTON SOCIETY
Box 31
Church Street Station
New York, N.Y. 10008

ECLIPSE JAZZ
UNIVERSITY ACTIVITIES CENTER
2nd Fl. Michigan Union
Univ. of Michigan
Ypsilanti, Mich.

FESTIVAL PRODUCTIONS, INC.
George Wein, Pres.
P.O. Box 1169
Ansonia Station
New York, N.Y. 10023
Tel. (212) 873-0733

FRIENDS OF JAZZ
Jewish Community Center
8201 Holmes Rd.
Kansas City, Mo. 64131

HIGHLIGHTS IN JAZZ
7 Peter Cooper Rd.
Apt. 11 E
New York, N.Y. 10010

HARTFORD JAZZ SOCIETY
73 Lebanon Street
Hartford, Conn. 06112

THE HOUSE THAT JAZZ BUILT
1312 Stebbins Avenue
Bronx, N.Y. 10459

INDEPENDENT LABEL ASSOCIATION
2125 Eighth Ave. S.
Nashville, Tenn. 37204
Tel. (615) 383-6002
R.J. Lindsey, Pres.

INDIANA CLUB OF TRADITIONAL
JAZZ
Eddy Banjura
1129 Elliot Drive
Munster, Indiana 46321

INDIANAPOLIS JAZZ SOCIETY
P.O. Box 1072
Indianapolis, Ind. 46206

INSTITUTE OF JAZZ STUDIES
Dan Morgenstern, Dir.
135 Bradley Hall
Rutgers University
Newark, N.J. 07102
Tel. (201) 648-5595

INSTITUTE OF HIGH FIDELITY INC.
489 Fifth Ave.
New York, N.Y. 10017
Tel. (212) 682-5131
Jerry Kalov, Pres.

INTERNATIONAL ART OF JAZZ
5 Saywood Lane
Stonybrook, N.Y. 11790

INTERNATIONAL JAZZ
FEDERATION, INC.
P.O. Box 777
Times Square Station
New York, N.Y. 10108
Tel. (201) 939-0836
John Lewis, Pres., Jan. A. Byrczek, Exec.
Dir.

INTERNATIONAL MUSICIANS
ALLIANCE
83 Francis Street
Brookline, Mass. 02146

INTERCOLLEGIATE MUSICAL
COUNCIL
Morehouse College
Music Dept.
Atlanta, Ga. 30314
Tel. (404) 681-2800

INTERNATIONAL MUSICIANS
ALLIANCE
Foundation for the Alliance of Cultural
Arts & Humanities, Inc.
24 Everett Square
Allston, Ma. 02134

INTERNATIONAL RHYTHM & BLUES
ASSOCIATION
2138 E. 75 St., Suite 928
Chicago, Ill. 60649
Tel. (312) 768-9448
William C. Tyson, Pres.

INTERNATIONAL SOCIETY OF
PERFORMING ARTS ADMIN'RS
c/o Columbia Music Festival Ass'n
1527 Senate St.
Columbia, S.C. 29201
Tel. (803) 771-6303

JAZZ AT HOME CLUB OF
PHILADELPHIA
P.O. Box 16713
Philadelphia, Pa. 19139

JAZZ COALITION
P.O. Box 8928 JFK Sta.
Boston, Mass. 02114

JAZZ COMPOSERS ORCHESTRA
ASSOCIATION
6 W. 95th Street
New York, N.Y. 10025

JAZZ DEVELOPMENT WORKSHOP,
INC.
Marcus Belgrave, Artistc Dir.
2757 Grand River
Detroit, Mich. 48226
Tel.: (313) 871-3646

JAZZ HERITAGE SOCIETY
190-25 Woodhill Avenue
Hollis, N.Y. 11423

JAZZ IN AZ
P.O. Box 13363
Phoenix, Arizona 85002

JAZZ IN THE VALLEY
P.O. Box 137
Cheyney, Pa. 19319

JAZZ INTERACTIONS
527 Madison Avenue
New York, N.Y. 10022

JAZZMOBILE
159 W. 127th Street
New York, N.Y. 10027

JAZZ GROUP OF COLUMBUS
2358 Hardesty Ct.
Columbus, Ohio 43204

JAZZ HERITAGE FOUNDATION
P.O. Box 19070
Los Angeles, Calif.

JAZZ INSTITUTE OF CHICAGO
P.O. Box 7231
Chicago, Illinois 60607

JAZZ FORUM OF ATLANTA
P.O. Box 54848
Atlanta, Ga. 30308

THE JAZZ IMAGE
Minnesota Public Radio
400 Sibley Street
St. Paul, MN. 55101

JAZZMANIA SOCIETY, INC.
Mike Morgenstern, Dir.
Yardbird Suite
14 E. 23rd Street
New York, N.Y. 10010
Tel. (212) 477-3077

JAZZ RESEARCH INSTITUTE
15 E. Kirby, Suite 207
Detroit, Mich. 48202
Tel. (313) 871-5519

JONESBORO JAZZ SOCIETY
635 W. Kingshighway
Paragould, Arkansas 72450

KANSAS CITY, INC.
1700 Trader's National Bank Bldg.
Kansas City, Mo. 64106

THE KONTEMPORARY JAZZ
SOCIETY
P.O. Box 2049
Princeton, N.J. 08540

LAS VEGAS JAZZ SOCIETY
3459 Nakona Lane
Las Vegas, Nevada 89109

LEFT BANK JAZZ SOCIETY
2559 Frederick Avenue
Baltimore, Md. 21223

LETTUMPLAY
706 Eleventh Street, N.W.
Suite 21-21A
Washington, D.C. 20005

THE LINCOLN JAZZ SOCIETY, INC.
217 N. 11th
Lincoln, NE. 68508

MANNA HOUSE WORKSHOP
338 E. 106th Street
New York, N.Y. 10029

MICHIANA FRIENDS OF JAZZ
1930 E. Donald Street
South Bend, Indiana 46613

MINISTRY WITH THE ARTS
COMMUNITY
Emmanuel Church
15 Newbury Street
Boston, Mass. 02116

MINNESOTA JAZZ SPONSORS, INC.
5704 Schaefer Rd.
Minneapolis, MN. 55436

MOBILE JAZZ FESTIVAL
P.O. Box 1098
Mobile, Alabama 36601

NATIONAL JAZZ ENSEMBLE
Chuck Israels, Dir.
155 Bank Street
New York, N.Y. 10014
Tel. (212) 989-4665

NATIONAL ACADEMY OF
RECORDING ARTS & SCIENCES
(NARAS)
4444 Riverside Dr., Suite 202
Burbank, Calif. 91505
Tel. (213) 843-8233

NATIONAL ASSOCIATION OF JAZZ
EDUCATORS
P.O. Box 724
Manhattan, Kan. 66502
Tel. (913) 776-8744
Matt Berton, Exec. Dir.

NATIONAL ASSOCIATION OF NEGRO
MUSICIANS INC.
4330 Fullerton
Detroit, Mich. 48238
Tel. (313) 934-7448
Brazeal W. Dennard, Pres.

NATIONAL ASSOCIATION OF
SCHOOLS OF MUSIC
11250 Roger Bacon Dr., No. 5
Reston, Va. 22090
Tel. (703) 437-0700
Warner Imig, Pres.

NATIONAL ENTERTAINMENT &
CAMPUS ACTIVITIES ASSOCIATION
P.O. Box 11489
Columbia, S.C. 29211
Tel. (803) 799-0768
Gary English, Exec. Dir.

NATIONAL FEDERATION OF MUSIC
CLUBS
310 S. Michigan Ave.
Suite 1936
Chicago, Ill. 60604
Tel. (312) 427-3683

NATIONAL MUSIC COUNCIL
250 W. 57 St., Suite 626
New York, N.Y. 10019
Tel. (212) 265-8132

NATIONAL SCHOOL ORCHESTRA
ASS'N
Blair Academy of Music
1208 18 Ave. S.
Nashville, Tenn. 37212
Tel. (615) 320-5737
John Bright, Pres.

NEW YORK ASSOCIATION OF
CONTEMPORARY JAZZ ARTS, INC.
225 First Avenue
New York, N.Y. 10003

NEW YORK JAZZ REPERTORY
COMPANY
311 W. 74th Street
New York, N.Y. 10023

NEW JERSEY JAZZ SOCIETY
P.O. Box 302
Pluckemin, N.J. 07978

NEW MEXICO JAZZ WORKSHOP
408 Arroyo Tenario
Santa Fe, New Mexico 87501

NEW MUSE COMMUNITY MUSEUM
OF BROOKLYN, INC.
1530 Bedford Avenue
Brooklyn, N.Y. 11216

NEW ORLEANS JAZZ CLUB
c/o Harry Souchon
2417 Octavia Street
New Orleans, La. 70115

NEW ORLEANS JAZZ CLUB OF
CALIFORNIA
P.O. Box 1225
Kerrville, Tex. 78028
Tel. (512) 896-2285
Bill Bacin, Pres.

NORTHEAST OHIO JAZZ SOCIETY
3661 E. 106th Street
Cleveland, Ohio 44105

NORTHEASTERN UNIV. JAZZ
SOCIETY
Music Dept.
307 E 11 Center
360 Huntington Avenue
Boston, Mass. 20115

OMAHA JAZZ SOCIETY
c/o John Swoboda
1214 Harney Street
Omaha, Ne. 68102

OPPORTUNITY RESOURCES FOR
THE ARTS
1501 Broadway
New York, N.Y. 10036
Tel. (212) 575-1688
Freda Mindlin, Exec. Dir.

OVERSEAS PRESS CLUB OF
AMERICA
Hotel Biltmore, 19th Fl.
55 E. 43rd Street
New York, N.Y. 10017

PACE
3361 Southwest 3 Avenue
Miami, Fla. 33145

PAN JEBEL, INC.
P.O. Box 713
Radio City Station
New York, N.Y. 10019

POTOMAC RIVER JAZZ CLUB
c/o Esther C. West
4040 Uline Avenue
Alexandria, Virginia 22304

PRESERVATION FOR THE
PRESERVATION OF BIG BAND
MUSIC
P.O. Box 1861
Scottsdale, Ariz. 85252

THE RAINBOW GALLERY
1500 Sixth Street
Minneapolis, MN.

THE SANTA MONICA JAZZ CLUB
P.O. Box 84235
Los Angeles, Calif. 90073

STRATA ASSOCIATES, INC.
John Sinclair, Dir.
15 East Kirby
Detroit, Mi. 48202
Tel.: (313) 781-3644

THE SOUNDS OF JAZZ
136-16 220th Street
Laurelton, N.Y. 11413

STUDIO RIVBEA
24 Bond Street
New York, N.Y. 10012

STUDIO WE
193 Eldridge Street
New York, N.Y. 10002

ST. LOUIS JAZZ QUARTET
c/o Terrence Kipipenberger
7150 Princeton
St. Louis, Mo. 63130

TEXAS JAZZ FESTIVAL SOCIETY
3629 S. Saxet Drive
Corpus Christi, Texas 78481

THEATER ARTS PROJECT
Town Hall — 16 Main Street
Mattapoisett, Ma. 02739

THE WESTWOOD JAZZ CAMP
Box 29
New England, North Dakota 58647

UNITED STATES INFORMATION
AGENCY
ICS/DA
Washington, D.C. 20547
Tel. (202) 632-6720

UNIVERSAL JAZZ COALITION
156 Fifth Avenue — No. 817
New York, N.Y. 10010

UNA NOCHE PLATEADA
314 South Convent Avenue
Tucson, Arizona 85701

UPTOWN JAZZ JUNTA
Manhattanville Street
P.O. Box 811
New York, N.Y. 10027

VIRGIN ISLAND JAZZ SOCIETY
No. 2 Herman Hill
St. Croix, Virgin Islands 00864

WOMENS JAZZ FESTIVAL, INC.
9003 Belleview
Kansas City, Mo. 64114

WPFW-FM PACIFICA WASHINGTON
Pacifica Foundation
Central Station - Box 28324
Washington, D.C.

Appendix 19

SECTIONS 506(a) AND (b) OF COPYRIGHT LAW OF THE UNITED STATES OF AMERICA *
(United States Code, Title 17—Copyrights)

CRIMINAL OFFENSES

(a) CRIMINAL INFRINGEMENT.—Any person who infringes a copyright willfully and for purposes of commercial advantage or private financial gain shall be fined not more than $10,000 or imprisoned for not more than one year, or both: *Provided, however,* That any person who infringes willfully and for purposes of commercial advantage or private financial gain the copyright in a sound recording afforded by subsections (1), (2), or (3) of section 106 or the copyright in a motion picture afforded by subsections (1), (3), or (4) of section 106 shall be fined not more than $25,000 or imprisoned for not more than one year, or both, for the first such offense and shall be fined not more than $50,000 or imprisoned for not more than two years, or both, for any subsequent offense.

(b) FORFEITURE AND DESTRUCTION.—When any person is convicted of any violation of subsection (a), the court in its judgment of conviction shall, in addition to the penalty therein prescribed, order the forfeiture and destruction or other disposition of all infringing copies or phonorecords and all implements, devices, or equipment used in the manufacture of such infringing copies or phonorecords.

* Act of October 19, 1976, effective January 1, 1978 (Public Law 94-553, 90 Stat. 2541 et seq.)

FORM OF LICENSE AGREEMENT FOR ALL PRINTED EDITIONS

Date:

Music Publisher
Brill Building
New York, N.Y.

Gentlemen:

The following is the agreement between you and us.

1. You hereby grant to us the exclusive right and license during the term hereof to print, publish and sell, at our own cost and expense, your copyrighted musical composition (herein called "composition") entitled: _____
and written by: _____
in any and all editions thereof as we may elect, in the United States, its territories and possessions, and the Dominion of Canada, at such prices and on terms and discounts as we in our sole discretion may determine from time to time.

2. As and for compensation for said right and license, we shall pay you royalties computed at the following rates:

(a) Forty (40¢) cents for each regular sheet music copy sold by us, paid for and not returned.

(b) For all other separately printed copies, including organ solos, band arrangements, choral arrangements, etc., ten (10%) percent of the retail selling price of all copies thereof sold by us, paid for and not returned.

(c) For the use of the composition in folios, that proportion of 12½% of the retail selling price of the copies thereof, sold by us, paid for and not returned, as the composition bears to the total number of copyrighted musical works contained therein.

3. The foregoing royalties include all payments to be made to writer(s) of the composition, for which payments you shall be responsible.

4. We shall account to you on a semiannual basis for all royalties payable to you and shall simultaneously pay you all sums due to you. Each accounting shall set forth in detail the computation of the payments due and shall include, without limitation of the generality of the foregoing, the types of editions, the number of copies printed and the royalty rates applied. You agree that our accountings to you hereunder shall be deemed conclusive and binding upon you unless, within one year from the date of each accounting, we shall receive written notice from you specifying all disputes, errors and omissions asserted by you. You shall have the right to examine our books and records and those of our affiliates during reasonable hours, on ten (10) days written notice, regarding all matters hereunder.

5. For the purpose of computation of royalties, each edition shall not consist of more than twenty-five (25) songs without your consent.

6. Each copy of the composition as published by us shall bear your name as the copyright owner, with the form of copyright notice prescribed by you.

7. The title of the composition shall not be in the main title of the folio without your consent.

8. You warrant and represent that you are the sole owner of the composition and the copyrights thereon for the licensed territory, that you have the sole right and authority to enter into this agreement, and that the composition is original and does not infringe upon the rights of third parties. You agree to indemnify and save us harmless of and from any and all liabilities, damages, costs and expenses, including reasonable attorneys' fees, suffered or incurred by us by reason of a breach or claim of breach of your covenants and warranties hereunder. We agree to give you immediate written notice of any adverse claim and to permit you to defend in our behalf by a counsel chosen by you.

9. If we fail to account and make payments hereunder and such failure is not cured within ten (10) days after written notice thereof is sent to us by registered mail, or if we fail to perform any other obligations required of us hereunder and such failure is not cured within thirty (30) days after written notice to us by registered mail, or in the event we go into compulsory liquidation or bankruptcy or make an assignment for the benefit of creditors or make any composition with creditors, or any insolvency or composition proceeding shall be commenced by or against us, then and in any of such events you, in addition to such other rights and remedies which you may have at law or otherwise under this agreement, may elect to cancel or terminate this agreement without prejudice to any rights or claims you may have, and all rights hereunder shall forthwith revert to you and we may not thereafter exercise any rights hereunder and shall destroy all printed copies in our possession. Your failure to terminate this agreement upon any default or defaults shall not be deemed to constitute a waiver of your right to terminate the same upon any subsequent default.

10. This agreement and our rights hereunder shall be in full force and effect for a period of three (3) years from the date hereof and shall continue in effect thereafter until terminated by you or us by a ninety (90) day prior written notice by registered mail which may become effective at the close of such period or thereafter. You agree that notwithstanding such termination by you, for a period of one (1) year after termination, we shall continue to have the right to market and sell any and all copies of the composition then on hand, provided and on condition that within thirty (30) days following the termination date we supply you with a written inventory of the number of copies of each edition then on hand.

11. This agreement shall not be construed as one of partnership or joint venture.

12. This agreement shall be construed and interpreted under the laws of the State of New York applicable to agreements wholly to be performed therein.

Please indicate your acceptance of the foregoing by signing at the place indicated below.

Very truly yours,

PRINT PUBLISHER

BY _____

AGREED TO AND ACCEPTED:

MUSIC PUBLISHER

BY _____

Appendix 21

FORM OF SELLING AGENCY AGREEMENT FOR ALL PRINTED EDITIONS
(invoices Issued in Name of Agent)

Date:

Music Publisher
Brill Building
New York, N.Y.

Gentlemen:

The following is the agreement between you and us:

1. You hereby appoint us and we agree to act as your sole and exclusive selling agent and distributor in the United States of America, its territories and possessions, and the Dominion of Canada, on the terms and conditions herein set forth, for printed editions of musical compositions in your catalog.

2. You agree to furnish us with copies of the printed editions in your catalog for our sale and distribution. You will pay directly all expenses involved in the production of the printed editions, including engraving, autographing, artwork, type and printing. We agree to cooperate with you in connection with such production, including the making available of our production facilities. You will cause copies of the printed editions to be reproduced by printers to be designated for such purpose by us, in such quantities as we shall require.

3. We shall bear the costs of shipping copies of printed editions to purchasers thereof and shall attend to billing, warehousing, shipping, collections and all other matters incidental to the distribution and sale of printed editions.

4. You agree that all copies of printed editions shall be sold and distributed through us at such list prices and on such terms and conditions as we in our sole discretion establish from time to time in the exercise of good faith, including but not limited to special "rack" jobber and other discounts.

5. We shall render statements within sixty (60) days after June 30th and December 31st showing the number of copies sold and paid for. Subject to the deduction of our commissions and subject to our establishing a reasonable reserve against contingent returns, we shall simultaneously remit to you the balance of the net moneys actually received by us from the paid sales of the printed editions.

6. As compensation for our services hereunder, you agree to pay us commissions in a sum equal to the following percentage of the gross wholesale selling price to jobbers on all paid sales of the printed editions:
Twenty (20%) percent. You hereby irrevocably authorize and empower us to retain and deduct our said commission in our accountings to you.

7. You shall have the right, by representatives of your own choosing, to examine during ordinary business hours all of our books and records and those of our affiliates relating to matters hereunder.

8. We agree that all copies of the printed editions printed under our control shall bear your name as the copyright proprietor, with a copyright notice prescribed by you. We also agree to place copies of each such edition on sale in Canada prior to or simultaneously with the inception of sales in the United States of America, to secure a Certificate of Sale for the printed edition and to deliver the Certificate to you together with 25 copies of the printed edition. You shall be responsible for securing your registration of the copyright thereof in the United States of America.

9. You hereby agree that all copies of the printed editions which may be printed during the term hereof shall be prominently imprinted with the following notice:

Sole Selling Agent: Independent Distributor
106 Carmody Street
New York 1, N.Y.

10. We agree to use our best efforts in the marketing and promotion of the printed editions through circulars, trade lists and other customary modes of promotion, so as to acquaint the entire trade with its availability. No charge shall be made to you for promotion.

11. You warrant that you are the sole owner of the printed editions which are the subject of this agreement, that you have the sole right and authority to enter into this agreement and that the printed editions will not infringe upon the rights of third parties. You agree to indemnify and save us harmless from liabilities, damages, costs and expenses, including reasonable counsel fees, suffered or incurred by us by reason of a breach or claim of breach of your covenants and warranties hereunder. We agree to give you immediate written notice of any adverse claim and to permit you to defend on our behalf by a counsel chosen by you.

12. If we fail to account and make payments hereunder and such failure is not cured within ten (10) days after written notice thereof is sent to us by registered mail, or if we fail to perform any other obligations required of us hereunder and such failure is not cured within thirty (30) days after written notice to us by registered mail, or in the event we go into compulsory liquidation or bankruptcy or make an assignment for the benefit of creditors or make any compositions with creditors, or any insolvency or composition proceeding shall be commenced by or against us, then and in any of such events you, in addition to such other rights and remedies which you may have at law or otherwise under this agreement, may elect to cancel or terminate this agreement without prejudice to any rights or claims you may have, and all rights hereunder shall forthwith revert to you and we may not thereafter exercise any rights hereunder and shall thereupon return the inventory of your printed editions to you. Your failure to terminate this agreement upon any default or defaults shall not be deemed to constitute a waiver of your right to terminate the same upon any subsequent default.

13. This agreement shall continue for a term of one (1) year from the date hereof and shall continue thereafter unless and until terminated at the end of such one (1) year period or subsequently by a written notice of termination given by either party by registered mail at least sixty (60) days prior to the termination date. At or before the termination date we shall return the inventory of your printed editions to you, together with statements as at such date. If our present management or ownership is changed, you may terminate this agreement at any time thereafter upon sixty (60) days written notice by registered mail.

14. This agreement shall not be construed as one of partnership or joint venture.

15. This agreement shall be construed and interpreted under the laws of the State of New York applicable to agreements wholly to be performed therein.

Please signify your acceptance of the foregoing by signing at the place indicated below.

Very truly yours,

INDEPENDENT DISTRIBUTOR

BY _____

AGREED TO AND ACCEPTED:

MUSIC PUBLISHER

BY _____

Appendix 22

FORM OF CATALOG SELLING AGENCY AGREEMENT FOR ALL PRINTED EDITIONS
(Invoices Issued in Name of Principal)

Date:

Music Publisher
Brill Building
New York City, New York

Gentlemen:

The following is the agreement between you and us:

1. You hereby appoint us, and we agree to act as, the sole and exclusive selling agent and distributor for printed editions in your catalog, for the territory of the United States, its territories and possessions, and the Dominion of Canada.

2. For the purpose of this agreement, your catalog shall consist of any and all printed editions, containing your musical compositions, that you may own or otherwise control during the term hereof.

3. You agree to furnish us with copies of the printed editions in your catalog for our sale and distribution. You will pay directly all expenses involved in the production of the printed editions, including engraving, autographing, artwork, type and printing. We agree to cooperate with you in connection with such production, including the making available of our production facilities.

4. We agree to maintain a separate set of accounts receivable books for your firm. Such books and records will contain complete information covering all transactions in connection with the sale and distribution of your printed editions. You hereby authorize us to have printed, at your cost, the necessary invoices bearing the name of your firm and our address.

5. We shall send to you monthly statements showing the number sold of each type of printed edition, together with checks received by us for sales of your printed editions. You agree to pay us, after the tenth of each month, the amount due us as compensation, in accordance with the provisions of Paragraph 7 hereof, for printed editions sold and paid for through the end of the previous month. We shall also render to you a monthly statement for money expended for postage, and you will issue a separate certified check made payable to "Postmaster" for the amount due, to be sent to us with the payment of our compensation. You shall have the right, by representatives of your own choosing, to examine during ordinary business hours all of our books and records and those of our affiliates relating to matters hereunder.

6. We agree to use our best efforts in the marketing and promotion of your printed editions through circulars, trade lists and other customary modes of promotion, so as to acquaint the entire trade with their availability. No charge shall be made to you for promotion.

7. In full consideration for our services and expenses other than postage, you agree to pay us as follows:

Twenty (20%) per cent of all moneys received from the sale of printed editions in your catalog.

8. You warrant that you are the sole owner of the printed editions which are the subject of this agreement, that you have the sole right and authority to enter into this agreement with respect to such printed editions, and that the printed editions will not infringe upon the rights of third parties. You agree to indemnify and save us harmless of and from any and all liabilities, damages, costs and expenses, including reasonable counsel fees, suffered or incurred by us by reason of a breach or claim of breach of your covenants and warranties hereunder. We agree to give you immediate written notice of any adverse claim and to permit you to defend on our behalf by a counsel chosen by you.

9. Each copy of your printed editions printed under our control shall bear your name as the copyright proprietor with a notice prescribed by you. We agree to place copies of each such edition on sale in Canada prior to or simultaneously with the inception of sales in the United States of America, to secure a Certificate of Sale for the printed edition and to deliver the Certificate to you together with 25 copies of the printed edition. You shall be responsible for securing your registration of the copyright thereof in the United States of America.

10. If we fail to account and make payments hereunder and such failure is not cured within ten (10) days after written notice thereof is sent to us by registered mail, or if we fail to perform any other obligations required of us hereunder and such failure is not cured within thirty (30) days after written notice to us by registered mail, or in the event we go into compulsory liquidation or bankruptcy or make an assignment for the benefit of creditors or make any compositions with creditors, or any insolvency or composition proceeding shall be commenced by or against us, then and in any of such events you, in addition to such other rights and remedies which you may have at law or otherwise under this agreement, may elect to cancel or terminate this agreement without prejudice to any rights or claims you may have, and all rights hereunder shall forthwith revert to you and we may not thereafter exercise any rights hereunder and shall thereupon return the inventory of your printed editions to you. Your failure to terminate this agreement upon any default or defaults shall not be deemed to constitute a waiver of your right to terminate the same upon any subsequent default.

11. This agreement shall be for a period of two (2) years and shall continue thereafter unless and until terminated at the end of such two (2) year period or subsequently by a written notice of termination given by either party by registered mail at least sixty (60) days prior to the termination date. At or before the termination date we shall return the inventory of your printed editions to you, together with statements as at such date. If our present management or ownership is changed, you may terminate this agreement at any time thereafter upon sixty (60) days written notice.

12. This agreement shall not be construed as one of partnership or joint venture.

13. This agreement shall be construed and interpreted under the laws of the State of New York applicable to agreements wholly to be performed therein.

Please signify your acceptance of the foregoing by signing at the place indicated below.

Very truly yours,

SELLING AGENT

BY _____

AGREED TO AND ACCEPTED:

MUSIC PUBLISHER

BY _____

Appendix 23

FORM OF LICENSE AGREEMENT FOR SONG LYRIC REPRINT RIGHTS

Date:

Song Lyric Magazine
Tenth Avenue
Nashville, Tennessee

Gentlemen:

The following is our agreement:

1. We hereby grant to you and your affiliates the non-exclusive license to print and vend in song lyric publications in the United States, its territories and possessions, and the Dominion of Canada, the lyrics for the following musical composition(s) for a period of one (1) year from the date hereof:

2. You agree to pay us for the rights herein granted, provided the lyrics of said musical composition(s) are available to you during the period of this agreement, the sum of_____Dollars per song, receipt of which is hereby acknowledged.

3. In the event that during the period of this agreement said musical composition(s) is (are) included among the top ten most popular songs in the country on the Billboard Hot 100 Chart of Hits, you shall pay us the additional sum of_____Dollars per song, on such Chart, provided said lyrics are available to you at such time.

4. We warrant and represent that the lyrics furnished to you are new and original, that they do not infringe upon the rights of third parties and that we have the sole right and authority to enter into this agreement. We agree to indemnify and save you harmless of and from any and all liabilities, damages, costs and expenses, including reasonable counsel fees, suffered or incurred by you by reason of a breach or claim of breach of our covenants and warranties hereunder. You agree to give us immediate written notice of any adverse claim and to permit us to defend on your behalf by a counsel chosen by us.

5. You agree that all copies of the lyrics of our composition(s) printed hereunder shall carry an appropriate copyright notice, furnished by us, showing our ownership of the copyright of the said composition(s).

6. This agreement shall be binding on the parties hereto and their successors and assigns. You agree to remain liable at all times for performance of your covenants hereunder.

Very truly yours,

MUSIC PUBLISHER

BY _____

AGREED TO AND ACCEPTED:

SONG LYRIC MAGAZINE

BY _____

Appendix 24

FORM OF BACKGROUND MUSIC TRANSCRIPTION LICENSE BY PUBLISHER
(Used by The Harry Fox Agency, Inc.)

AGREEMENT made as of   by and between

(hereinafter referred to as "   ") and THE HARRY FOX AGENCY, INC., 110 East 59th Street, New York, New York 10022 (hereinafter referred to as "AGENT").

WITNESSETH:

WHEREAS, AGENT is the licensing and collecting agent for numerous music publisher-principals (hereinafter individually and collectively referred to as the "Publishers") who own or control the rights hereinafter licensed in their respective musical compositions;

WHEREAS,   is engaged in the business of producing background music services and furnishing such services to its customers;

WHEREAS,   in order to record the musical compositions owned by the Publishers and to reproduce and distribute the recordings, is required under copyright law to obtain a license from the Publishers and accordingly desires to obtain such a license from the Publishers for the use of their respective musical compositions; and

WHEREAS, AGENT has been authorized and instructed by its principals, the Publishers, to issue a license to   :
NOW, THEREFORE, it is agreed as follows:
1. This agreement is being entered into by AGENT as the authorized agent, and acting for and on behalf of its principals, the Publishers.

2. For the purposes hereof the Publishers shall be and be deemed those publishers listed in "The Harry Fox Music Publishers Directory" as it is from time to time amended and supplemented, excluding therefrom however those publishers who are the subject of notices to   from AGENT excluding such publishers from the operation of this agreement. The right to exclude publishers from the operation of this agreement (hereby reserved) may be exercised from time to time by AGENT pursuant to instructions from, and acting on behalf of, such publishers so excluded, provided that any such exclusion shall not apply to any compositions licensed and recorded under this agreement prior to the date of the delivery of the notice to   relating to their exclusion.

3. The term of this Agreement shall be for a period of ( ) years commencing   and terminating   (hereinafter referred to as the "Term").

4. The territory within which the rights hereinafter licensed may be exercised by   is limited to the United States of America, its territories and possessions and Puerto Rico (hereinafter referred to as the "Territory").

5. For the purposes hereof, the following *non-exclusive* rights are hereby granted to   by the Publisher with respect to the "licensed compositions" (as such term is hereinafter defined) during the Term and for use within the Territory:

(a) The right to mechanically reproduce (i.e. make recordings of) the licensed compositions in whole or in part for the purposes of using such recordings in and only in connection with the background music services furnished by   to its customers.

(b) The right to make and use copies of such recordings in connection with background music services only and the right to make and furnish copies of such recordings to its customers for use in connection with such background music services only.

(c) The rights herein granted to record and make copies of recordings hereunder embodying performances of the licensed compositions shall include recordings on wire, tape, discs or any other devices now or hereafter known but are limited to audio devices only not accompanied by the recording of visual images.

(d) The right granted in paragraph 5(a) to mechanically reproduce includes the right to record and use the music of a licensed composition without the lyrics thereof (i.e. an instrumental arrangement).

(e) Neither the title nor lyrics of the licensed compositions shall be changed, substituted for, added to or translated without the written consent of its respective Publishers.

(f) The public performance of the licensed compositions, as embodied in the recordings, by   is expressly conditioned upon such performers thereof having valid performing rights licenses from the respective Publishers, the American Society of Composers, Authors and Publishers (ASCAP) or Broadcast Music, Inc. (BMI) or any other person authorized to issue such licenses.

6. For the purposes hereof "licensed compositions" shall be and be deemed to mean those musical compositions with respect to which:

(a) the rights hereunder licensed are owned or controlled by the Publisher, *and*

(b) AGENT has not indicated a restriction on such use by the respective Publishers within 20 days after the receipt of such notice from   , the right to restrict such use hereby being reserved by and on behalf of the Publishers.

7. In consideration of the license hereby granted,   agrees to pay AGENT for and on behalf of its principals, the Publishers, for each respective licensed composition used by   hereunder during the Term as follows:

(a) The sum of $6.00 per year for each separate recording thereof in   active library as of   . In this connection,   agrees to furnish a list of such licensed compositions to AGENT within thirty (30) days from the date of the execution of this agreement, which list shall be accompanied by   payment therefor pursuant to this sub-paragraph (a).

(b) In connection with its use of the licensed compositions and the payments to be made hereunder by   ,   agrees to render statements to AGENT within thirty (30) days after the end of each six (6) month period of the Term (i.e. the periods ending March 31, and September 30th). Such statements shall identify all of the licensed compositions recorded and put into use in   music service during the applicable periods of the Term, shall show the dates of such first use and shall be accompanied by the applicable payments hereunder. AGENT shall have the right by its authorized representatives to inspect, copy and make abstract of the books and records of   during reasonable business hours to verify the accuracy of   statements and payments hereunder.

8. The license hereunder is limited to its express terms and all rights in the licensed compositions not expressly licensed hereunder are hereby expressly reserved by and for the Publishers.

9. This license is non-assignable by   except to a wholly owned subsidiary or parent or entity which purchases all or substantially all of   assets or the capital stock of   or its parent corporation, provided, however, that in no event shall   be relieved of its obligations hereunder without the express written consent of AGENT.

10. In the event that   shall fail to make any payment or comply with any other provision required to be performed by   in this agreement, AGENT shall, without prejudice to any other right of AGENT or its publisher-principals under this Agreement, have the right to revoke this agreement and the rights herein granted by written notice thereof sent to   by certified mail. In the event that   does not cure such failure within fifteen (15) days from the date of the mailing of such notice,   shall be and be deemed to be a willful infringer of copyright with respect to the licensed compositions as to which it has not paid the amounts due hereunder or with respect to which it has otherwise failed to comply with its obligations under this Agreement.

11. This agreement and the license of rights hereunder shall automatically terminate upon the filing by   of a petition in bankruptcy, or insolvency, or after any adjudication that   is bankrupt or insolvent, which adjudication is not vacated within 60 days, or upon the filing by   of any petition or answer seeking reorganization, readjustment or arrangement of business under any federal or state law relating to bankruptcy, or insolvency, or upon the appointment of a receiver for any of the property of   , or upon the making by   of any assignment for the benefit of creditors or upon the institution of any proceedings for the liquidation of   business or for the termination of its corporate character. Termination of this agreement shall be without prejudice for monies due to or to become due to AGENT and without prejudice to any other right of AGENT or the Publisher under this agreement. Termination shall not affect the license for any composition for which the fee has been paid.

12. Nothing herein contained shall constitute a waiver or release of any right, claim or cause of action against which AGENT or the Publishers may have at law or in equity against   with respect to any act or omission on the part of   not expressly licensed hereunder, all being hereby reserved.

13. This agreement sets forth the entire understanding of the parties with respect to the subject matter hereof, may not be altered or amended except in a signed written instrument and shall be governed and construed by and under the laws of the State of New York.

IN WITNESS WHEREOF, the parties hereto have caused this Agreement to be executed as of the   day of

By ————————————————————

THE HARRY FOX AGENCY, INC.

By ————————————————————
　　　　　Albert Berman, President

Appendix 25

ASCAP BACKGROUND MUSIC SERVICE LICENSE AGREEMENT

AGREEMENT made between the AMERICAN SOCIETY OF COMPOSERS, AUTHORS AND PUBLISHERS (hereinafter called "SOCIETY") and

a   Corporation (hereinafter called "LICENSEE"), as follows:

1. SOCIETY grants to LICENSEE and LICENSEE accepts, for the period commencing

and ending   , a non-exclusive license to publicly perform, or cause to be publicly performed, in the United States, its territories and possessions, non-visually, by means of "Background Music Service" (as hereinafter defined) and not otherwise, in the premises of "Subscribers of LICENSEE" (as hereinafter defined) and not elsewhere, non-dramatic renditions of the separate musical compositions of which SOCIETY shall, during the term hereof, have the right to license such performing rights. This license does not extend to or include the public performance of any rendition or performance of any opera, operetta, musical comedy, play or like production as such, in whole or in part.

Except as expressly herein otherwise provided, nothing herein contained shall be construed as authorizing LICENSEE to grant to others any right to reproduce or perform by any means, method or process whatsoever, any of the musical compositions licensed hereunder, or as authorizing "Subscribers of LICENSEE" (as hereinafter defined) to perform or reproduce compositions licensed hereunder by any method or process whatsoever except the reproduction and performance of such compositions by means of equipment at the premises of such "Subscribers of LICENSEE" (as hereinafter defined) designated in the agreement between each such respective Subscriber and LICENSEE.

The term "Background Music Service" as used in this agreement shall mean the transmission to the premises of "Subscribers of LICENSEE" (as hereinafter defined) of renditions of musical compositions, by means of

(a) wires or other conductors from a central studio or studios operated by LICENSEE and located at   ; or
(b) FM radio broadcasts from Station   , located at

or both, and the reproduction or performance of such renditions by means of equipment located in such premises.

Should LICENSEE's Background Music Service emanate from another FM radio station in lieu of or in addition to the one identified above, LICENSEE shall promptly identify such other FM radio station by written notice to SOCIETY and thereafter this agreement shall be deemed amended by the substitution or addition of the name of such other FM radio station for the station named hereinabove.

The term "Subscribers of LICENSEE", as used in this agreement, shall mean all persons, firms and corporations subscribing to the said Background Music Service.

This license shall not extend to or be deemed to include or authorize (a) the public performance of any musical composition licensed hereunder by any means, method or process whatsoever, other than those described above in this Paragraph "1"; or (b) the recording of, or the manufacture of, any recordings, or any other device used as a means of reproducing any musical composition of which the right of performance is licensed under this agreement.

2. This license shall not under any circumstances extend to (a) any ballroom, roller or ice-skating rink; or (b) any premises to which an admission fee is charged, provided, however, that this limitation shall apply only to the area of such premises from which the event or entertainment for which admission is charged is intended to be observed or heard and this license shall extend to any individual restaurant or store within any such premises where no separate admission fee is charged for admittance to such restaurant or store; or (c) transmission by any television station or any radio station to premises other than premises of Subscribers of LICENSEE; or (d) any community antenna operation.

3. A. LICENSEE warrants, represents and agrees that the fees set forth in Paragraph "6" of this agreement will be paid by LICENSEE with respect to all premises to which any Background Music Service is furnished directly or indirectly by LICENSEE or any enterprise which controls, is controlled by, or is under the same control as, LICENSEE.

B. LICENSEE further warrants and represents that each and every one of its agreements with its Subscribers hereafter made as well as all renewals or extensions of existing agreements, will contain the following provision:

"The SUBSCRIBER shall not transmit the programs nor use the service outside the premises designated in this agreement."

4. LICENSEE warrants, represents and agrees and it is a condition of this license that no commercial announcements or advertising, of any kind, will be transmitted to or reproduced or disseminated in the premises of Subscribers of LICENSEE.

5. LICENSEE agrees to furnish to SOCIETY during the term of this agreement, commencing with the receipt of a written request therefor from the SOCIETY, a copy of the daily log, list or record of musical compositions transmitted during the term hereof by LICENSEE to such premises, showing the title of each composition and the composer and author thereof.

It is agreed that until ninety (90) days after such time as SOCIETY shall notify LICENSEE in writing to the contrary, it will be sufficient for LICENSEE to furnish to SOCIETY the printed form of program furnished by LICENSEE to its Subscribers.

6. In consideration of the license herein granted, LICENSEE agrees to pay to SOCIETY with respect to each premises of each Subscriber of LICENSEE to which LICENSEE's Background Music Service is furnished, the following:

A. $27 per year for each premises of each Subscriber (other than the premises specifically mentioned in Sub-Paragraphs "B" and "C" of this Paragraph "6") including but not being limited to: hotels, motels, night clubs, restaurants, bars, grills, taverns, cocktail lounges and other establishments in which food and/or beverages are served, and stores, shops, supermarkets, automobile showrooms, gasoline service stations and other establishments where goods or services are sold or offered to the public at retail.

B. $27 per year for the first unit in each shopping center plus $15 per year for each additional unit in such shopping center.

Where LICENSEE's Background Music Service is furnished either to a Subscriber operating a shopping center where LICENSEE's Background Music Service is furnished to more than one unit, or to a Subscriber or Subscribers operating two or more such units within a shopping center, LICENSEE agrees that the amounts provided in this Sub-Paragraph "B" shall be paid with respect to each such unit in each such shopping center. For example if LICENSEE's Background Music Service were furnished to a total of 40 units in a total of 10 shopping centers, the fee would be:

$27.00 for the first unit in each of the 10 shopping centers	$27 × 10 =	$270
$15.00 for each of the remaining 30 units	$15 × 30 =	450
	Fee	$720

Each unit to which LICENSEE's Background Music Service is furnished by means of a speaker or speakers located immediately outside so as to render performances audible within such premises shall be treated the same as if the speaker or speakers were located inside such premises.

A "shopping center" as used in this agreement is a group of stores usually but not necessarily having common ownership, a related architectural style, and a common parking lot and not generally located in the central business area of a city. A group of stores shall not be deemed to be a shopping center merely by virtue of the fact that they are adjacent to one another. A "unit" in such a shopping center is a store or shop, supermarket, automobile showroom, gasoline service station or other establishment where goods or services are sold or offered to the public at retail.

C. A sum equal to 3½% of the gross amount paid for the installation and use of equipment in, and the servicing of, and the furnishing of programs to the premises of Subscribers of LICENSEE for the following premises (excluding premises described in Sub-Paragraphs "A" and "B" of this Paragraph "6"): an office, factory or plant; a bank; an office or a professional building; a doctor's, dentist's, or other professional office; a hospital, clinic, nursing or rest home or rehabilitation center; a funeral home or mortuary; a library, school, college or university; a church; a private club owned and operated by the members as a non-commercial venture; an apartment house or residence; a governmental office; a park or recreation area owned and operated by the government excluding private or commercial concessions or leased areas; a garage; a security or commodity broker; an insurance or real estate agency; a finance or loan office; a savings and loan association; a warehouse; a trucking terminal which is limited to operators of such trucks and maintenance men and to which other members of the public are not generally admitted; a research organization or laboratory; a room occupied solely as a rest room (or lounge); a room occupied solely as a reception or information area or an employees' cafeteria in such respective premises.

Where merchandise, services or any thing or service of value is received in lieu of or in addition to cash consideration for the installation and use of equipment in, and the servicing of, and furnishing of programs to any premises described in this Sub-Paragraph "C", the same shall be described and the reasonable value thereof determined and accounting made to SOCIETY on the same basis as if a regular billing had been made by LICENSEE therefor in a sum equal to such value, provided however, that the fee for each such premises shall in no event be less than Fifteen Dollars ($15) per year.

The term "gross amount paid for the installation and use of equipment in, and the servicing of and furnishing of programs to the premises of Subscribers of LICENSEE", as used in this Sub-Paragraph "C" of this Paragraph "6", shall be deemed to include all payments made (other than a bona fide payment for the actual sale price of equipment), whether in money or in any other form, directly or indirectly, for installation and use of LICENSEE's facilities, and for any and all services (including programs) furnished to the premises of such Subscribers of LICENSEE in connection therewith, and whether such payment shall have been made directly to LICENSEE or to any other person, firm or corporation. No deductions shall be permitted except the following:

(1) the part of the cost of initial installation at such premises which represents the actual amount expended by LICENSEE for labor or materials other than the actual equipment installed by LICENSEE at such premises for which LICENSEE bills the Subscriber at the approximate cost of such labor or materials or a lesser amount;

(2) the amount of tax collected (whether or not separately billed) by LICENSEE from Subscribers with respect to premises described in this Sub-Paragraph "C" solely for payment under Section 4251 of the 1954 Internal Revenue Code and any similar tax that may be imposed by Federal, State or Municipal Governments if such tax is imposed upon Subscribers and is actually collected from Subscribers and paid by LICENSEE to the Federal or a State or Municipal Government;

(3) the fees under this Sub-Paragraph "C".

D. For each premises for which a fee is payable under Sub-Paragraph "A" or "B" of this Paragraph "6", and for which the agreement between the Subscriber of LICENSEE and LICENSEE shall commence on any day from the first through the fifteenth day of any month, or terminate on any day from the sixteenth through the last day of any month, the fee shall be paid in full for such month. For each such premises for which such agreement shall commence on any day from the sixteenth through the last day of any month, or terminate on any day from the first through the fifteenth day of any month, no fee shall be payable for such month.

E. The minimum fee under this agreement shall be Ten Dollars ($10) per month; provided, however, that if LICENSEE has not been engaged in the background music business for six (6) months, this provision shall not apply until LICENSEE shall have completed six (6) months in said business.

7. LICENSEE agrees to render monthly statements to SOCIETY on or before the last day of each month, covering the period of the preceding calendar month, setting forth separately the gross amounts paid for the installation and use of equipment in, and the servicing of, and furnishing of programs to the premises of Subscribers of LICENSEE without exception, for (a) all premises of all Subscribers and (b) all premises described in Paragraph "6.C."; the number of premises within Sub-Paragraph "6.A."; the number of shopping centers within Sub-Paragraph "6.B.", indicating as to each the number of units to which LICENSEE's Background Music Service is furnished; and the amount payable under Paragraph "6" of this agreement. Whenever any deduction is made for the amount expended for labor or materials as provided in Paragraph "6.C.", an itemized statement of the amounts so expended shall be set forth. Said statements shall be rendered under oath on forms supplied gratis by SOCIETY, and shall be accompanied by a remittance in full of the amount due SOCIETY under the terms hereof.

Accountings and payments shall be made on a billing basis with the right of reduction or rebate for bad accounts. All billings made subsequent to the termination of this license with respect to installations, servicing or the furnishing of programs during the term hereof shall be accounted for by LICENSEE as and when such billings shall be made by LICENSEE; and it is agreed that all such billings shall be made by LICENSEE not later than thirty (30) days after the termination of this license.

8. SOCIETY shall have the right by its duly authorized representatives, at any time during customary business hours, to examine the books and records of account of LICENSEE to such extent as may be necessary to verify any and all statements rendered and accountings made hereunder.

SOCIETY shall give LICENSEE not less than thirty (30) days' written notice of its intention to make such an examination. If, within ten (10) days after receipt of such written notice, LICENSEE shall give SOCIETY written notice of its desire to have the examination conducted by an independent certified public accountant, then (a) the examination shall be made by any nationally known certified accounting firm or by any independent certified public accountant residing in the state or within 100 miles of LICENSEE's principal place of business, selected by SOCIETY and (b) the total cost of such accounting firm or such an independent certified public accountant, including fees and expenses, shall be borne as follows: SOCIETY shall bear the first Two Hundred and Fifty Dollars ($250) of such cost, and the balance shall be borne equally by LICENSEE and by SOCIETY.

LICENSEE shall give SOCIETY's auditor (including any independent certified public accountant SOCIETY may select) full access to all relevant records of LICENSEE including the names and addresses of, and any other pertinent information concerning, the Subscribers of LICENSEE. SOCIETY agrees to instruct auditors in its employ not to make any list of the names and addresses of Subscribers of LICENSEE except insofar as necessary for the verification of LICENSEE's statements and accountings to SOCIETY, and to destroy any such list upon completion of the audit or, if a deficiency be found as to which such data may be relevant, upon the payment or other disposition of such audit deficiency. SOCIETY agrees to instruct any independent certified public accountant selected by SOCIETY not to furnish any list of the names and addresses of Subscribers of LICENSEE or any copy thereof, to SOCIETY or to anyone else.

9. SOCIETY reserves the right, at any time and from time to time, in good faith, to restrict the performance of compositions from musical comedies, operas, operettas, and motion pictures, or any other composition being excessively performed, only for the purpose of preventing harmful effect upon such musical comedies, operas, operettas, motion pictures or compositions, in respect of other interests under the copyrights thereof; provided, however, that the maximum number of compositions which may be at any time thus restricted shall not exceed three hundred (300) and moreover that limited licenses will be granted upon application entirely free of additional charge as to restricted compositions, if and when the copyright owners thereof are unable to show reasonable hazards to their major interests likely to result from such performances; and provided further that SOCIETY shall not exercise such right to restrict any such composition for the purpose of permitting the fixing or regulating of fees for the recording or transcribing of such composition; and provided further that in no case shall any charges, "free plugs" or other consideration be required in respect of any permission granted to perform a restricted composition; and provided further that in no event shall any composition, after the initial radio or television broadcast thereof, be restricted for the purpose of confining further performances thereof to a particular program or licensee.

SOCIETY reserves the further right, at any time and from time to time, in good faith, to restrict the performance of any compositions, over and above the number specified in the previous paragraph, only as to which any suit has been brought or threatened on a claim that such composition infringes a composition not contained in SOCIETY's repertory or on a claim that SOCIETY does not have the right to license the performing rights in such composition.

10. Upon any breach or default by LICENSEE of any terms herein contained, SOCIETY may give LICENSEE thirty (30) days notice in writing to cure such breach or default, and in the event such breach or default has not been cured within the said thirty (30) days, SOCIETY may then forthwith terminate this license.

11. SOCIETY agrees to indemnify, save and hold LICENSEE and the respective premises of Subscribers of LICENSEE harmless, and defend LICENSEE and such premises from and against any claim, demand or suit that may be made or brought against it with respect to renditions given on LICENSEE's programs during the term hereof in accordance with this license, of the separate musical compositions copyrighted or composed by members of SOCIETY and in SOCIETY's repertory.

In the event of the service upon LICENSEE or any such premises of any notice, process, paper or pleading, under which a claim, demand or action is made or begun against LICENSEE or any such premises on account of any such matter as is hereinabove referred to, LICENSEE shall promptly give SOCIETY written notice thereof and simultaneously therewith deliver to SOCIETY any such notice, process, paper or pleading, or a copy thereof, and SOCIETY at its own expense shall have sole charge of the defense of any such action or proceeding. LICENSEE, however, shall have the right to engage counsel of its own, at its own expense, who may participate in the defense of any such action or proceeding and with whom counsel for SOCIETY shall cooperate. LICENSEE shall cooperate with SOCIETY in every way in the defense of any such action or proceeding, and in any appeals that may be taken from any judgments or orders entered therein, and shall execute all pleadings, bonds or other instruments, but at the sole expense of SOCIETY, that may be required in order properly to defend and resist any such action or proceeding, and prosecute any appeals taken therein.

In the event of the service upon LICENSEE of any notice, process, paper or pleading under which a claim, demand or action is made or begun against LICENSEE on account of the rendition of any musical composition contained in SOCIETY's repertory but not copyrighted or composed by members of SOCIETY, SOCIETY agrees at the request of LICENSEE to cooperate with and assist LICENSEE in the defense of any such action or proceeding, and in any appeals that LICENSEE may elect to take from any judgments or orders entered therein.

12. All notices required or permitted to be given by either of the parties to the other hereunder shall be duly and properly given if mailed to such other party by registered or certified United States mail, addressed to such other party at its main office for the transaction of business.

13. If LICENSEE shall cease to operate the Background Music Service referred to in this agreement and if LICENSEE shall have discharged all the obligations of LICENSEE to SOCIETY under this agreement, then LICENSEE shall have the right to assign this agreement for the balance of its term upon the express condition that such assignee shall accept such assignment and shall agree to assume and to carry out and perform all the terms and conditions of this agreement on the part of LICENSEE to be kept and performed for the balance of the term of this agreement. Upon such acceptance and assumption, LICENSEE shall be relieved of any future obligations hereunder. Except as hereinabove expressly provided, LICENSEE shall have no right to transfer or assign this agreement, the rights granted hereunder being personal to LICENSEE.

IN WITNESS WHEREOF this agreement has been duly executed by SOCIETY and LICENSEE, this   day of   ,19

AMERICAN SOCIETY OF COMPOSERS,
AUTHORS AND PUBLISHERS

By ....

....
LICENSEE

American Society of Composers,
   Authors and Publishers
575 Madison Avenue
New York, New York 10022

Gentlemen:

   This refers to the Background Music Service agreement entered into simultaneously herewith.

   With respect to Paragraph "4" of said agreement, it is understood that in the event we decide in the future to furnish a music service with commercial announcements, you shall offer, upon application by us to you, the then current form of license agreement offered to others similarly situated who furnish such a music service. If that form of agreement is acceptable to us, you and we agree to execute it promptly effective from the date we begin furnishing a music service with commercial announcements to any Subscriber. If that form of agreement is not acceptable to us, we shall promptly advise you of that fact and it is understood that our application to you shall be treated as an application under the Consent Decree in *United States of America v. American Society of Composers, Authors and Publishers,* and if we are unable to agree on reasonable rates as provided in that Consent Decree, we may apply thereunder to have the Court determine a reasonable fee for such a music service.

   If, notwithstanding the provisions of Paragraph "4" of said agreement, any Subscriber shall insert commercial announcements in conjunction with our Background Music Service, such insertion shall not be deemed to be a breach of said agreement provided that we shall pay to you for each such Subscriber the sum of three dollars ($3.00) per month per floor for each month during which any such insertion shall be made, in lieu of all other fees payable under said agreement.

   Nothing contained herein, or in Paragraph "4" of said agreement, shall be construed to deprive the Subscribers of LICENSEE of the right to insert public address announcements concerning goods or services sold or offered to the public at the premises of such Subscribers, where no compensation (in money or any other form) is paid to anyone, directly or indirectly, for such announcements. The fees provided in said agreement, rather than those provided in the preceeding paragraph, shall apply to the premises of Subscribers who insert such public address announcements.

   Your signature in the space provided below shall constitute this a valid and enforceable agreement modifying as herein provided the terms and conditions of the said Background Music Service agreement.

Very truly yours,

ACCEPTED AND AGREED TO:

AMERICAN SOCIETY OF COMPOSERS,
   AUTHORS AND PUBLISHERS

By _____

Appendix 26

BMI BACKGROUND MUSIC SERVICE LICENSE AGREEMENT

BMI

AGREEMENT, made at New York, N.Y. on .... between BROADCAST MUSIC, INC. (BMI), a corporation organized under the laws of the State of New York, with principal offices at 320 West 57th Street, New York, N.Y. 10019, and

....
(Legal Name of Licensee)

doing business as ....
(Trade Name)

....

Please check appropriate box and complete
☐ A corporation organized under the laws of ....
☐ A partnership composed of ....
☐ An individual residing at ....

(hereinafter called LICENSEE) with offices located at ....

City of .... State of .... Zip ....

WITNESSETH:

WHEREAS, BMI is engaged in licensing music for public performance and,

WHEREAS, LICENSEE is engaged in the business of operating a background music or storecast music service (hereinafter "music service") which leases, either directly or through sub-distributors, a musical program service primarily to individual places of entertainment, resort, residence, business, industry and others which are not under LICENSEE'S direct or indirect ownership or control (each of which is hereinafter individually called a "serviced premises"),

IT IS HEREBY AGREED AS FOLLOWS:

1. The initial term of this agreement shall be the period beginning on .... and ending on December 31, 1985 and shall continue thereafter for additional terms of one (1) year each, unless cancelled by either party as of December 31, 1985 or at the end of any subsequent one-year period upon not less than sixty (60) days' advance notice by ordinary first-class U.S. mail.

2. (a) "Background music" as used herein shall mean and be limited to non-dramatic performances of recorded music, whether vocal or instrumental, and regardless of the means employed by LICENSEE to provide such music to a serviced premises. It is understood that such "background music" is intended to be used as an accompaniment to routine activities, including, but not limited to, work, shopping, conversation, dining and relaxation, as long as such music is not intended to accompany dancing or to serve as an adjunct to any other physical activity or form of entertainment.

(b) "Serviced Premises" as used herein shall mean a single hotel, restaurant, bar, grill, tavern, factory, office, bank, store, professional office, residence, educational or other like and unlike premises, but shall not under any circumstances extend to (i) any ballroom, discotheque, dance studio or skating rink; or (ii) any premises to which an admission fee is charged, but only with respect to the portion of the premises from which the event or entertainment for which admission is charged is intended to be observed or heard; provided, however, that any individual restaurant, store, or other portion of such premises where no separate admission fee is charged shall be covered by this license.

(c) "Industrial Serviced Premises" as used herein shall mean and be limited to offices, factories, plants, banks, thrift institutions, businesses and other like premises. In determining whether a like premises is an "Industrial Serviced Premises," the test shall be that the music service is primarily confined to the personnel employed on the serviced premises, or in retail establishments that the music service is primarily confined to personnel areas during the hours when the store is open to the public or furnished through the store premises during such times when the store is not open to the public.

(d) "Non-Industrial Serviced Premises," as used herein shall mean all premises which are not "Industrial Serviced Premises" as defined in Subparagraph 1(c).

(e) "Shopping Center" as used herein is one constructed and operated as a coordinated group of stores, with music service to more than one premises within the center. This definition shall not be deemed to exclude a coordinated group of stores that may incidentally contain one or more offices.

(f) "Sub-distributors" as used herein shall mean only those persons, firms or corporations authorized by LICENSEE to furnish its music service.

(g) "Storecast Music" as used herein shall mean and be limited to non-dramatic performances of recorded music interspersed with advertising announcements for which consideration is received from the advertisers for the

PLEASE COMPLETE WHITE AREAS ONLY

placing of the advertisement and serving as an accompaniment to shopping in a retail store where merchandise is sold or services rendered to the public and audible solely to persons physically on the serviced premises and, by means of loud-speakers, in the immediate vicinity of such serviced premises. It is understood that if no consideration is received from the advertiser for the placing of advertisements, the providing of a music service which includes commercial announce-ments shall be considered a background music service.

3. This license shall be deemed to embrace:

☐ LICENSEE'S owned music service operations only;

Please check appropriate box

☐ LICENSEE'S owned music service operations as well as those of *all* of its sub-distributors and accordingly LICENSEE hereby assumes all obligations under this agreement of those sub-distributors;

☐ LICENSEE's owned music service operations as well as those of *some* of its sub-distributors and accordingly LICENSEE hereby assumes all obligations under this agreement of those sub-distributors.

4. BMI hereby grants to LICENSEE a non-exclusive license to perform publicly and to cause or permit the public performance by background music or storecast music on one or more serviced premises of all musical works, the right to grant public performances of which BMI shall during the term hereof control. LICENSEE's performances shall be audible only within and immediately adjacent to the serviced premises supplied by LICENSEE. In no event shall this license extend to any other type of performances whatsoever or to any cable television system (other than as a means to provide a background music or storecast music service to LICENSEE's serviced premises) or to transmission by any radio or tele-vision station to a place other than on LICENSEE's serviced premises.

5. LICENSEE agrees to pay to BMI for the license granted herein the fees stated on the license fee schedule below for the applicable contract year of this agreement; provided, however, that the payment to BMI for all serviced premises to which music service (other than storecast music) is furnished shall not be less than twenty (20) times the applicable annual minimum fee for the relevant year.

LICENSE FEE SCHEDULE

CONTRACT YEAR	TYPE OF SERVICED PREMISES	ANNUAL FEE PER SERVICED PREMISES	ANNUAL MINIMUM FEE PER SERVICED PREMISES**
1982	INDUSTRIAL	One percent (1%) of the gross amount charged or billed* to each premises	$7.50
	NON-INDUSTRIAL	One-and-one-half percent (1.5%) of the gross amount charged or billed* to each premises	$7.50
	SHOPPING CENTERS	One-and-one-half percent (1.5%) of the gross amount charged or billed* to each premises	$7.50 for the first premises; $4.50 for each additional premises
	SERVICED PREMISES OF ANY TYPE USING STORECAST MUSIC	$7.50 per floor supplied, plus $.90 per loudspeaker installed for outside audibility	NONE
1983	INDUSTRIAL	One percent (1%) of the gross amount charged or billed* to each premises	$8.75
	NON-INDUSTRIAL	One-and-one-half percent (1.5%) of the gross amount charged or billed* to each premises	$8.75
	SHOPPING CENTERS	One-and-one-half percent (1.5%) of the gross amount charged or billed* to each premises	$8.75 for the first premises; $5.25 for each additional premises
	SERVICED PREMISES OF ANY TYPE USING STORECAST MUSIC	$8.75 per floor supplied, plus $1.05 per loudspeaker installed for outside audibility	NONE
1984, 1985 and all subsequent calendar years	INDUSTRIAL	One percent (1%) of the gross amount charged or billed* to each premises	$10.00
	NON-INDUSTRIAL	One-and-one-half percent (1.5%) of the gross amount charged or billed* to each premises	$10.00
	SHOPPING CENTERS	One-and-one-half percent (1.5%) of the gross amount charged or billed* to each premises	$10.00 for the first premises; $6.00 for each additional premises
	SERVICED PREMISES OF ANY TYPE USING STORECAST MUSIC	$10.00 per floor supplied, plus $1.20 per loudspeaker installed for outside audibility	NONE

*See definition in Paragraph 9

**Not applicable to small profes-sional offices, residences, hospitals, or government offices

6. (a) The fees due BMI under this agreement shall be payable quarterly, no later than the twenty-fifth (25th) day of January, April, July and October of each year of the term hereof. Each such quarterly payment shall represent one-

fourth (1/4th) of LICENSEE's total annual fees, but if the first calendar year of the initial term of this agreement is less than a full calendar year, LICENSEE should pro-rate the payment due hereunder for the initial partial quarter of such calendar year.

(b) LICENSEE and BMI acknowledge that because fees are payable in advance they must be estimated. The estimated payment for a quarter shall be the amount actually found to be due to BMI for the preceding quarter adjusted to reflect the difference between the estimated fees paid for such preceding quarter and the actual fees due for such preceding quarter. Estimated advanced payments and adjustments of previous estimates shall be calculated on quarterly report forms which shall be provided by BMI to LICENSEE for such purpose.

7. LICENSEE may make deductions for bad accounts, provided LICENSEE, at the time of taking such deductions, shall furnish BMI with specific information as to each deduction, but in no event shall LICENSEE make such deductions until the accounts have been charged off on the books of LICENSEE as bad debts.

8. (a) LICENSEE agrees to furnish BMI with a complete list of all its serviced premises no later than simultaneously with the first quarterly report provided for by Paragraph 6 hereof. Said list shall indicate in respect to each serviced premises of LICENSEE, the name and location by city and state (with a separate listing for each serviced premises which constitutes part of a master account) of said serviced premises, and (unless all of said serviced premises are supplied only with storecast music) whether the serviced premises is classified as an "Industrial Serviced Premises," "Non-Industrial Serviced Premises," or a serviced premises in a shopping center, and the amount payable under this agreement for each listed serviced premises. Once the initial list of its serviced premises has been furnished by LICENSEE to BMI, LICENSEE, at least once in each subsequent year of this agreement within ten (10) days of BMI's request therefor, shall set forth changes in the initial list of serviced premises by specifically listing (in the same manner as the initial list) each additional serviced premises and each serviced premises which has terminated background music or storecast music service during the previous year and the date of termination of such service. In the event that it is reasonably necessary for BMI to obtain the date of commencement of service for a particular listed additional serviced premises in order to properly determine retroactive payments which may be due BMI by such premises for a period prior to the commencement of service by LICENSEE thereto, LICENSEE agrees to provide such date to BMI, within ten (10) days of BMI's written request therefor.

(b) If LICENSEE operates its music service through sub-distributors as defined herein, LICENSEE shall supply BMI, simultaneously with LICENSEE's first quarterly report under Paragraph 6, with a list by name and address of each such sub-distributor, with subsequent additions and deletions thereto at least once in each year of this agreement within ten (10) days of BMI's request therefor, and shall state whether such sub-distributor is one for whom LICENSEE is assuming the obligations contained in this agreement or whether it is one for whom LICENSEE is not assuming such obligations.

9. The phrase "gross amount charged or billed" to each serviced premises as used herein shall be deemed to mean all direct and indirect payments (whether in money or any other form) made by a serviced premises to LICENSEE or to any other person, firm or corporation in connection with LICENSEE's supplying of a background music or storecast music service. In making payments, LICENSEE may exclude only the following (it being understood that such exclusions will not affect the minimum fees payable to BMI hereunder):

(a) bad debts as provided in Paragraph 7 hereof;

(b) the actual sale price of any equipment sold to a serviced premises;

(c) monies received for the lease of communications equipment which is extraneous to the supplying of background music or storecast music service (except that if any cable television system or microwave multi-point distribution system is used as a means of distributing background music or storecast music to LICENSEE's serviced premises, the converter or other technology facilitating such distribution shall not be deductible), but for any such deduction LICENSEE shall supply BMI, simultaneously with its report for the quarter in which such deduction is taken, the name and address of each such lessee;

(d) the amount of any sales, use or excise tax collected from a serviced premises and remitted by LICENSEE to any Federal, State or local taxing authority;

(e) the fees paid to BMI pursuant to this agreement;

(f) any billing for service and maintenance of equipment owned by or leased to a serviced premises, provided that under no circumstances, in the case of leased equipment, shall that portion of a monthly fee charged to a serviced premises for music service be less than $40; and further provided that the amount charged for music service and the amount charged for service and maintenance must be clearly stated on the face of any agreement with a serviced premises and a copy of the page of such agreement setting forth such separate charges shall be provided to BMI by LICENSEE simultaneously with its report for the quarter in which such deduction is first taken;

(g) all one-time charges for service and maintenance work actually performed on equipment, so long as such charges are billed not later than ninety (90) days following completion of the work;

(h) any penalties for late payment or finance or interest charges imposed upon a serviced premises by LICENSEE.

10. BMI shall have the right by its authorized representatives, at any time during customary business hours and upon reasonable advance written notice, to examine the books and records of account of LICENSEE to such extent as may be necessary to verify any and all statements rendered and accountings made hereunder. BMI shall consider all data and information coming to its attention as a result of any such examinations contained in any statements as completely confidential. Nothing in this Paragraph shall be construed as granting BMI the right to make copies of LICENSEE's books and records and the names and addresses of the serviced premises of LICENSEE, unless LICENSEE specifically grants BMI the right to do so upon BMI's request therefor.

11. BMI agrees to indemnify, save harmless and defend LICENSEE, its officers and employees and the proprietors of the serviced premises supplied by it hereunder, from and against any and all claims, demands or suits (and liabilities, expenses and costs associated therewith, including without limitation, except to the extent BMI elects to control the matter and supplies counsel of its own choosing, the reasonable fees of counsel of the indemnified party's choosing) that may be made or brought against them, or any of them, with respect to the performance of any material licensed under this agreement. Such indemnity shall be limited to all works which are licensed by BMI at the time of performance on the serviced premises. Such indemnity shall not apply to works performed at the serviced premises of LICENSEE after written request by BMI that they refrain from such performances. BMI's Clearance Department will, upon request, advise LICENSEE whether particular musical works are available for performance as part of BMI's repertory. LICENSEE agrees to give BMI immediate notice of any such claim, demand or suit, either against it or against any serviced premises supplied by it, to deliver to BMI any papers pertaining thereto, and to cooperate and to cause the serviced premises to cooperate with respect thereto, and BMI shall have full charge of the defense of any claim, demand or suit. LICENSEE, however, shall have the right to engage counsel, at its own expense, who may participate in the defense of any such action or proceeding and with whom counsel for BMI shall cooperate.

12. In the event that LICENSEE maintains, transmits or furnishes to any serviced premises during any period of the term, any record, log or other tabulation or musical compositions, LICENSEE agrees to furnish BMI with a copy thereof on a quarterly basis.

13. In the event that BMI, at any time during the contract term, shall issue licenses on a formula or other basis more favorable to similar background music or storecast music licensees than are contained herein, such more favorable license agreements shall be tendered to LICENSEE.

14. It is agreed that LICENSEE may assign this agreement to any subsidiary, affiliated or associated company of LICENSEE or in connection with any sale, merger, reorganization or consolidation in which LICENSEE is a party.

15. Any notice required or permitted to be given under this agreement shall be in writing and shall be deemed duly given when sent by ordinary first-class U.S. mail to the party for whom it is intended, at its address hereinabove stated, or any other address which either party hereto may from time to time designate for such purpose, and when any such notice is so mailed, it shall be deemed to have been given upon the fifth calendar day following the day of mailing thereof.

16. (a) All disputes of any kind, nature or description arising in connection with the terms and conditions of this agreement shall be submitted to arbitration in the City, County, and State of New York under the then prevailing rules of the American Arbitration Association by an arbitrator or arbitrators to be selected as follows: Each of the parties shall, by written notice to the other, have the right to appoint one arbitrator. If, within ten (10) days following the giving of such notice by one party, the other shall not, by written notice, appoint another arbitrator, the first arbitrator shall be the sole arbitrator. If two arbitrators are so appointed, they shall appoint a third arbitrator. If ten (10) days elapse after the appointment of the second arbitrator and the two arbitrators are unable to agree upon the third arbitrator, then either party may, in writing, request the American Arbitration Association to appoint the third arbitrator. The award made in the arbitration shall be binding and conclusive on the parties and judgment may be, but need not be, entered in any court having jurisdiction. Such award shall include the fixing of the costs, expenses, and attorney's fees of arbitration, which shall be borne by the unsuccessful party.

(b) If LICENSEE elects to waive the terms set forth in 16(a) above, LICENSEE must cross out 16 (a) and initial the box to the left.

17. Upon any breach or default of any of the terms or conditions herein contained, BMI may, at its sole option, and in addition to any and all other remedies which it may have, cancel this license if such breach or default is continuing thirty (30) days after LICENSEE's receipt of written notice thereof. No waiver by BMI of full performance of this license by LICENSEE in any one or more instances shall be deemed a waiver of the right to require full and complete performance of this agreement thereafter or of the right to cancel this agreement.

18. This agreement constitutes the entire understanding between the parties with respect to the subject matter hereof. This agreement cannot be waived or added to or modified orally and no waiver, addition, or modification shall be valid unless in writing and signed by the parties. This agreement, its validity, construction and effect shall be governed by the laws of the State of New York.

IN WITNESS WHEREOF, this agreement has been executed in duplicate originals by the duly authorized representatives of BMI and LICENSEE all as of the date first above written.

BROADCAST MUSIC, INC.

....
LICENSEE (Legal Name)

By: ....
(Signature)

By: ....
(Signature)

....
(Print Name of Signer)

....
(Print Name of Signer)

....
(Title of Signer)

....
(Title of Signer)

Appendix 27

FORM OF TELEVISION FILM SYNCHRONIZATION LICENSE

TV License No.:   Date:
Composition:

To Licensee:

1. In consideration of the sum of _____payable upon the execution hereof, we grant you the non-exclusive right to record on film or video tape the above identified musical composition(s) in synchronization or timed relation with a single episode or individual program entitled _____ for television use only, subject to all of the terms and conditions herein provided.

2. (a) The type of use is to be _____

(b) On or before the first telecast of the said film, you or your assigns agree to furnish to us a copy of the cue sheet prepared and distributed in connection therewith.

3. The territory covered by this license is the world.

4. (a) This license is for a period of _____from the date hereof.

(b) Upon the expiration of this license all rights herein granted shall cease and terminate and the right to make or authorize any further use or distribution of any recordings made hereunder shall also cease and terminate.

5. This is a license to record only and does not authorize any use of the aforesaid musical composition(s) not expressly set forth herein. By way of illustration but not limitation, this license does not include the right to change or adapt the words or to alter the fundamental character of the music of said musical composition(s) or to use the title(s) thereof as the title or sub-title of said film.

6. Performance of the said musical composition(s) in the exhibition of said film is subject to the condition that each television station over which the aforesaid musical composition(s) is (are) to be so performed shall have a performance license issued by us or from a person, firm, corporation, society, association or other entity having the legal right to issue such performance license.

7. No sound records produced pursuant to this license are to be manufactured, sold and/or used separately or independently of said film.

8. The film shall be for television use only but may not be televised into theatres or other places where admission is charged.

9. All rights not herein specifically granted are reserved by us.

10. We warrant only that we have the legal right to grant this license and this license is given and accepted without other warranty or recourse. If said warranty shall be breached in whole or in part with respect to (any of) said musical composition(s), our total liability shall be limited either to repaying to you the consideration theretofore paid under this license with respect to such musical composition to the extent of such breach or to holding you harmless to the extent of the consideration theretofore paid under this license with respect to such musical composition to the extent of said breach.

11. This license shall run to you, your successors and assigns, provided you shall remain liable for the performance of all of the terms and conditions of this license on your part to be performed and provided further that any disposition of said film or any prints thereof shall be subject to all the terms hereof, and you agree that all persons, firms or corporations acquiring from you any right, title, interest in or possession of said film or any prints thereof shall be notified of the terms and conditions of this license and shall agree to be bound thereby.

MUSIC PUBLISHER

By _____

Appendix 28

FORM OF SOUNDTRACK LIBRARY SYNCHRONIZATION LICENSE

Library, Inc. hereby grants to the undersigned Licensee as the authorized representative of the producer, or as the producer, of the production entitled _____(the music cue sheet of which Licensee agrees to furnish to Library, Inc.) the non-exclusive irrevocable right, license, privilege and authority to use the recordings listed below for the sole, limited and restricted purpose of including said recordings and mechanically reproducing the same in connection with the said production as an integral part thereof and the exhibition or broadcast of said production as a (television) (theatrical) (industrial) film in the following territory only:

| | | PUBLISHER |
NUMBER TITLE	COMPOSER	(PERFORMANCE RIGHTS)
_____	_____	_____
_____	_____	_____
_____	_____	_____
_____	_____	_____

This is a license to record only and the public performance for profit of the said production is subject to the rights, if any, of the various composers or performing rights societies or other owners of the performing rights in the music to collect performing fees therefor. Library, Inc. represents and warrants only that it is the sole owner or authorized agent of the owner of the recordings covered by this license and agrees to repay the consideration paid for this license if said warranty shall be breached. Licensee agrees that this license is granted without any other warranty or recourse.

(LICENSEE)   LIBRARY, INC.

BY _____   By _____

Appendix 29

MINIMUM COMPENSATION AND PUBLICATION ROYALTY PROVISIONS IN PRODUCERS-COMPOSER AND LYRICISTS GUILD OF AMERICA MINIMUM BASIC AGREEMENT OF 1967
(Expired October 31, 1971)

ARTICLE 20 MINIMUM COMPENSATION

(a) Definition of a qualified composer and song writer:

(1) A qualified composer of underscoring is a composer who has screen credit for one feature length picture, three one-half (½) hour or one one-hour (1) or more in length television motion picture, or 52 weeks of employment in the motion picture industry, as a composer of underscoring.

(2) A qualified song composer is a composer who has two published songs or who composed two separate songs each of which is completely contained in a motion picture produced and released in the American motion picture industry or who has had 52 weeks of employment in the American motion picture industry as a composer of either or both song music or song lyrics.

(b) Wage Scale Minimum Compensation:

(1) There are no minimum compensation requirements with respect to unqualified composers.

(2) The minimum compensation per week for a qualified composer for composition only, shall be:

	Television Motion Pictures	*Theatrical Motion Pictures*
Term contract:	$357.50	$393.25
Week to week:	$385.00	$423.50

The above salary shall commence and apply when an assignment is made under the Producer's direction and control. The above television weekly rate shall apply in term or week-to-week employment in any week in which no work hereunder is performed in a theatrical motion picture; in any week in which such work is performed in both theatrical and television motion pictures the theatrical motion picture rate will apply for that week. For these purposes, a term contract is a personal service contract for a term of at least ten out of thirteen weeks or any like ratio for a longer period. A week-to-week contract is a personal service contract for a term of less than ten out of thirteen weeks. A composer employed on a weekly basis, may be terminated at any time after one week.

If any composer under a week-to-week or term contract shall render services after the expiration of the period for which his specified compensation is provided in the employment contract and no additional amount is specified for such additional period, then in such event the composer shall receive the weekly rate specified in such contract for each week, or, for purpose only of prorating days worked in a partial workweek (of less than six (6) days), one-fifth (1/5) for each such a day worked during which the composer shall render such additional services. In any week of employment when the Producer may under this agreement employ the composer for less than one full week (i.e. after one week or after the term of the agreement), if the composer shall render services in composition and also other services not covered by this agreement his minimum compensation for composition shall be prorated in proportion to the amount of time required by Producer for composition.

(3) In the alternative, when the employment for composition, excluding songs, is for television films only, and it is non-exclusive employment, the minimum compensation shall be:

a) Not less than $192.50 for a half-hour show.
b) Not less than $385 for a one-hour show.
c) Not less than $550 for a one and one-half hour show.
d) Five minutes or less of new music, not less than $100.

The above rates of $192.50 for a half-hour show, $385 for an hour show, and $550 for a one and one-half hour show shall be applicable where more than five minutes of new music is composed for a program.

Where more than five minutes of new music is composed and more than one composer is employed, the combined payments to such composers shall be not less than $200 for a half-hour show or $385 for an hour show. In no event shall a composer who composes five minutes or less of new music, under such circumstances, be paid less than $100 if he composed "a five minute or less fragment."

(4) The minimum compensation for employment for the composition of songs shall be governed by the theatrical rate provisions of (b) (2) of this article only.

(5) Any amounts paid to the composer in excess of the minimum compensation, as provided above, may be applied to any other payments (except royalties provided for by Article 21) required under this agreement.

(6) Theatrical Exhibition of Television Films:

In the event a television motion picture or pictures containing music composed on or after the effective date of this agreement, under the provisions of Article 20 (b) (3) above, is exhibited theatrically (as one or in combination) Producer shall pay to the composer or composers of such music, so used, in such exhibition, the following applicable single amount for an unlimited number of such exhibitions:

The amount, if any, that (i) $385 exceeds the compensation paid such composer or composers for a half hour show so used; or (ii) $770 exceeds the compensation paid such composer or composers employed for a one hour show so used; or (iii) $1,100 exceeds the compensation paid such composer or composers employed for a one and one-half hour show so used; or (iv) $40 exceeds the compensation paid such composer or composers employed for each minute for a five-minute or less fragment so used. . . .

ARTICLE 21 PUBLICATION ROYALTIES

Should the Producer, or any subsidiary or affiliated company, or any assignee or licensee of Producer, exploit the music or musical composition (hereinafter referred to as the "composition") then the Producer, or such subsidiary or affiliated company, or such assignee or licensee, shall pay directly to the composer an amount of royalty with respect to such composition not less than the following, and Producer's contract with such subsidiary or affiliated company, or assignee or licensee, shall so require and if Producer's contract does so provide then Producer shall not be responsible for payment of the royalties hereunder:

(a) Five cents (5¢) per copy in respect of regular piano copies sold and paid for in the United States and Canada.

(b) Fifty percent (50%) of all net sums received by the publisher in respect of regular piano copies, orchestrations, band arrangements, octavos, quartets, arrangements for combinations of voices and/or instruments, and/or other copies of the composition sold in any country other than the United States and Canada; provided, however, that if the publisher should sell such copies through, or cause them to be sold by, a subsidiary or affiliate or any assignee or licensee which is actually doing business in a foreign country, then in respect of such sales, the publisher shall pay to the composer not less than ten percent (10%) of the wholesale selling price in respect of each such copy sold and paid for.

(c) Ten percent (10%) of the wholesale selling price (after trade discounts if any) of each copy sold and paid for in the United States and Canada, or for export from the United States, of orchestrations, band arrangements, octavos, quartets, arrangements for combinations of voices and/or instruments, and/or other copies of the composition (other than regular piano copies).

(d) (i) If the composition, or any part thereof, is included in any song book, song sheet, folio or similar publication issued by the publisher containing at least four (4), but not more than twenty-five (25) musical compositions, the royalty to be paid by the publisher to the composer shall be an amount determined by dividing ten percent (10%) of the wholesale selling price (after trade discounts, if any) of the copies sold, among the total number of copyrighted musical compositions included in such publication. If such publication contains more than twenty-five (25) musical compositions, said ten percent (10%) shall be increased by an additional one-half percent (½) for each additional musical composition.

(ii) If, pursuant to a license granted by the publisher to a licensee not controlled by or affiliated with it, the composition, or any part thereof, is included in any song book, song sheet, folio or similar publication, containing at least four (4) musical compositions, the royalty to be paid by the publisher to the composer shall be that proportion of fifty percent (50%) of the gross amount received by it from the licensee, as the number of uses of the composition under the license and during the license period, bears to the total number of uses of the publisher's copyrighted musical compositions under the license and during the license period. Such royalties shall be computed and paid within thirty (30) days after the expiration of the term of each license, but if any such license term is in excess of one year, such royalties shall be computed and paid annually.

(iii) In computing the number of the publisher's copyrighted musical compositions under subdivision (ii) hereof, there shall be excluded musical compositions in the public domain and arrangements of musical compositions in the public domain if no royalties are payable with respect to such arrangements by the publisher.

(iv) Royalties on publications containing less than four (4) musical compositions shall be payable at regular piano copy rates.

(e) As to "professional material" not sold or resold, no royalty shall be payable.

(f) Fifty percent (50%) of all net sums actually received by the publisher in respect of any licenses (including statutory royalties) authorizing the manufacture of parts of instruments serving to mechanically reproduce the composition; or to use the composition in synchronization with sound motion pictures produced by anyone other than: (i) the Producer, its subsidiary, and affiliated companies; (ii) any company using the composition in a motion picture financed substantially by or to be distributed by the Producer; and (iii) the producer for whom the composition was originally composed, and its subsidiary and affiliated companies; or to reproduce it upon electrical transcription for broadcasting purposes; except that the composer (s) shall not be entitled to any share of the monies distributed to the publisher by any performing rights society anywhere in the world, or other source, which makes a distribution to composers either directly or through another performing rights society or other person, company, society, association or organization.

(g) If the publisher administers licenses authorizing the manufacture of parts of instruments serving to mechanically reproduce said composition, or the use of said composition in synchronization or in timed relation with sound motion pictures produced by anyone other than: (i) the Producer, its subsidiary, and affiliated companies; (ii) any company using the composition in a motion picture financed substantially by or to be distributed by the Producer; and (iii) the producer for whom the composition was originally composed, and its subsidiary and affiliated companies; or its reproduction upon electrical transcriptions, or any of them, through an agent, trustee or other administrator acting for a substantial part of the industry and not under the exclusive control of the publisher (hereinafter sometimes referred to as licensing agent), the publisher in determining his receipts, shall be entitled to deduct from gross license fees paid by the licensees, a sum equal to the charges paid by the publisher to said licensing agent.

(h) "Publisher" as used in this Article 21 shall mean the original Publisher.

The foregoing rates shall apply only in cases in which all of the music and lyrics of the composition have been composed by one composer, or in cases in which a musical composition has been composed for which no lyrics have been written.

As to songs, if one person composes the music and another the lyrics, the foregoing rates shall apply, but one-half shall be allocated to the composer of the music and one-half to the author of the lyrics (no allowance being made for the title). If there shall be more than one composer or more than one lyricist, then they shall agree between themselves upon the division of their half of the above royalties, but in the absence of such agreement, their half shall be divided equally between them.

The royalties hereinabove provided for shall be payable only in connection with compositions originally created by the composer, it being agreed that no royalties shall be payable with reference to arrangements, orchestrations, translations or other adaptations or modifications of compositions written by others.

No royalties shall be payable for any uses made by the Producer or by the independent producer for whom the composition was originally composed (or by its or their associated, affiliated, parent or subsidiary corporations or by any persons, firms or other corporations with whom or with which any of said corporations may have contracts or arrangements for the production, performance, television, exhibition or distribution of motion pictures) in motion pictures (theatrical or television) or in connection with any advertising, publicising or exploitation thereof. Nothing in this agreement shall be construed to obligate the Producer or its licensees or assigns to publish, record, reproduce or otherwise exploit any music or musical composition.

Appendix 30

FORM OF A NECAA ARTIST/AGENCY REPORT

Check appropriate category:

☐ Contemporary Music   ☐ Performing Arts: Music   ☐ Theatre
☐ Coffeehouse   ☐ Performing Arts: Dance   ☐ Novelty/Variety
☐ Country Music   ☐ Performing Arts: Mime

Artist: _____ Agency: _____ Agent: _____

Performance Date: _____ Reporting Date: _____ Date Contract Signed by School: _____

School: _____ City: _____ State: _____

Person Filling Out Report: _____ Position: _____

For questions 1—8 place an X in the appropriate box.
Complete additional questions on back.

1. Artist's Cooperation and Attitude

5 Excellent Fulfilled all items of contract; complete cooperation with school; excellent attitude on and off stage

4 Good Fulfilled all items of contract; cooperated with school; good attitude on and off stage

3 Average Fulfilled terms of contract; made no effort beyond these to ensure a good performance or create a good working relationship with the school.

2 Fair Minor violations of contract terms; uncooperative; poor attitude on and off stage.

1 Poor Major violations of contract terms; completely uncooperative; extremely hard to work with because of very negative attitude.

2. Artist's Professionalism

5 Excellent Excellent showmanship, extremely smooth performance; very professional conduct; excellent variety; excellent stage presence; able to handle technical difficulties very well.

[4] Good Good showmanship; smooth performance; professional

5. Information Regarding Artist's Arrival

5 Excellent School notified of artist's expected time of arrival, and transportation and accommodation arrangements in advance; school contacted upon artist's arrival in town.

4 Good School notified of artist's expected time of arrival, and transportation and accommodation arrangements in advance; school not contacted upon artist's arrival in town.

3 Average School given no advance information regarding artist's arrival; school contacted upon artist's arrival in town.

2 Fair School given no advance information regarding artist's arrival; school contacted immediately prior to performance.

1 Poor School given no advance information regarding artist's arrival; school not contacted before artist's arrival at performance site.

6. Cooperation of Artist's Representative

5 Excellent Extremely cooperative; very professional attitude and conduct; excellent communication with school, regarding technical requirements; excellent job of communicating information from school to artist and from artist to school by representative; made very useful suggestions to ensure a successful engagement.

4 Good Very cooperative; good professional attitude and conduct; good communication with school regarding technical requirements; good job of communicating information from school to artist and from artist to school by representative; made useful ceptable conduct; average variety; average stage presence; unable to handle technical difficulties acceptably.

[2] Fair Poor showmanship; breaks in smoothness of performance; unprofessional conduct; fair variety; fair stage presence; unable to handle technical difficulties.

[1] Poor Complete lack of showmanship; numerous breaks in smoothness of performance; very unprofessional conduct; lack of variety; lack of stage presence; unable to handle technical difficulties.

3. Artist's Musical Accomplishment

[5] Excellent Excellent musical ability; powerful presentation; excellent musical coordination with back-up; complete familiarity with repertoire; excellent musical blending of repertoire numbers; extremely flexible in adapting to audience mood.

[4] Good Good musical ability; good coordination with back-up; familiar with repertoire; good musical blending of repertoire numbers; adapts to audience mood.

[3] Average Musically correct; coordinated with back-up; familiar with repertoire; good musical blending of repertoire numbers; adapts to audience mood.

[2] Fair Noticeable musical flaws; weak presentation; fair coordination with back-up; unfamiliar with sequence of numbers and with some individual numbers.

[1] Poor Numerous and extreme musical flaws; very weak presentation; extremely poor coordination with back-up; very unfamiliar with sequence of numbers and individual numbers.

[n/a] Not Applicable Performance did not include live music.

4. Audience Reaction

[5] Excellent Extremely enthusiastic; excellent rapport throughout entire performance.

[4] Good Good enthusiasm; good rapport throughout performance.

[3] Average Moderate enthusiasm; moderate rapport at several points during performance.

[2] Fair Very little enthusiasm; very weak rapport during performance.

[1] Poor No enthusiasm; complete lack of rapport during performance.

school; average job of communicating information from school to artist and from artist to school by representative.

[2] Fair Uncooperative; unprofessional attitude and conduct; inadequate communication regarding technical requirements with school; fair job of communicating information from school to artist and from artist to school by representative.

[1] Poor Extremely uncooperative; very unprofessional attitude and conduct; no communication regarding arrival times and technical requirements.

7. Cooperation of Artist's Personal Manager and Artist's Road Personnel

[5] Excellent Extremely cooperative; very professional attitude and conduct; excellent communication with school; works extremely well with local personnel.

[4] Good Very cooperative; good professional attitude and conduct; good communication with school; works well with local personnel.

[3] Average Cooperative; professional attitude and conduct; adequate communication with school; works well with local personnel.

[2] Fair Uncooperative; unprofessional attitude and conduct; inadequate communication with school; experienced some difficulty in working with local personnel.

[1] Poor Extremely uncooperative; very unprofessional attitude and conduct; extremely poor communication with school; could not work with local personnel.

[n/a] Not Applicable.

8. Publicity Materials Supplied

[5] Excellent Excellent quality; more than sufficient quantity; extremely effective.

[4] Good Good quality; sufficient quantity; effective.

[3] Average Good quality; adequate quantity; effective.

[2] Fair Adequate quality; inadequate quantity; minimally effective.

[1] Poor Poor quality; insufficient quantity; ineffective.

9. Rider accepted by artist? Yes _____ No _____ If no why? _____

10. Were there any requirements or requests made by the artist which, in your opinion some buyers would find difficult to supply? Yes _____ No _____

If yes what were they? _____

11. Were there any problems in starting the show on time due to either the performer or the school? Yes _____ No _____ If yes, explain _____

12. Approximate attendance _____ Facility Capacity _____ Ticket Price(s) _____ Did actual attendance meet your expectations?

Yes _____ No _____ . If no, what do you see as the problem? _____

13. Was the actual length of performance that which you contracted for? Yes _____ No _____ If no, why? _____

14. Was the act willing to do extra activities? Master classes _____ Teasers _____ Press Conference _____ Lecture/demonstrations _____

15. If rehearsal required, did act show up? Yes _____ No _____ Was act on time for rehearsal? Yes _____ No _____

16. Were there any security problems which might be attributed to the act? Yes _____ No _____ If yes, explain _____

17. Contractual fee $ _____ Percentage (if applicable) _____ Were there any special considerations which affected the price? _____

18. Payment by: Check _____ Cash _____ Were there any objections to the manner of payment? Yes _____ No _____

19. If deduction made from artist's payment, how much and for what reason? _____

20. Additional comments regarding the engagement (Lengthy comments will be edited for publication.) _____

_____

_____

Complete this form after each event and return to NECAA National Office as soon as possible.

Send more forms

SAMPLE SOUNDTRACK LIBRARY RATE CARD

XYZ PRODUCTION MUSIC
Schedule of Rates for Music Licensing

TELEVISION PRODUCTIONS,
INDUSTRIAL, RELIGIOUS, EDUCATIONAL, AND OTHER
NONTHEATRICAL FILMS

A. Basic rate is $60 per track (i.e., per needle down) of music used or portion thereof and a maximum payment for any one film as follows:

Maximum Per Film	Playing Time
$190.00	10 minutes or less
220.00	15 minutes
325.00	20 minutes
425.00	30 minutes
475.00	45 minutes
700.00	60 minutes

Note: The rates given above cover television or nontheatrical licensing, but not both. To obtain both television and nontheatrical clearance, an additional sum equal to one-third of the original payment shall be due.

B. Rates for Theatrical Productions, Subscription TV and Audio/Visual Cassettes available upon request.

C. Transcribed Radio Programs: $60 per track or portion thereof used.

D. Sound Disks for Slide Films: $40 per track, or portion thereof used. Maximum scale same as item A.

E. Narrative Disks: $60 per track, or portion thereof used.

Appendix 32

TYPICAL PAGE FROM AUDARENA STADIUM LISTING
PUBLIC ASSEMBLY FACILITIES
INDEX

NEW YORK

limited floor load. $1,500 vs. 12½% avg. daily rental fee. **Other Facilities**–130 restaurant capacity; 160-200 cocktail lounge capacity; 11 meeting rooms with 50-10,000 capacity; 1,000 hotel rooms nearby; 1,800 on site parking; 1,500 parking capacity within walking distance. 500,000 population within market area; 15 miles to nearest airport. Home of Niagara Univ. Teams.
Niagara University–14109, (716) 285-1212. Mgr.: Peter Lonergan. **Student Center Arena**–3,500 permanent seats. 94' x 52' floor area. Permanent stage. **Other Facilities**–Conc. stand; 1,000 on site parking.

OLEAN—Olean Recreation Center–East State St. 14760, (716) 372-1484. Mailing Address: Municipal Building. Mgr.: David A. Forney. **Arena**–1,700 seats. 30' ceiling. 28,800 sq. ft. floor area. Concrete floor. 200' x 85' ice rink. 480 volts. 16' freight doors. Utilities: Water, gas. Rental fee available upon request. **Bradner Stadium**–5,000 permanent seats. Night lighting. Rental fee available upon request.

ONEONTA—Hartwick College–13820, (607) 432-4200. Chrmn.: Thomas H. Green. **Gym**–2,200 permanent seats. Air Cooled. 120' x 100' floor area. $100 avg. daily rental fee. **Elmore Field Stadium**–2,800 permanent seats. College use only. **Other Facilities**–2 conc. stands; 2,000 on site parking; 2,000 within walking distance.
State Armory–4 Academy St., 13820, (607) 432-5240. Mgr.: Gordon Beams. 1,000 portable seats. 120' x 90' floor area. **Exhibit Area**–5,130 sq. ft. $200 avg. daily rental fee.

ORCHARD PARK—Rich Stadium–1 Bills Dr., 14127, (716) 648-1800. Mgr.: Donald W. Guenther. Promo Dir.: Dennis R. White. 80,020 permanent seats. Night lighting. **Other Facilities**–38 conc. stands; 16,000 on-site parking. Home of Buffalo Bills.

OSWEGO—New York State University–13126, (315) 341-2500. Athletic Dir.: John Spring. **Golden Romney Fieldhouse**–5,000 permanent seats. Portable stage. 200' x 85' ice rink. **Laker Hall Gym**–5,000 permanent seats. 285' x 160' floor area. Portable stage.
Oswego Speedway–Hall Road, 13126, (315) 458-2051. Mgr.: Dick O'Brien. Asst. Mgr.: George Caruso, Jr. Conc. Mgr.: George Caruso, Sr. Promotion: Dick O'Brien. 12,000 permanent, sheltered seats. ⅝ mile paved oval track. Night lighting. Auto racing.

OZONE PARK—Aqueduct Racetrack–11417, (212) 641-4700. Mailing address: Box 90, Jamaica. Pres.: James Heffernan. Conc. Mgr.: Araserv. Mktg. Dir.: Howard Giordano. 32,332 seats (20,000 permanent & sheltered, 15,000 portable). 5,000 standing room. Horse racing. Rental fee negotiable. **Other Facilities**–62 conc. stands. CC-TV/projection facilities. 16,000 on site parking. 10,000,000 population within primary market area.

PIKE—Wyoming County Fair–Box 187, 11427, (716) 493-5169. Gen. Supt./Sec.: Donald G. Robinson, Sr., 88 N. Main St., Castile. **Exhibit Area**–15,520 sq. ft. 10'15" ceilings. 7' x 8' & 10' x 12' loading doors. Utility services: Water, electricity. **Indoor Arena**–1,000 seats. **Outdoor Arena**–6,100 seats (5,600 permanent, 500 portable).

PLATTSBURGH—Crete Memorial Civic Center–Cumberland Head Corners, 12901, (518) 563-4431. Mailing address: City Hall. Mgr.: Cassidy A. Clark. Concessions Mgr.: Timothy Murtha. **Exhibit Area**–27,800 sq. ft. total; 23,800 sq. ft. main hall. 39' ceiling. A/C. Freight bay. 15' x 16' loading doors. **Arena**–3,400 seats (1,800 permanent, 1,600 portable). 39' ceiling. A/C. 23,600 sq. ft. floor area. 40' x 60' portable stage. 85' x 200' ice rink. Portable basketball & utility floors. $350 avg. daily rental fee. **Other Facilities**–2 conc. stands; 4 meeting rooms; 2,000 hotel rooms nearby; 1,000 on site parking; 5,000 parking capacity within walking distance. 60,000 population within primary market area; 6 miles to nearest airport.
New York State University–12901, (518) 564-2000. Athletic Dir.: Dr. Ernest Rangazas. **Fieldhouse**–4,500 permanent seats. Portable stage. 200' x 85' ice rink. **MacDonough Stadium**–2,000 permanent seats. **Hawkins Theatre**–850 seats. Dressing rooms.

POTSDAM—Clarkson College of Technology–13676, (315) 268-6622. Chrmn. P.E.: John Hantz. **Alumni Gym**–1,750 seats. 15,000 sq. ft. floor area. **Walker Arena**–Mgr.: John Serwatka. 1,600 seats. 200' x 85' ice rink. **Snell Stadium**–1,000 permanent seats. Baseball.

NY State University–13676, (315) 268-2700. **Hosmer Hall**–(315) 268-2969. Mgr.: Robert Mero. 1,400 permanent seats. 7 dressing rooms. A/C. **John W. Maxcy Hall**–(315) 268-3004. Mgr.: Will Eschen. Dir. of Student Activities: Mike Lebeda. Promo Dir.: Louis E. LaGrand. **Gym**–3,200 permanent seats. Portable stage. **Arena**–2,400 permanent seats. 40' ceiling. 95' x 200' floor area. 20' x 50' portable stage. 85' x 185' ice rink. $35 avg. hourly rental fee. **Ballpark**–500 permanent seats. ¼ mile all-weather, 8-lane track. $25 per hr. avg. daily rental fee. Track events. **Other Facilities**–3 meeting rooms with 35-45 capacity; CC-TV/projection facilities; 100 hotel rooms nearby; 300 on site parking. 35,000 population within market area. Home NY State Univ. at Potsdam & local high school teams.

POUGHKEEPSIE—Marist College–12601, (914) 471-3240. Mgr.: Ronald Petro. **James J. McCann Recreation Center**–3,075 seats (2,075 permanent, 1,000 portable). 24' ceiling. 29,000 sq. ft. floor area. 40' x 40' portable stage. Home of Marist College teams.
Mid-Hudson Civic Center–Civic Center Plaza, 12601, (914) 454-5800. Mgr.: James G. Doyle. Asst. Mgr.: Susan Ryerson. Oper. Mgr.: Brendon Brady. Promo Dir.: Rose Promo Dir.: Rose Ann Shankman. **Theatre**–3,038 seats. 8 dressing rooms. A/C. 70' x 36' stage. 70' prosc. 14 lines. 400, 3 phase, 4 leg. House services: All. $1,000 avg. daily rental fee. House promotes & co-promotes. **Arena**–3,500 seats (1,000 permanent, 2,500 portable). 28' ceiling. A/C. 17,000 sq. ft. floor area. 80' x 40' portable stage. 200' x 85' ice rink. 400, 3 phase, 4 leg. Unlimited floor load. $750 avg. daily rental fee. **Exhibit Area**–25,000 sq. ft. 16,800 sq. ft. main hall. Concrete floor. Unlimited floor load. 28' ceiling. A/C. Freight bay. 12'8" x 12' freight doors. 8,000 sq. ft. tenant storage area. Utilities: Water, gas, air. 400 3 phase, 4 leg. Unlimited floor load. $750 avg. daily rental fee. **Other Facilities**–4 conc. stands; 1,600 banquet capacity; 6 meeting rooms with 30-200 capacity; CC-TV/projection facilities; 700 on-site parking; 4,500 parking within walking distance. 900 hotel rooms nearby. 500,000 population within primary market area; 4 miles to nearest airport.

RHINEBECK—Dutchess Co. Fair–Box 389, 12572,)914) 876-4001. Mgr.: Thomas J. Odak. **Grandstand**–2,000 seats. ½-mile track. **Exhibit Areas**–251,000 sq. ft. 8,500 on-site parking.

ROCHESTER—Community War Memorial–100 Exchange Street, 14614, (716) 546-2030. Mgr.: Bernard A. Hoepel. Conc. Mgr.: John Osowski. **Exhibit Area**–50,000 sq. ft. 6,000 lbs. psf. floor load. 10' ceiling. 2 freight bays. 8' x 10' loading doors. Utilities: Water, electricity, & steam. $950 avg. daily rental fee. **Arena**–9,300 seats (5,774 permanent, 3,526 portable). 56' ceiling. A/C. 126' x 236' floor area. 40' x 100' permanent stage. 36' x 36' portable stage. 85' x 200' ice rink. Portable basketball floor. 2500 KVA wattage. 4,500 lbs. psf. floor load. $3,000 (min.) vs 15% avg. daily rental fee. **Other Facilities**–19 conc. stands; 2,500 banquet capacity; 12 meeting rooms with 70-550 capacity; CC-TV/projection facilities; 2,000 hotel rooms nearby; 1,400 on site parking; 3,500 parking capacity within walking distance. 200,000 population within market area; 9 miles to nearest airport. Home of Rochester Americans Hockey Team.
Holleder Memorial Stadium–999 Ridgeway Ave., 14615, (716) 232-2420. Mailing address: 812 Wilder Bldg. Mgr.: John T. Mazzola or Rochester Lancers Soccer. 26,000 seats (22,000 permanent, 4,000 portable). Athletic events, concerts. Night lighting. Rental fee available upon request. **Other Facilities**–4 conc. stands; 2,500 on-site parking; 2,000 in walking distance; 5 miles to nearest airport. Home of Rochester Lancers Soccer Club, Ltd.
Monroe County Fair–(716) 334-4000. Mailing address: Box 22848, 14692. Exec. Dir.: G. Robert Alhart. **Dome Center**–4,700 seats (2,064 permanent, 2,636 portable). 16' x 35' ceilings. A/C. 56' x 40' portable stage. 200' x 85' ice rink. Unlimited floor load. $1,300 avg. daily rental fee. **Exhibit Areas**–71,000 sq. ft. 50,000 sq. ft. main hall. 16' ceiling. 14' x 14' loading doors. Unlimited floor load. A/C. $950 avg. daily rental fee. **Grandstand**–4,000 permanent seats. ½ mile clay track. **Other Facilities**–50 capacity cocktail lounge; 2 conc. stands; 2,000 banquet capacity, 4 meeting rooms with 50-250 capacity; 4,000 on-site parking; 1,200 hotel rooms nearby. 850,000 population within primary market area.
Nazareth Arts Center–4245 East Ave., 14618, (716) 586-2420. Mgr.: Joe Baranowski. Promo Dir.: Meg Quinn. 1,153 permanent seats. 50' x 38' permanent stage. A/C. $425 per performance or 4 hrs. avg. rental fee.

Rochester Institute of Technology—Frank Ritter Memorial Arena—1 Lomb Memorial Drive, 14623, (716) 475-2222. Mgr.: Edward F. Ziegler. 2,250 permanent seats. 35' ceiling. 15,500 sq. ft. floor area. Portable stage. 85' x 185' ice rink. $600 avg. daily rental fee.

Silver Stadium—500 Norton St., 14621, (716) 467-3000. Asst. Mgr.: Bill Berlecky. 14,000 seats (12,000 permanent, 2,000 portable). 2,000 standing room. 10,000 seats sheltered. Night lighting. Minimum with percentage rental fee. Home of Rochester Red Wings.

Temple Civic Center—875 E. Main St., 14605, (716) 271-3250. Mgr.: Leonard Parker. 2,574 permanent seats. 5 dressing rooms. 104' x 40' permanent stage. 50' prosc. Avg. daily rental fee available upon request.

University of Rochester—River Campus, 14627, (716) 275-2121. Pres.: Robert L. Sproull. **Fieldhouse**—300 portable seats. Alexander Palestra Gym—3,000 permanent seats. 80' ceiling. 88' x 50' floor area. Portable stage. Univ. use only. **Fauver Stadium**—Mgr.: David Ocoor. 6,000 seats. **Other Facilities**—4 conc. stands; 500 on-site parking; 1,000 within walking distance.

RYE—Playland Ice Casino—10580, (914) 967-2040. Mgr.: Norbert Bouchard. 1,200 permanent seats. 208' x 80' ice rink. **Studio Rink**—45' x 145'. **Beginners Rink**—75' x 24'. $40 to $70 per hour rental fee. **Other Facilities**—Conc. stand; meeting room with 60 capacity; 2,300 on site parking.

ST. BONAVENTURE—St. Bonaventure University—14760, (716) 375-2501. Dir.: Fr. Brennan Fitzgerald. Asst. Mgr.: Kevin McNamee. **Gym**—6,500 seats. 4 dressing rooms. 81,000 sq. ft. floor area. 40' x 20' portable stage. 200 amps, 3 phase. $500 avg. daily rental fee. **Other Facilities**—200 capacity restaurant; 2 conc. stands; 500 banquet capacity. Home of the St. Bonaventure University basketball team.

SARATOGA—Albany-Saratoga Speedway—U.S. Rt. 9, 12220, (518) 587-0220. Mailing Address: Box 438, Ballston Spa. Mgr.: C. J. Richards. Asst. Mgr.: T. S. Richards. Conc. Mgr.: J. L. Richards. Promo. Dir.: C. J. Richards. 8,000 seats. 10,000 standing room. 3/10 mile clay oval track. Night lighting. $1,000 avg. daily rental fee.

SARATOGA SPRINGS—Saratoga Performing Arts Center—12866, (518) 584-9330. Exec. Dir.: Herbert A. Chesdrough. Promo Dir.: Laura Lowe. 5,103 permanent, 33,000 lawn seats. A/C. 70' x 100' stage. 100' x 60' prosc. 102 lines. House Main, 2000 amps; Stage Main, 1600 amps KVA wattage. House promotes & co-promotes. Rental fee available upon request. **Other Facilities**—400 restaurant capacity; 100 cocktail lounge capacity; 3 conc. stands; 400 banquet capacity; meeting room with 50 capacity; 1,500 hotel rooms nearby; 5,000 on-site parking; 5,000 parking within walking distance. 20,000 population within primary market area.

Saratoga Racetrack—12866, (516) 488-6000. Pres.: James Heffernan. 18,000 permanent, sheltered seats. Horse racing. **Other Facilities**—2 restaurants, cocktail lounge, conc. stands. 7,000 on-site parking.

SCHAGHTICOKE—Schaghticoke Fair—Verbeck Ave., 12154, (518) 753-4411. Mgr.: Samuel Hamilton. **Grandstand**—3,000 seats. **Exhibit Areas**—12,000 sq. ft. 8,500 on-site parking.

SCHNECTADY—Union College—12308, (518) 370-6000. Athletic Dir.: Richard Sakala. **Fieldhouse**—3,000 portable seats. 70' ceilings. 200' x 160' floor area. Portable stage. **Achilles Rink**—2,900 permanent seats. 200' x 85' ice rink. **Stadium**—3,500 permanent seats. 400 meter asphalt track. Football, baseball, track.

SLOANSVILLE—Chariot Park—(518) 853-3304. Mailing address: Box 200, Esperance, 12160. Mgr.: James L. Gage. Asst. Mgr.: James Gage, Jr. **Grandstand**—1,500 permanent seats. 5,000 standing room. ¼ mile oval track & motocross course. **Other Facilities**—3 conc. stands; 3,000 on-site parking; 25 miles to nearest airport.

SOUTHAMPTON—Southampton College—Montawk Hwy., 11968, (516) 283-4000. Mgr.: Alan Green. Asst. Mgr.: JoAnne Sullivan. **Fine Arts Theatre**—500 permanent seats. 80' x 60' permanent stage. A/C. House services: Sound, lighting, janitorial. **Gym**—2,500 seats. 55' ceiling. 113,200 sq. ft. floor area. Portable stage. Unlimited floor load. **Wood Hall**—50 restaurant capacity; 40 cocktail lounge capacity; 300 banquet capacity; 20 meeting rooms with 5-500 capacity; CC-TV/projection facilities. 600 on site parking. Home of Southampton College teams.

STATEN ISLAND—Wagner College—631 Howard Ave., 10301, (212) 390-3000. Pres.: Dr. John Satterfield. **Fredrick Sutter Gym**—1,600 permanent seats. 70' ceiling. 94' x 50' floor area. Portable stage. $150 avg. daily rental fee. **Stadium**—15,000 seats. ¼ mile cinder track. Football, track. **Auditorium**—350 seats. 2 dressing rooms. 65' x 30' stage. Complete House services. $500 avg. daily rental fee. House promotes & co-promotes. **Other Facilities**—900 banquet capacity. Cafeteria. 1,000 on-site parking.

STONY BROOK—New York State University at Stony Brook—11790, (516) 246-5000. Athletic Dir.: John Ramsey. **Gym**—2,200 permanent seats. 94' x 50' floor area. Portable stage.

SUFFERN—Rockland Community College—145 College Road, 10901, (914) 356-4650. Pres.: Dr. Seymour Eskos. **Fieldhouse**—4,000 portable seats. 35' ceiling. 86,211 sq. ft. floor area. $1,500 avg. daily rental fee.

SYRACUSE—Civic Center of Onondaga County—411 Montgomery St., 13202, (315) 425-2155. Dir.: Dr. Joseph Golden. Dir. of Programming: Carol T. Jeschke. Promo Dir.: Russ Thomas. **Crouse-Hinds Concert Theater**—2,117 seats. 15 dressing rooms. 107' x 48' stage. 60' x 40' prosc. 80 lines. 208 volts. House promotes & co-promotes. Rental fees avail. upon request. **Carrier Theater**—463 seats. 25' x 57' stage. 37' x 20' prosc. 10 lines. 15 dressing rooms. House promotes & co-promotes. **Bevard Community Room**—150 seats. 2,400 sq. ft. Rental fees avail. upon request. 400 hotel rooms nearby; 3,000 parking in walking distance; 1.5 million population in market area; 12 miles to nearest airport.

Le Moyne College—Le Moyne Heights, 13214. (315) 446-2882. Athletic Dir.: Thomas J. Niland, Jr. **Gym**—3,000 seats (2,200 permanent, 800 portable). 40' ceiling. 20,000 sq. ft. floor area. Portable stage. $200 avg. daily rental fee. Conc. stands; 420 on site parking; 600 within walking distance.

Mac Arthur Stadium—13208, (315) 474-7833. Mgr.: Russo. 10,500 seats (8,046 permanent, 2,094 portable). 2,000 standing room. 4,000 sheltered. Night lighting. Home of Syracuse Chiefs Baseball Club.

New York State Fair—State Fairgrounds, 13209, (315) 487-7711. Bus. Mgr.: Bill MacIntyre. **Coliseum**—4,500 permanent seats. 100' x 200' floor area. 30' x 45' portable stage. $600 avg. daily rental fee. **Grandstand**—15,000 seats. 1 mile track. $3,000 min. against % of daily rental fee. **Center of Progress Bldg.**—(315) 487-7743. Dir. Roger J. Mara. 85,000 sq. ft. Unlimited floor load. 78' ceiling. Three 22' x 20' loading ramps. 7,000 storage area. $1,500 avg. daily rental fee. **Other Facilities**—Restaurant; 4 conc. stands; 12 meeting rooms with 40-800 capacity; 4,000 on-site parking; 15,000 within walking distance; 4,000 hotel rooms nearby. 600,000 population within primary market area.

Onondaga Community College—(315) 469-7741. Mailing address: c/o Onondaga Student Services Assoc., Rt. 173, Syracuse, 13215. Pres.: Dr. Andreas Paloumpus. Vice Pres./Treas.: Peter Anderson. **Auditorium**—388 seats. Dressing room. 20' x 18' stage. **Other Facilities**—5 + hotels nearby; 800 on-site parking; 2,300 parking capacity within walking distance.

Onondaga County War Memorial—515 Montgomery St., 13202, (315) 425-2650. Dir.: Donald A. "Pete" Napier. Asst. Mgr.: Dennis W. Snow. Concessions: Gladieux Food Service. **Exhibit Area**—65,000 sq. ft. 20,000 sq. ft. main hall. Concrete floor. Unlimited floor load. A/C. 2 freight bays. 16' x 16' freight doors. 3,000 sq. ft. storage area. Utilities: Water, air. **Arena**—8,200 seats. (5,500 permanent, 2,700 portable.) 65' ceiling. A/C. 18,000 sq. ft. floor area. 80' x 30' permanent stage. 14' x 60' portable stage. 90' x 200' ice rink. Portable insulated floor. Unlimited floor load. $1,200 avg. daily rental fee.

Syracuse University—13210, (315) 423-2054. Mgr.: Joseph G. Szombathy. **Manley Fieldhouse**—9,500 permanent seats. 76' ceiling. 75,000 sq. ft. floor area. **Exhibit Area**—75,000 sq. ft. 76' ceiling. Freight bay. 20' x 12' freight doors. Rental fee negotiable. **Other Facilities**—Portable conc. stand. 1,000 banquet capacity. Meeting rooms with 50-75 capacity. CC-TV/projection facilities. 1,200 on site parking. 1,000 hotel rooms within a mile. 400,000 population within primary market area. **Stadium**—26,300 permanent seats. 850 on site parking. **Carrier Dome**—(315) 423-4634. Mailing address: 310 Steele Hall, Syracuse University. Mgr.: Thomas F. Benzel. Asst. Mgr.: David Skiles. **Exhibit Areas**—83,000 sq. ft. Tartan floor. 160' ceiling. Freight bay. 14' x 18' loading doors. Utilities: Water. 120/208 volts. **Arena**—50,000 permanent seats. 160' ceiling. 83,000 sq. ft. floor area. 120/208 volts. **Stadium**—50,000 sheltered seats. Night lighting. 200 meter indoor track. **Other Facilities**—18 conc. stands; CC-TV/Projection facilities; 3,800 hotel rooms nearby; 4,000 on-site parking. 650,000 population in market area; 12 miles to nearest airport. Home of Syracuse University teams.

TARRYTOWN—Dick Clark Westchester Theatre—600 White Plains Road, 10591, (914) 631-3313 or 631-9100. Bldg. Mgr.: Bobby Schiffman. Conc. Mgr.: Doug Licursi. Promo. Dir.: Joe Carlucci. 3,574 seats. 4 dressing rooms. A/C. 60' x 45' stage. 10 lines. $3,500 avg. daily rental fee. All house services. House promotes & co-promotes.

TROY—Rensselaer Polytechnic Institute—12180, (518) 270-6262. Mgr.: Andrew J. Maloney. Asst. Mgr.: John Holstein. **Houston Fieldhouse at RPI**—7,200 seats (4,900 permanent, 2,200 portable). 40' ceiling. 12,070 sq. ft. floor area. 20' x 60' portable stage. 185' x 85' ice rink. 40,000 sq. ft. exhibit area. Rental fees avail. upon request. **Other Facilities**—2 conc. stands; 5,000 banquet capacity; 600 on site parking.

Troy Arena—1 Main Street, 12180, (518) 273-8400. Mgr.: Ted C. Bayly. 6,000 permanent seats.

UNIONDALE—Nassau Veterans Memorial Coliseum—Mitchel Field Complex, 11553, (516) 794-9300. V. Pres./Gen. Mgr.: Antonio G. Travares. Promo. Dir.: Carl Hirsh. Dir. of Oper. Ray Westergard. 17,000 seats (14,750 permanent, 2,250 portable). 72' ceiling. A/C. 85' x 200' floor area. 42' x 64' portable stage. 200' x 85' ice rink. Portable basketball, track floors. $8,500 vs. 17½ avg. daily rental fee. **Exhibit Area**—60,000 sq. ft. Unlimited floor load. 20' ceiling. A/C. 6 freight bays. 12' x 16' loading doors. Utilities: Electric, water, telephone. $.04 per sq. ft. or $1,200 avg. daily rental fee. **Other Facilities**—250 restaurant capacity; 10 conc. stands. 5,000 banquet capacity; 6,500 on-site parking. 750 hotel rooms nearby. 11,000,000 population within primary market area. Home of NY Islanders.

UTICA—Utica Memorial Auditorium—One Kennedy Plaza, 13501, (315) 798-3356. Mailing address: 400 Oriskany St. West. Dir. of Operations: Joseph Critelli. Conc. Mgr.: Richard Plumb. **Exhibit Area**—25,000 sq. ft. 24,000 sq. ft. main hall. Concrete floor. Unlimited floor load. 38' ceiling. A/C. 2 freight bays. 13' x 12' freight doors. Utilities: Water, gas, air. Rental fees avail. upon request. **Arena**—5,986 seats (4,030 permanent, 1,956 portable). 6 dressing rooms. A/C.

38' ceiling. 24,000 sq. ft. floor area. 80' x 40' portable stage. 40' x 20' prosc. 3 lines. 185' x 85' ice rink. Portable basketball & dance floors. 400 amps 208/ 115 v. Unlimited floor load. Rental fees avail. upon request. **Other Facilities**— 2,000 banquet capacity; 10 conc. stands; 4 meeting rooms with 50-100 capacity; 800 hotel rooms nearby; 250 on site parking; 800 parking capacity within walking distance. 350,000 population within market area; 12 miles to nearest airport. Home of Mohawk Valley Thunderbirds, Utica Mohawks, local college hockey, local high school basketball, pro boxing & wrestling & amateur boxing. **State Armory**—Parkway East, 13501, (315) 724-6518, 724-4533. Supt.: W. L. Helligas. Asst. Mgr.: Robert B. Leone. 3,500 portable seats. $650 avg. daily rental fee. **Exhibit Area**—27,200 sq. ft. 200' x 100' set up area. Unlimited floor load. 60' ceiling. $650 daily rental fee. **Other Facilities**—650 on site parking; 1,200 parking within walking distance.

VERNON—Utica-Rome Auto Speedway—13476, (315) 829-3813. Mgr.: Clifford Baker. 6,000 permanent seats. Night lighting. Rental fee available upon request. Auto racing (oval, drag).

WALTON—Delaware County Fair—13856, (607) 829-8776. Sec.: Arnold Froelich. **Exhibit Area**—9,000 sq. ft. **Grandstand**—2,000 sheltered seats.

WANTAGH—Jones Beach Theatre—11793, (516) 221-2070. Mgr.: Sterling Mace. 8,206 seats. 12 dressing rooms. 120' x 20' stage. 80' prosc. **Other Facilities**— Restaurant; conc. stand; 1,400 banquet capacity; 20,000 on-site parking.

WATERLOO—Seneca County Fair—13148, (315) 568-5505. Sec.: Richard Compo, RD 3, Box 3106, Seneca Falls. **Grandstand**—4,000 seats.

WATERTOWN—Jefferson Community College—Box 473, 13601, (315) 782-5250. Mgr.: Donald J. Hughes. **Theatre**—500 seats. 3 dressing rooms. 39'6" x 24' stage. 12' prosc. Two 90 amp KVA wattage. Avg. daily rental fee less than $100 if non-profit agency.
Jefferson County Fair—Box 750, 13601, (315) 686-5166. Mgr.: Arch Brick. **Grandstand**—2,000 permanent, sheltered seats. **Exhibit Area**—10,000 sq. ft. 400 on-site parking.

WATKINS GLEN—Watkins Glen Auto Racetrack—Box 1, 14891, (607) 535-4500. Exec. Dir.: Malcolm Currie. 6,000 permanent seats. 14,148 around track seating. 3 3/7 miles track. Auto racing. Rental fee negotiable.

WEEDSPORT—Weedsport Speedway—Rt. 31, Box 657, 13166, (315) 834-6606. Mgr.: Glenn Donnelly. Asst. Mgr.: Andrew Fusco. Conc. Mgr.: Aaron Freshman. Promo Dir.: Jack Burgess. 5,000 permanent seats. 1,000 standing room. Night lighting. Avg. daily rental fee available upon request. Auto racing. **Other Facilities**—400 capacity restaurant; 3 conc. stands; 400 banquet capacity; 2 meeting rooms with 16-100 capacity; CC-TV/projection facilities; 150 hotel rooms nearby; 3,000 on site parking. 750,000 population within market area; 25 miles to nearest airport.

Index